German-Bohemians
The Quiet Immigrants

Bronze statue of German-Bohemian immigrants, by German sculptor, Leopold Hafner, standing in German Park in downtown New Ulm

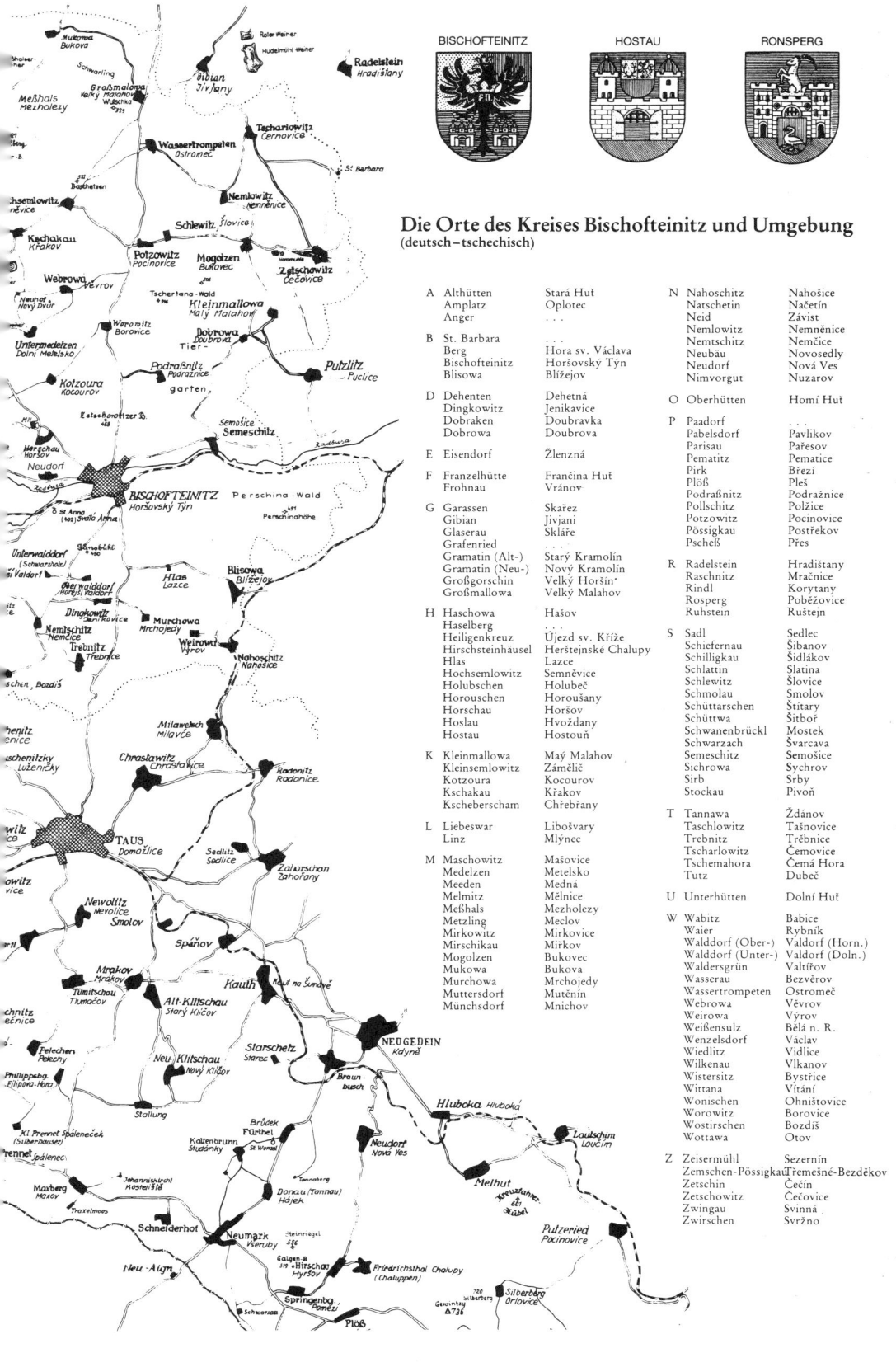

BISCHOFTEINITZ   HOSTAU   RONSPERG

Die Orte des Kreises Bischofteinitz und Umgebung
(deutsch–tschechisch)

A	Althütten	Stará Huť
	Amplatz	Oplotec
	Anger	
B	St. Barbara	. . .
	Berg	Hora sv. Václava
	Bischofteinitz	Horšovský Týn
	Blisowa	Blížejov
D	Dehenten	Dehetná
	Dingkowitz	Jenikavice
	Dobraken	Doubravka
	Dobrowa	Doubrova
E	Eisendorf	Žlenzná
F	Franzelhütte	Frančina Huť
	Frohnau	Vránov
G	Garassen	Skařez
	Gibian	Jivjani
	Glaserau	Skláře
	Grafenried	. . .
	Gramatin (Alt-)	Starý Kramolín
	Gramatin (Neu-)	Nový Kramolín
	Großgorschin	Velký Horšín˙
	Großmallowa	Velký Malahov
H	Haschowa	Hašov
	Haselberg	
	Heiligenkreuz	Újezd sv. Kříže
	Hirschsteinhäusel	Herštejnské Chalupy
	Hlas	Lazce
	Hochsemlowitz	Semněvice
	Holubschen	Holubeč
	Horouschen	Horoušany
	Horschau	Horšov
	Hoslau	Hvoždany
	Hostau	Hostouň
K	Kleinmallowa	Maý Malahov
	Kleinsemlowitz	Záměličč
	Kotzoura	Kocourov
	Kschakau	Křakov
	Kscheberscham	Chřebřany
L	Liebeswar	Libošvary
	Linz	Mlýnec
M	Maschowitz	Mašovice
	Medelzen	Metelsko
	Meeden	Medná
	Melmitz	Mělnice
	Meßhals	Mezholezy
	Metzling	Meclov
	Mirkowitz	Mírkovice
	Mirschikau	Mírkov
	Mogolzen	Bukovec
	Mukowa	Bukova
	Murchowa	Mrchojedy
	Muttersdorf	Mutěnin
	Münchsdorf	Mnichov
N	Nahoschitz	Nahošice
	Natschetin	Načetín
	Neid	Závist
	Nemlowitz	Nemněnice
	Nemtschitz	Nemčice
	Neubäu	Novosedly
	Neudorf	Nová Ves
	Nimvorgut	Nuzarov
O	Oberhütten	Horní Huť
P	Paadorf	. . .
	Pabelsdorf	Pavlikov
	Parisau	Pařesov
	Pematitz	Pematice
	Pirk	Březí
	Plöß	Pleš
	Podraßnitz	Podražnice
	Pollschitz	Polžice
	Potzowitz	Pocinovice
	Pössigkau	Postřekov
	Pscheß	Přes
R	Radelstein	Hradištany
	Raschnitz	Mračnice
	Rindl	Korytany
	Rosperg	Poběžovice
	Ruhstein	Ruštejn
S	Sadl	Sedlec
	Schiefernau	Šibanov
	Schilligkau	Šidlákov
	Schlattin	Slatina
	Schlewitz	Slovice
	Schmolau	Smolov
	Schüttarschen	Štitary
	Schüttwa	Šitboř
	Schwanenbrückl	Mostek
	Schwarzach	Švarcava
	Semeschitz	Semošice
	Sichrowa	Sychrov
	Sirb	Srby
	Stockau	Pivoň
T	Tannawa	Žďánov
	Taschlowitz	Tašnovice
	Trebnitz	Třebnice
	Tscharlowitz	Čemovice
	Tschemahora	Čemá Hora
	Tutz	Dubeč
U	Unterhütten	Dolní Huť
W	Wabitz	Babice
	Waier	Rybník
	Walddorf (Ober-)	Valdorf (Horn.)
	Walddorf (Unter-)	Valdorf (Doln.)
	Waldersgrün	Valtířov
	Wasserau	Bezvěrov
	Wassertrompeten	Ostromeč
	Webrowa	Věvrov
	Weirowa	Výrov
	Weißensulz	Bělá n. R.
	Wenzelsdorf	Václav
	Wiedlitz	Vidlice
	Wilkenau	Vlkanov
	Wistersitz	Bystřice
	Wittana	Vitání
	Wonischen	Ohnišťovice
	Worowitz	Borovice
	Wostirschen	Bozdiš
	Wottawa	Otov
Z	Zeisermühl	Sezernín
	Zemschen-Pössigkau	Třemešné-Bezděkov
	Zetschin	Čečín
	Zetschowitz	Čečovice
	Zwingau	Svinná
	Zwirschen	Svržno

German-Bohemians
The Quiet Immigrants

La Vern J. Rippley
with
Robert J. Paulson

St. Olaf College Press
Northfield, Minnesota

for the

German-Bohemian Heritage Society
New Ulm, Minnesota

Copyright © 1995 St. Olaf College Press 55057-1098
German Bohemian Heritage Society, Box 822, New Ulm,
Minnesota 56073

Library of Congress Cataloging-in-Publication Data

Rippley, La Vern J.
Library of Congress Catalog Card Number: 94-12045
    German-Bohemians. The Quiet Immigrants / La Vern J. Rippley
with Robert J. Paulson
ISBN 0-9622931-4-8

Mathilda Rewitzer Helget watering her vegetable and flower garden at 327 N. Washington in New Ulm. The German-Bohemians brought their love of flowers from the Old Country. RP

Honorary Contributors

Following are the names of those who contributed $50 toward the publication of this book:

Arbes, Walter and Florence – Courtland
Bauer, George and Louise – New Ulm
Bayerl, Richard and Mary – Northville MI
Beranek, Daniel and Trudy – New Ulm
Berres, Robert and Alice – Edina
Bleich, Howard and Doreen – Nipawin, Sask. Canada
Brown, William and Patricia – La Mesa CA
Cosgriff, J. A. Jr. M. D. – Olivia
Dahmen, Margaret – Sleepy Eye
Domeier, Donald and Avona – Sleepy Eye
Domeier, Marlene – New Ulm
Dorner, Peter and Lois – Oregon WI
Eckstein, A. J. and Harriet – New Ulm
Eckstein, Patrick J. and Nicole – New Prague
Ellwanger, James and Gloria – San Antonio TX
Fahrbach, Patricia – Albuquerque NM
Feddema, Richard and Rita – Richfield
Fischer, Elmer J. – New Ulm
Fischer, Jerome and Diane – New Ulm
Franta, Cletus and Rosemary – New Ulm
Ginkel, James C. – New Ulm
Glotzbach, Mr. and Mrs. George – Lutherville MD
Goblirsch, Alphonse and Marcella – Lafayette
Grausam, Mike and Agnes – Sleepy Eye
Groebner, Gerald and Alvina – St. Paul
Groebner, Stuart P. and Collette – New Ulm
Gulden, Gerald and Shirleen – North Mankato
Gust, Charles and Mary – Stevens Point WI

Haala, David – Sleepy Eye
Haala, Linus – Springfield
Haala, Thomas and Nancy – New Ulm
Haas, Joseph and Ethel – Sleepy Eye
Halbert, Ralph and Mary – St. Paul
Hinsman, Darrell and Jeanie – New Ulm
Hobbs, Karen L. – Colorado Springs CO
Hoffman, Emmet – Minneapolis
Hornick, Ruth – Confrey
Howie, Rolland and Dorothy – Dennison
Johnson, Marianne H. – Hector
Karl, Lois J. – Okemos MI
Kastanek, Jrwin and Cathryn – Hillman
Kastanek-Hoppe, Charlotte E. – Clear Lake
Kestner, Martha R. – St. Paul
Kitzberger, William – New Ulm
Korenchen, Marie – New Ulm
Kral, Jerome and Dolores – Sleepy Eye
Kral, Mary J. – Rochester
Krause, Paul and Jeannette – Waseca
Kretsch, Eleanor – New Ulm
Kretsch, Patrick and Colleen – New Ulm
Kretsch, Paul and Janice – New Ulm
Lindmeyer, Louis and LuAnn – New Ulm
Linsmayer, J. Nicholas – Mendota Heights
Loseleben, Jay and Lynn – Camano Island WA
Madson, M. Leroy – Gardner ND
Manderfeld, Willard and Alice – New Ulm
Mathiowetz, Andrew and Veronica – Morgan
Meter, Kenneth A. – Minneapolis
Neils, Priscilla – New Hampton IA
Nimmerfroh, Laurence J. – Green Bay WI
Olson, Lorraine Groebner – New Ulm

Pankratz, Richard and Janice – Fall City WA

Paulson, Dorothy – St. Paul

Plombon, William J. and Mrs. – Stanley WI

Portner, George and Angeline – New Ulm

Pruente, Fred and Kate – Sonora CA

Raska, Walter and Jeanette – Plymouth

Ries, LaRay – Lisbon ND

Roth, Carlis and Doris – Sheldon IA

Rothmeier, Steven G. – St. Paul

Saffert, Ambrose and Hildegard – New Ulm

Schaefer, Donald Jr. and Diana – New Ulm

Schmid, Neoma M. – Sleepy Eye

Schnobrich, Gerald and Patricia – New Ulm

Schulte, Josephine H. – San Antonio TX

Seifert, Dr. James and Jane – New Ulm

Seifert, Leonard and Darlene – New Ulm

Simek, Virginia – St. Paul

Smith, Patrick and Catherine – Visalia CA

Steiner, John W. Rev. – Owen WI

Stephany, Jean L. – Redwood Falls

Tauer, Edward J. – Springfield

Tauer, Frederick and Janet – Sleepy Eye

Tauer, Ray and Peggy – Sleepy Eye

Teynor, Dr. Joseph W. and Barbara Lael – Edina

Tietel, Selma – New Ulm

Traurig, Leo and Patricia – New Ulm

Traurig, Thomas A. and Kathleen J. – Long Beach CA

Ubl, Thomas and Darlene – New Ulm

VanLerberg, Cleo Kathryn – Shawnee KS

Veeser, Verona R. – Stanley WI

Waibel, Willard and Dorothy – New Ulm

Warta, Denis and Dorothy – New Ulm

Warta, Norman and Lois – New Ulm

Waterman, Anna – Visalia CA

Welna, Eileen M. – St. Paul

Wendinger, Peter and Paul – New Ulm

Wilfahrt, Willard and Alice – Sleepy Eye

Winch, Bruce and Lynn – St. Cloud

Windschitl, Gerald and Carol – Andover

Windschitl, Patricia M. – Virginia Beach VA

Woratschka, Norbert and Arlene – New Ulm

Zupfer, Betty – Milroy

Zwach, Donald and Frances – Waseca

Photo Credits:

BC	Brown County Historical Society Collection
SA	*Sudetendeutscher Atlas*
LB	*Linz in Böhmerwald*
KM	Ken Meter
OD	Otto Dietz
RP	Robert Paulson
PB	*Pfarrgemeinde Berg*
BS	*Heimatkreis Bischofteinitz*
AP	Angeline Portner
DZ	Donald Zwach
LR	La Vern J. Rippley

Contents

Contents

Preface
German-Bohemians: The Quiet Immigrants

ON JULY 19-21, 1991 during New Ulm Minnesota's annual Heritagefest, the German-Bohemian Heritage Society celebrated by erecting a monument in German Park, downtown New Ulm, Minnesota. Positioned on a tapered granite pedestal, the three-figure bronze sculpture was created and poured in Germany by the artist Leopold Hafner of Aicha vorm Wald near Passau in Bavaria, who was born in Wallern in the Böhmerwald [Bohemian Forest].

While the artistic concept was assigned to Leopold Hafner, the preparation work including inscribing the granite was done by Wallace Bloedel of Bloedel Monument Company in New Ulm. Around the base of the statue are the over 350 family names of immigrants from the counties (Kreis) of Bischofteinitz, Mies and Tachau, an area of Western Czechoslovakia which is highlighted by a map on the back side of the granite pedestal. Also etched in granite are the townships where these rural settlers located in Minnesota. On the front side of the monument is the title "German-Bohemian Immigrants," supplemented by narrative descriptions on the east side about life in the old homeland, and on the west side about settlement and cultural transfers in the New World. The inscriptions reads as follows:

German-Bohemian Immigrant Monument in German Park, New Ulm, Minnesota.

East Side

This monument was erected in 1991 by the German-Bohemian Heritage Society to commemorate the immigrants to this region from the German speaking western rim of present-day Czechoslovakia. They emigrated from the counties of Bischofteinitz, Mies and Taus in the Province of Pilsen, as shown on the European map, and settled in the townships sketched on the U.S. map. Around the base in the granite slabs are inscribed the over 350 immigrant family names as they were approximately spelled when the families departed their old homeland. Known at the time of their departure as Bohemia, a crown colony in the Austro-Hungarian Empire, this region in the 20th century was included in the larger periphery of the Czech nation designated as the Sudetenland. More locally it was called the *Böhmerwald*, Bohemian Forest, a ridge of high hills that forms a natural border with Germany.

The immigrants came mostly from small villages, with the largest numbers from the village centers of Hostau, Muttersdorf, and Ronsperg. These were farm communities where the people lived and housed their stock, going out daily to work their scattered non-contiguous fields. Most villages had Catholic churches or chapels and the residents spoke a Bohemian dialect of German. From New Year's Day to Christmas each year they observed special traditions, spiced with large wedding celebrations and funerals attended by the entire communities. Music in every form – bands, singing societies and choirs – permeated all aspects of village life.

West Side

Many German-Bohemian traditions crossed the ocean to the New Ulm region. Some immigrants from German-speaking Bohemia were among the earliest farm settlers arriving by ship on the Minnesota river within two years after German Turners founded the city. Beginning in 1856 they farmed in Cottonwood, then extended their settlement northward into St. George, and westward into Sigel township, Sleepy Eye and to farther west. As more and more arrived (after 1872 by rail) they could no longer all farm. Beginning around 1880 they acquired homes especially in the southeast section of the city of New Ulm, an area they affectionately called the *Gänseviertel*, Goosetown. They also concentrated in the *Wallachei* (low land) region to the west. Farther north in the city, retired farmers built homes near Trinity Catholic Church. Younger city dwellers often labored in the roller mills, the breweries, and as carpenters, masons and cigar makers.

Among them in later years were also doctors, painters, musicians, butchers and blacksmiths. Many women earned extra money *Klöppling* (making lace) and sewing feather-filled bedding. The Bohemian heritage has been most strongly exhibited in the "old time" band traditions of southern Minnesota.

Bottom

[This statue was created by Leopold Hafner, a 1945 refugee from Wallern (Neuern), the district of Bohemia from which many local immigrants derived, but now of Aicha vorm Wald near Passau, Germany. His creation depicts the strong familial ties that bind residents in the local area to their heritage in the homeland.]

When the dedication of the German-Bohemian monument at German Park in New Ulm occurred on July 20, 1991, the results of three years of planning had come to fruition.[1] The idea for such a monument originated with Louis Lindmeyer Jr., then president of the German-Bohemian Society, in early 1988. Highly instrumental in bringing the project to a successful conclusion was Rudolf Kiefner of Wolfershausen near Kassel in central Germany. At the age of 11 in 1946, Rudolf with his expellee parents, the Josef Kiefners of Bischofteinitz, came to rest in the Wolfershausen village where fellow expellees named a new street on which they live Böhmerwaldstraße.[2]

By serving as chief liaison officer for emigres from the Bischofteinitz region who are scattered in exile mostly in western Germany, Canada and the United States, Kiefner had already been instrumental in erecting other shrines to his people. They stand today notably in Furth im Wald in Bavaria, the sister city of Bischofteinitz, where the altar in the *Kreuzkirche* [Holy Cross Church] commemorates the suffering of the Böhmerwald refugees and, also in Furth, a bronze statue of the patron saint for major towns in county Bischofteinitz, Ronsperg, Hostau, Eger and Karlsbad, namely St. John Nepomuk, whose statue graces a milepost column on the bridge.

Kiefner suggested that Hafner be the sculptor, not just because, like the German-speaking ancestors of today's inhabitants of Brown county, he was from the southern Böhmerwald, but also because he had won many awards in Germany for his resourceful art works. In particular he had become known for his bust of geneticist Gregor

Rudolf Kiefner, Heimatkreis Betreuer [Bohemian Homeland research coordinator] and instigator for the German-Bohemian monument, born in Ronsperg, Bohemia but after the 1945 expulsion at home near Kassel, post office Felsberg/Wolfershausen, in Central Germany. Kiefner died on February 2, 1993.

George Portner, Kurt Eisen, Paul Kretsch and Louie Lindmeyer, in regional costume of the Bischofteinitz area of Bohemia, taken during the fall 1990 ground breaking ceremony in German park, New Ulm.

Mendel in the Walhalla Hall of Fame at Regensburg, along with his plaque of the writer Ackermann aus Böhmen [Johannes von Tepl] both famous Germans from the Böhmerwald. More recently he has been acclaimed for his "Living Water" fountain at the pilgrimage church of Altötting, sculpted for the four Catholic dioceses of Freising, Passau, Regensburg and Salzburg.[3]

The notion of a monument captured the imaginations of the German-Bohemian Heritage Society members. An art object would commemorate ancestors! A piece of art would also bind the living descendants of a common migration together and help them clarify their identity. Always known for their art – art in the form of paintings (for instance by members of the Gag family) – the German-Bohemians were especially known for their music, the Hofmeister concert bands, and particularly old time music (by the likes of the Lindmeyer Band, Whoopee John Wilfahrt, Emil Domeier, the Helgets and others). What better method to characterize the German-Bohemian heritage than by a piece of art for the City of New Ulm!

Throughout the year 1990 a strategy for siting the monument was developed. Some suggested the open park land to the immediate south of Turner Hall. Others considered the Brown county courthouse site appropriate. The question of ownership and care made county commissioners doubt the wisdom of adding monuments near the courthouse. Finally it became clear that the City of New Ulm would be the appropriate owner and it was determined that the downtown space in German Park at the juncture of Second and German Streets would be the most suitable.

The general public was invited to dedication ceremonies on Friday, Saturday and Sunday, including the July 19th banquet at 6:30 in Turner Hall. At this event Kiefner directed the traditional Bohemian musical group, the *Egerländer Trachtengruppe* which subsequently performed during the weekend at New Ulm's Heritagefest. The unveiling took place at 1:30 on Saturday afternoon July 20. On Sunday morning July 21 at 9:30 in Holy Trinity Cathedral, the Twin Cities *Böhmerwald Singers* under the direction of Robert and Dorothy Paulson performed a traditional "Waldler Messe" [Forester's Mass] sung in the German-Bohemian dialect.

Since the dedication of the German-Bohemian Monument pride has increased among representatives of the German-bohemian her-

The monument ground breaking ceremony in German Park, L-R: Kurt Eisen, George Portner, Harriet Eckstein, Mayor Carl "Red" Wyczawski, La Vern Rippley, Robert Paulson, Wallace Bloedel, Daniel Beranek, Paul Kretsch and Louie Lindmeyer.

itage. From a German-Bohemian Heritage Society enrollment of 60 in the years preceding the dedication, the membership has grown to over 300. Positioned in German park, the monument commands respect not only of visitors but community leaders who have invited a board member of the German-Bohemian Heritage Society to help plan and raise funds for the renovation of German Park.

The purposes of the monument are many! On the one hand it is intended to instruct the public by calling attention to this immigrant group to the Brown county region. More importantly, it is designed to stir interest in the history of the German-Bohemians in Brown county. Invariably, New Ulm histories that have been written about the German-speaking immigrants emphasize the Turners (well educated refugees of the 1848 Revolutions in Germany) who settled and built the elitist 19th century society of New Ulm.[4] Quite forgotten have been the people and the contributions of this other group, those from the Bischofteinitz region in western Bohemia.

German speakers from Bohemia were not prolific with books or

Sculptor Leopold Hafner conversing with Wallace Bloedel of the gravestone monument company in front of the German-bohemian masterpiece during dedication cere-monies July 17, 1991.

articles about their history. Being from small towns and peasant stock, they seldom knew or cared where their origins lay in the Old Country. The geographic region from which they derive is located on the map of Europe at the most westward point in Czechoslovakian territory. On the German side of the German-Czech boundary beginning in the North are the Bavarian towns of Marktredwitz, Weiden, Cham, Furth im Wald and Bayrisch-Eisenstein extending to Passau in the South [with Regensburg the largest regional market center]. In the Czech Republic beginning in the North are Cheb (Eger) Marianské Lázně (Marienbad), Plzeň – the regional center (Pilsen), Hostouň (Hostau), Horšovský Týn (Bischofteinitz), Domažlice (Taus), Klatovy (Klattau) – a subregional center, Nýrsko (Neuern), Kašperske Hory (Bergreich-enstein), Volary (Wallern) and Ceský Budějovice (Budweis) – a major regional center in the South. The territory that lies immediately on the eastern side of this political demarcation along with its emigrants is the subject matter of this book. Politically until January 1, 1993 when Bohemia and Slovakia split, it was Czechoslovakia. What is now the Czech Republic for centuries before 1919 was Austrian Bohemia and as such belonged to the Holy Roman Empire of the German Nation. Since the Reformation, it was ruled for centuries by the Habsburg family from the capital at Vienna.[5]

This volume presents information about this small segment of German speakers to Minnesota. Not just a profile about how the German-Bohemians differed from their compatriots, the book also tells about their homeland, its traditions and its life styles. It speaks to the individual German-Bohemians as well as to the general audience, trying to offer a "voice to the voiceless." It identifies the origins, stipulates the characteristics and illuminates the customs of a people with Old World habits and New World adaptations. Because the immigrants were rural, relatively uneducated, and therefore not given to write diaries or keep documents about their history, the luxury of thorough documentation from their past is unavailable. What follows is an effort to render a meaningful analysis of a special people and their heritage. With this book, the attempt to symbolize an identity by means of a monument advances to a verbal description.

Acknowledgments

In a book of this nature one's debt to others can never be repaid. Prime mover for the book was Robert J. Paulson whose heritage shines through the text at various points. Paulson visited me at St. Olaf College several times during 1982-3 to show me slides and talk about the need for this project, of which I gradually became convinced. After several years of gestation our work procedure evolved. I would write the book and be responsible for all the normal scholarly, organizational and stylistic matters. I would assemble all the information if he would help collect it. Thus Paulson gathered historical data, the census, naturalization, photographic, and illustrative material while with him I also conducted interviews and generally spearheaded the technicalities of producing a book.

Others also deserve much credit. First among them is the late Rudolf Kiefner of Wolfershausen near Kassel, Germany, coordinator of Germans whose heritage derives form the Bischofteinitz district.

Also essential to the project were Johann Gröbner and Rudolf Womes, historian expellees to Germany from the villages from which many southern Minnesota German-Bohemians emigrated. Thanks to Hildegard Binder Johnson, Minnesota's foremost but now deceased German immigrant historian, emerita professor at Macalester College, for her inspiration. Elroy Ubl, New Ulm's unofficial historian deserves much credit as does the highly informative Marlene Domeier at her German Store, and the ever ready Darla Gebhard at the Brown County Historical Society, all in New Ulm. Each of the officers past and present of the German-Bohemian Heritage Society earned merit for their moral support, among them especially Paul Kretsch, Louis Lindmeier, Angeline and George Portner. In a special way, gratitude is owed to Emmett Hoffmann of Minneapolis for spearheading the drive to raise the first half of the volume's publication costs. Needless to say, for any errors that yet remain, I assume full responsibility.

La Vern J. Rippley
February 1995

Notes

1. The story of the monument's development is told in a booklet *The German-Bohemian Monument* published by the German-Bohemian Heritage Society in New Ulm, 1992.

2. Rudolf Kiefner died at his home on February 2, 1993.

3. Since expulsion with his family from the Böhmerwald in 1946, Hafner has been living with his family and creating works of art in his home studio situated in the Alter Pfarrhof Reuth (former Bishop's court of residence) adjacent to the town of Aicha vorm Wald in eastern Bavaria.

4. This group is compared to the Bohemians in Chapter Four.

5. Among many atlases that show the historical development of the area is Fr. Dörr and W. Kerl, *Ostdeutschland und die deutschen Siedlungsgebiete in Ost- und Südosteuropa in Karte, Bild und Wort* (Munich; Südwest Verlag, 1987), pp. 50 ff.; also Manfred Dloczik, Adolf Schlüttler, and Hans Sternagel, *Der Fischer Informationsatlas Bundesrepublik Deutschland, Karten, Graphiken, Texte und Tabellen* (Frankfurt/M: Fischer Taschenbuch, 1982), pp. 147 ff.

Introduction

German-Bohemians to Brown County–
The Case for "Chain Migration"

ERMAN-SPEAKERS MIGRATED to the United States in largest numbers during the 19th century. During the Napoleonic period from 1797-1815 there was little movement but in the 1830s emigration quickened. A much larger transatlantic trek of Germans ensued after the 1848 revolutions. This upheaval, coupled to economic depression continuing since the mid-1840s, led to the exit of over 250,000 Germans in a single year (1854), a crescendo that encompassed annual totals exceeding 100,000 in each of the years during the decade from 1845-1855. New crests of German emigration waves peaked during the 1870s and again in the 1880s with the departure of about 254,000 in the pinnacle year of 1882.[1] The debarkation of German-speakers in numbers exceeding seven million between 1840 and 1900 coincided with the opening of the frontier in Indiana, Illinois, Michigan, Wisconsin, Iowa, Kansas, Nebraska, and Minnesota.

During that period, economic conditions in the Old World drove the adventurous, the young, the unmarried, and frequently the rural inhabitants of Central Europe to seek better living conditions in the New World. Seldom was religious persecution, government intolerance, or even the military draft a significant factor in the decision of an individual to emigrate. Rather, it was the chance for economic improvement that induced young, single adventurers to try something new, which in turn influenced those who had remained behind to follow. Called of late "chain migration," relatives and often married villagers missing among earlier "pioneer" emigrants soon joined their family members and acquaintances in the New World. In many respects, the subject matter of this book is a discussion that falls into the category of a "chain migration." After a few emigrants from extreme western Bohemia arrived in America, they found their way to southern Minnesota, specifically Brown county. Soon thereafter and continuing for a half century, acquaintances from the same region followed. The families who came to New Ulm from Bohemia, therefore, were anything but those immigrants whom Oscar Handlin described as the uprooted in his book by the same name.[2] They were *not uprooted* but *transplanted* from an environment that was to some degree replicated from the Old World to the New. Not that New Ulm was unique in this respect. All across America, chain migration communities were durable if they enjoyed the size necessary to maintain a cross section of daily life that in at least some respects replicated the Old World format. Chain migration was more the rule than the exotic exception.[3]

By the eve of World War I, 94% of immigrants arriving in US ports were joining friends or family. Not only were their destinations pinpointed, many of the new arrivals actually had someone at the port to meet them on arrival. Some 31% even received prepaid fares from relatives or friends already in America.[4] In this respect, Germans exceeded the national average, because 37% percent of their newcomers in 1910 were holding prepaid tickets. This means that German speakers were more likely to be joining relatives in ethnic communities than was true of the national immigration. Often religion was a strong factor in holding transplanted communities together and in the New Ulm German-Bohemian community there was uniformity of religion: All were Catholic. No ethnic communities survived long in rural or small town American society if they did not have the unifying force of a church.[5]

Migrants to ethnic communities in the New World, such as the German-Bohemians in New Ulm, differed from individuals who sought their fortunes independently of ethnic precursors. The individuals who chose to emigrate were self-selected, self-motivated, able to fend for themselves, and therefore likely to assimilate faster into their New World. As contrasted to chain migrants, individuals were usually unmarried, younger adults, males in ratios of up to 75%, had more wealth, had received a better education before leaving and enjoyed higher occupational achievement. By contrast, those migrants who left the European community for the re-established "village" in America tended to arrive with families, therefore were married, as a group showed much broader age distribution, revealed a more closely balanced sex ratio, had lower wealth status, less education, and poorer occupational levels.[6] Not genuine pioneers, chain migrants took less risks. They were driven more by economic conditions than by adventure and were generally less likely to rise to new heights in America. Often the risk takers (in contrast to the chain migrants) headed straight for the cities where they more quickly made their mark economically. Consequently they more swiftly rose above and were earlier to leave the ethnic community as exemplified by the Turner groups at New Ulm.

Chain migrants were less apt to seek acculturation. They were less likely to marry outside their "cocoon" and were less inclined toward assimilation with American society.[7] This principle can be illustrated by comparison to Scandinavian immigrants. Of all the Scandinavian countries, Denmark was the best off economically in the Old World. In addition, Denmark supplied individuals rather than chain migrants. As a result, Danish migration on a percent of population basis was less than half the rate for Sweden and only about one third that of Norway. As a consequence the Danes in Minnesota, being individuals seeking adventure and economic betterment rather than replicated Old World traditions in New World ethnic communities, readily dispersed upon arrival. Swedes and Norwegians, on the other hand, were more likely to re-establish their traditional lifestyles. In 1905 in Minnesota there were 33 townships that had 75% or more people of Norwegian stock. In the same year there were 26 such townships for Swedes. But there were no such townships at all where Danish stock reached a 75% level of the total population, and only six where it even had a majority. Further demonstrating this phenomenon were the Finns who, despite their relatively small percentage of Minnesota immigrants, nevertheless dominated 17 townships at or above the 75% level.[8] The Finns were chain migrants. So were Swedes and Norwegians, but not the Danes. This pattern holds true also in the matter of intermarriage. Danes had the highest out marriage rates for both sexes among all immigrants to Minnesota.

Retention of mother tongue is another indicator of chain migra-

3

tion. Among Scandinavians in Minnesota the Danes were the quickest to abandon their native language. The Swedes came next while Norwegians and especially Finns were most retentive of mother tongue. Not just the German-Bohemians but also Minnesota Germans from the Reich tended to cluster. In her article on intermarriages between Germans and other nationalities in Minnesota in 1860 and 1870, Hildegard Johnson shows that the Germans were unlikely to intermarry even when their partners were Irish co-religionists. Thus, even the requirement that members marry within the Catholic faith (a much stronger demand than existed between prospective Protestant partners) was insufficient to induce exogamy.[9] In 1870 there were in Minnesota nearly 15,000 German heads of a family with only 1,850 (or about 12% of the total) married to non-German-born spouses. As reductive of exagomy as this 12% figure is by itself, it diminishes considerably if consideration is given to spouses who were first generation Americans born of German-speaking parents (e. g. in Pennsylvania, Ohio, Illinois or Wisconsin where the German population was strong and therefore German language retentive).

Nor can the Irish connection to German Catholics explain away the tendency toward endogamy. For instance in Winona and Blue Earth counties where the German Catholic population was strong, there were virtually no German-Irish marriages. In the 99% German communities of Minnesota, such as Hampton in Dakota county, there were no exogamous intermarriages at all. Those Minnesota Germans who did marry outside their ethnic background were most likely to marry American born spouses, followed by French and only then by Irish. The few German-French marriages are likewise dubious inasmuch as French Alsatians were German-speakers and thus not ethnically French. At any rate, while the statistical intermarriage rate for Germans in Minnesota in 1870 stood at 12%, the rate of exogamy for the New Ulm area Germans was just 8.7%. And if the 8.7% is factored with the aforementioned provisos, then exogamy for Brown county German-Bohemians is practically nil.

With regard to language retention, Germans in Minnesota were rated as most energetic in keeping their mother tongue. Among ingredients that contributed to their language retention were those listed by Heinz Kloss in his article on German language maintenance in the United States: religio-societal insulation, timing of immigration, language islands, affiliation with denominations offering parochial schools, and pre-immigration experience with language maintenance efforts.[10] All of these factors were exemplified by the German-Bohemians in Brown county. The Bohemians were all Catholic, they arrived early enough to avoid immediate competition with non-German-speaking arrivals, and they formed a language island that was large enough to resist assimilation. They also had parochial Catholic schools and a tradition of clinging to their German language in an Old World territory where from time to time Czech vied with German to become the official language of government.

Minnesota Germans preserved their language through schools, both public and private. In 1917 when the Minnesota Commission of Public Safety inquired into the advisability of shutting down the schools where the German language was the vehicle of instruction, Archbishop Ireland of St. Paul persuaded the Safety commissioners to reserve judgement.[11] During the period of the Commission's investigation, however, state superintendent of public education Carl Gustav Schulz brought forth data to demonstrate the widespread use of German in the Minnesota schools. In Stearns county, for example, 100 of the public one-room school houses were using German as the vehicle of instruction. Only ten used Norwegian, and two Polish. In the private sector, however, over which the superintendent had no control and had only limited information, there were 307 parochial schools in 1917 with a total enrollment of 38,853 pupils. Less than one third (94) used English exclusively. Nearly two thirds (195) used German primarily with only occasional periods when English was the vehicle of instruction. A mere ten used Polish, four were French. There was one each in Norwegian, Dutch, Danish and Czech. Clearly the maintenance of language on a quality basis was stronger among German speakers than for any nationality group in Minnesota.

The chapters that follow are intended to illustrate how the German-Bohemians in Brown county revealed patterns of chain rather than individual migration. Their enclave fostered language retention, religious homogeneity, endogamy, family transplants, retention of Old World lifystyles, and a somewhat slower than normal rate of asimilation with American society.

5

West Newton residents relaxing in front of St. George store after cutting ice from a nearby lake.

Notes

1. See the graphs with discussion of the causes in La Vern J. Rippley, *The German-Americans* (Lanham, MD: University Press of America, 1984), pp. 73 ff.

2. Oscar Handlin, *The Uprooted: The Epic Story of the Great Migration that Made the American People* (Boston: Little, Brown, 1951).

3. See in general Kathleen Neils Conzen, *Making Their Own America. Assimilation Theory and the German Peasant Pioneer* (New York: Berg, 1990), commentary by Jörg Nagler, 38-44. Other examples are Russell Gerlach, *Immigrants in the Ozarks* (Columbia, MO: 1977); Robert C. Ostergren, *A Community Transplanted. The Trans-Atlantic Experience of a Swedish Immigrant Settlement in the Upper Middle West* 1835-1915 (Madison: University of Wisconsin Press, 1988); Watler D. Kamphoefner, *The Westfalians. From Germany to Missouri* (Princeton, NJ: Princeton University Press, 1987); James M. Bergquist, "German Communities in American Cities: An Interpretation of the Nineteenth-Century Experience," *Journal of American Ethnic History* (1984) 4: 9-30; Gary Foster, Richard Hummel and Robert Whittenbarger, "Ethnic Echoes through 100 Years of Midwestern Agriculture," *Rural Sociology* (1987) 52: 365-78; Stanley Nadel, *Little Germany. Ethnicity, Religion, and Class in New York City, 1845-80* (Urbana: University of Illinois Press, 1990); Sonya Salamon, "Ethnic Communities and the Structure of Agriculture," *Rural Sociology* (1985) 50: 323-40 and others. Maps showing rural ethnic groups in America help pinpoint settlements that resulted from chain migration. For example, U. S. Bureau of the Census, *Statistical Atlas, Twelfth Census of the United States,* 1900 (Washington, D. C.: 1903), plates 55-75; Richard Hartshorne, "Racial Maps of the United States," *Geographical Review* (April, 1938) 28: 276-88; Neale Carman, *Foreign-*

Language Units of Kansas, Vol 1, *Historical Atlas and Statistics* (Lawrence: University of Kansas Press, 1962); Terry G. Jordan, *German Seed in Texas Soil: Immigrant Farmers in Nineteenth Century Texas* (Austin: University of Texas Press, 1966); La Vern J. Rippley, *The Immigrant Experience in Wisconsin* (Boston: Twayne, 1985) appendix maps; Karl B. Raitz, "Ethnic Maps of North America," *Geographical Review* (July, 1978) 68: 335-50; and James Paul Allen and Eugene James Turner, *We the People: An Atlas of America's Ethnic Diversity* (New York: Macmillan, 1988), pp. 51 ff. The role of "chain migration" is explained theoretically by Walter Kamphoefner, "Entwurzelt oder verpflanzt," in Klaus Bade, ed. *Auswanderer - Wanderarbeiter - Gastarbeiter: Bevölkerung, Arbeitsmarkt und Wanderung in Deutschland seit der Mitte des* 19. *Jahrhunderts* (Ostfildern: Scripta Mercaturae, 1984), I: 321-49.

4. Reported in Walter D. Kamphoefner, *The Westfalians: From Germany to Missouri,* p. 188 based on *Reports of the Immigration Commission,* Vol 3 "Statistical Review of Immigration," pp. 360-365.

5. Among other studies eemplifying this pattern, see Rudolph J. Vecoli, "Contadini in Chicago: A Critique of *The Uprooted,*" *Journal of American History,* 51 (1964), 404-417 and ibid., "The Formation of Chicago's Little Italies," *Journal of American Ethnic History,* 2 (1983), 1-20; June G. Alexander, "Staying Together: Chain Migration and Patterns of Slovak Settlement in Pittsburgh Prior to World War I," *Journal of American Ethnic History,* 1 (1981), 56-83; Hildegard Binder Johnson, "The Location of German Immigrants in the Middle West," *Annals of the Association of American Geographers,* 41 (1951), 1-41. See also *Reports of the Immigration Commission* (1911) 3, "Statistical Review of Immigration," 360-365; S. Baily, "The Village Outward Approach to the Study of Social Networks: A Case Study of the Agnonesi Diaspora Abroad, 1885-1989," and D. N. Marquiegui, "Spanish Migration Chains from Soria to Lujan," *Studi Emigrazione,* 29 (March, 1992).

6. Kamphoefner, *Westfalians* p. 190; Peter Marschalck, Deutsche *Überseewanderung im* 19. *Jahrhundert* (Stuttgart: Klett, 1973), p. 71 and Wolfgang Kollmann and Peter Marschalck, "German Emigration to the United States," in *Perspectives in American History,* V (Cambridge, MA: Harvard University Press, 1974), pp. 499-554.

7. Richard M. Bernard, *The Melting Pot and the Altar: Marital Assimilation in Early Twentieth Century Wisconsin* (Minneapolis: University of Minnesota Press, 1980). See also Stanley Nadel, *Little Germany.* German chain immigrants tended not just to marry other Germans but even to select marriage partners from the identical region or duchy in Germany.

8. June Holmquist, ed. *They Chose Minnesota: A Survey of the State's Ethnic Groups* (St. Paul: Minnesota Historical Society, 1981), pp. 229, 259, 279-80, 300-301. Also concerning the matter of transplantation from European village to American farm, see Jon Gjerde, *From Peasants to Farmers: The Migration from Balestrand, Norway to the Upper Middle West* (Cambridge: Cambridge University Press, 1985).

9. Hildegard Binder Johnson, "Intermarriages between German Pioneers and other Nationalities in Minnesota in 1860 and 1870," *The American Journal of Sociology,* 51 (January 1946), 299-304.

10. Heinz Kloss, "German-American Language Maintenance Efforts," in Joshua A. Fishman, ed. *Language Loyalty in the United States* (The Hague: Mouton, 1966), pp. 206-252.

11. I have dealt with this issue at some length in "Conflict in the Classroom: Anti-Germanism in Minnesota Schools, 1917- 1919," *Minnesota History,* 47 (Spring, 1981), 170-183, especially 175-176.

One

German-Bohemians:
Their Origins

HO WERE THE German-Bohemians? What was the historical situation out of which their culture developed? What regional politics resulted from the German-Czech duality?

Bohemia until 1919 was home to a politically shifting people who got their name from the Celtic tribe, the *Boii*. Although the Latin name of the country survives in German [*Böhmen*], the current Slavic inhabitants of the area call it in Czech [*Vechy*]. This more or less geographical and historical unit in central Europe is bounded on the south by Austria, on the west by the German state of Bavaria, on the north by the German state of Saxony and on the east by Polish (formerly German) Silesia.

Within the Czech Republic, Bohemia includes the former kingdom of Moravia. To a degree, mountain ranges shape natural boundaries on both the southwest [called *Böhmerwald*, the Bohemian Forest) and on the northwest [called the *Erzgebirge* , Iron Ore Mountains]. To the Northeast lie the Sudety Mountains, a range that has varying local names as the border weaves back and forth between Bohemia and Germany to the point where it meets the Moravian border. Called *Ceskomoravska Vysocina* (Bohemian-Moravian Hills), this modest mountain range separates the Bohemian from the Moravian basins, which explains the semi-independence of each territory throughout their common history. Bohemia and Moravia together formed the

Czech half, while Slovakia comprised the eastern half of the central European republic before the two agreed to split on January 1, 1993.

The Bohemian basin is drained by the Vltava (Moldau) river which empties into the Elbe and then the North Sea, putting Bohemia in a German watershed. Bohemia has always shown greater affinity toward the German sphere of influence. The Moravian basin drains south into the Danube, linking it geographically to Austria-Hungary. In Bohemia and Moravia the climate is temperate, ranging from an average of 68 degrees Fahrenheit in July to an average 29 degrees in January. Rainfall is adequate for most crops. The surrounding well-worn mountains are covered mostly with coniferous and some deciduous [especially beech] trees, and they contain deposits of coal, iron, copper, silver and other minerals.

Bohemia has a rich tradition of folk culture which varies from village to village and valley to valley, not to mention from one region to another. Folk tales, folk costumes, folk music and folk art are highly variable. Several creative artists have incorporated a folk idiom into their major works, notably the composers Antonin Dvorak, Bedrich Smetana, and Jaromir Weinberger. In architecture, Bohemia was deeply influenced by the baroque but has developed its own forms of glass, complicated patterns of embroidery and bobbin knitting.

Czech political history begins with rulers deriving from the mythical plowman Premysl, hence the Premslid dynasty which commenced in the ninth century. Its most famous representative was Duke Saint Wenceslaus [907-929].[1] Arriving from Constantinople in 863, two Greek brothers, Cyril and Methodius, preached in Slavic and translated the sacred books thus establishing what is known today as the Church Slavonic language. With Rome's approval, they set up a diocese, initiating the struggle between the Latin Germanic and Orthodox Slavic rites that has continued ever since. This age old tug of war between the Eastern and Western Churches is mirrored in the political arena where Western (German) Kaisers have maneuvered against Eastern (Russian) Tsars and the Red Army for spheres of influence. The resulting gerrymandering persisted through the Nazi annexation of the Sudetenland in the 1930s, the Stalinist occupation of 1948, and the Soviet re-invasion of 1968. The 1993 split between Bohemia and Slovakia mirrors this East [Slovaks] West [Czechs] dichotomy.

From 973 until the 13th century the Latin rite steadily gained strength as exemplified by the bishopric of Prague becoming subordinate to the Archbishop of Mainz in Germany, as well as by Bohemia uniting with Moravia in support of German Emperor Frederick I Barbarossa. This resulted in the Golden Bull of Frederick II in the year 1212, which normalized Bohemia as an autonomous unit within the Holy Roman Empire of the German Nation. In 1355, Prague became the brain center of the empire when Charles IV of the Luxemburg dynasty became Holy Roman Emperor.

During this era, German-speaking newcomers were encouraged to immigrate into Bohemia and found urban centers, especially under the Premyslid reign (circa 1200-1300) of Kings Ottokar and Wenceslaus. In greatest demand were skilled German craftsmen for silver mining, city administration, and rural land management. Also, larger estate owners and monastic institutions imported German managers to oversee their estates. Thus arose in Bohemia an urban and landed German-speaking middle class that acquired privileges more through savoir faire – the result more of their knowledge of German, the language of bureaucracy – than through colonial prerogative. Once in charge, German-speaking civil servants saw to it that additional farmers and artisans were imported from Germany. Often these newcomers amalgamated quickly with the local population. They also took up residences as peasants and townsfolk in the less attractive border districts, in a short time turning them into prosperous agricultural regions. During the latter 1200s, Bishop Bruno promoted extensive German colonization also in the Olmütz (Olomouc) region of northern Moravia, which the German settlers almost immediately renamed the province of Schönhengst.

These borderlands would give rise in the twentieth century to the term "Sudeten Germans," which once applied only to a northern Bohemian mountain range but became generic for the entire outer rim of Czechoslovakia as defined by the 1938 Munich accords reached between Hitler and the European allies.[2] Accordingly, the lands in which the German-speaking element was predominant were ceded by Czechoslovakia to Germany in what has come to be known as the Munich Pact of September 30, 1938. To the popular mind the annexation became synonymous with appeasement: Britain and France avoided war at the expense of the Czechoslovak Republic. Of the Sudeten territories acquired by the Third Reich, small sections were

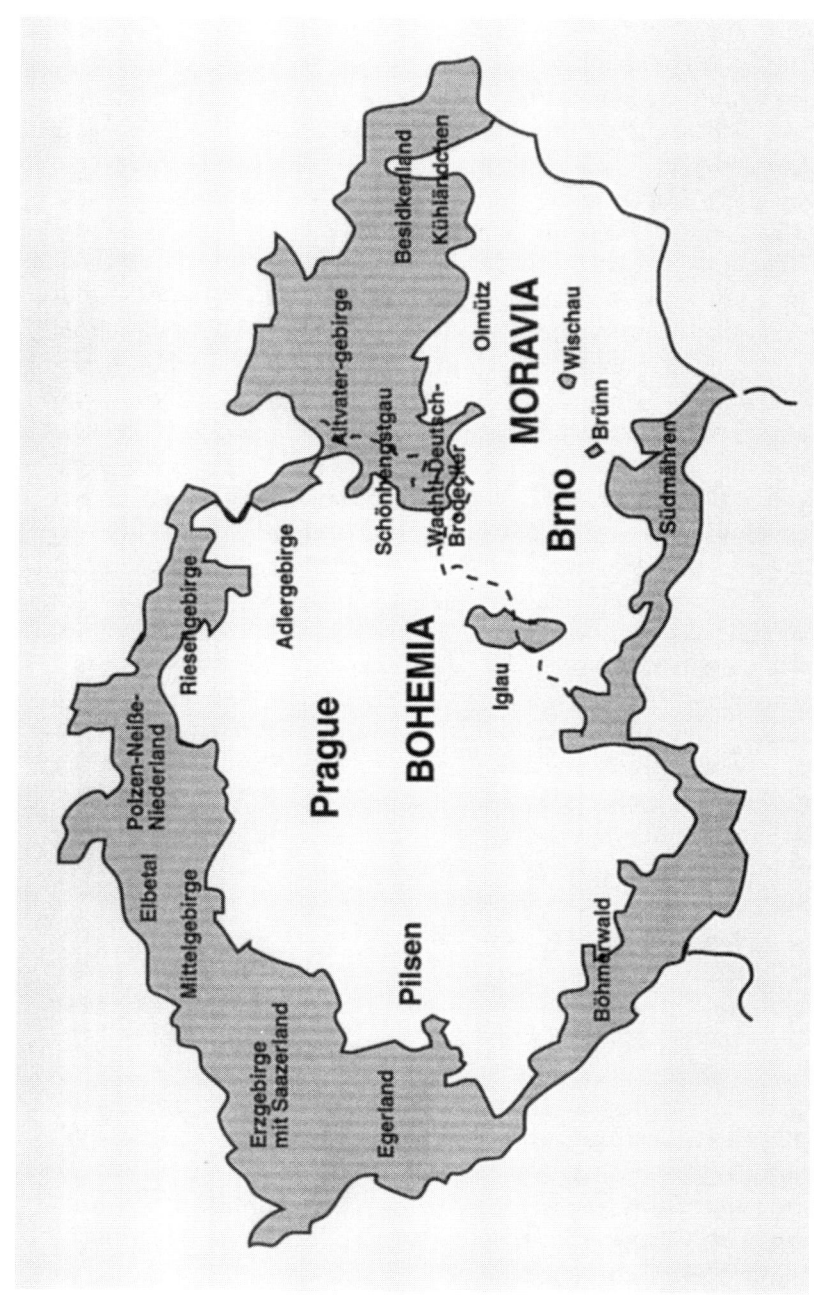

Political and language map of Bohemia and Moravia, since January 1, 1993 the Czech Republic. Note that the slightly shaded areas around the entire periphery designate the regions in which German was the dominant language spoken by the inhabitants. KM

added to Bavaria and the Ostmark (Austria) whereas the chief section was converted into the Reichsgau Sudetenland, with a population exceeding three million. The following March 1939 the thus-shrunken Bohemia became a protectorate of the Third Reich until 1945. The roots of this 1938 annexation and the 1946 expulsion of German speakers from the area lie buried deep in Central European history.

Following the Premyslid dynasty came the golden age of the Luxemburg emperors (c.1300-1400), during which German scholars, artisans and architects of the Gothic style came to Prague where they left their distinguishing mark. Bohemia at the time witnessed the initial cross currents of religious reform. Lax and corrupt church and civil authorities occasioned growing antagonisms between the King and the archbishop of Prague. The rights of vernacular language speakers became one of the earliest and most persistent bones of contention between the Germans and the Bohemians – one that would last throughout their next 800 year of co-existence.[3] The religious reform movement in Bohemia took a dramatic leap forward in 1402 when Czech nationalist Jan Hus was appointed to the Prague pulpit. Hus quickly rallied the Czech-speaking masses and successfully attracted academic supporters to his reform. John Wycliffe, an English reformer among the Czech masters, joined with Hus, triggering a reaction from German members of the local university who won support from Czech conservative prelates led by the bishop of Litomysl. For this bishop's role in Czech history, the name Litomysl became symbolic among immigrants to the United States. In Minnesota, Litomysl is the name for the Czech community south of Owatonna in Steele County.[4]

For over a decade in the early 1400s, Czechs feuded with Germans who campaigned vigorously against Hus until they officially succeeded in banning his sermons. Because Hus nevertheless inveighed against the policy of Pope John XXIII to grant indulgences for contributions to the papal treasury, he was burned at the stake on July 6, 1415. Rather than extinguishing the Hussite heresy it spread like a populist conflagration through the Czech-speaking population of Bohemia arousing the antagonism of Germans who clung tenaciously to both the Holy Roman emperor and the pope, thereby heightening local ethnic-linguistic strife. During the decades that followed, there were periodic invasions by German princes with support from the papacy or the emperor. Most Germans were easily expelled by the Hussites who were now united in both religion and language against their "external" foe. In due course, the reformers established a rallying center which they gave the biblical name of Tabor, with the result that for the next fifty years, Prague (German) stood against Tabor (Czech). In the exhausting struggle that ensued, both political and religious power slipped from the Holy Roman emperor and the Catholic bishop to the local lords, knights, and rural borough chiefs. In succeeding periods of intrigue, papal rulers, German kings, Hungarian princes and royal Poles all sought to extend their influence into a fractured Bohemia.

In 1517 a new threat to religious tolerance in Bohemia arose in Germany when Martin Luther posted his 95 theses in the town of Wittenberg, proving within a few short years that he was no ordinary heretic. The king of Bohemia at this time was Ferdinand I of Habsburg, a profoundly Catholic monarch, whose brother, Charles V (of Austria and Spain), did battle for the empire and the church. Lutheranism nevertheless found adherents both among the Unity of Czech Protestant Brethren as well as among German-speaking inhabitants of Bohemia. In an effort to subdue the Lutheran elements in his domain, Ferdinand in 1556 introduced the Society of Jesus (Jesuits) into Bohemia. When his son Maximilian succeeded Ferdinand in 1564, the Catholic Habsburgs came under siege from both the Czech Hussites and the German Lutherans. In 1576 Maximilian passed the scepter to his son Rudolf who, in a bold move to re-establish stability, transferred the court from Vienna to Prague.[5]

Raised in Spain and staunchly Catholic, Rudolf (1576-1612) with support of the Jesuits, prosecuted the Counter-Reformation in Bohemia. However, the Unity by this time had already produced a Czech language translation of the bible and thus Rudolf decided to grant freedom of worship to the Bohemian Unity of the Brethren. The agreement was a model of religious cooperation – differences were to be settled by negotiation rather than by measures taken on the battlefield. However, it portrayed Rudolf as a weak ruler who was soon deposed by rivals for the throne. Ferdinand of Styria (Austria) succeeded him and in 1618 accused a Protestant faction of violating the *Majestät* agreement. When Ferdinand put two local Czech governors on trial, then had them thrown from a window of the Royal Chancellery (May 23, 1618), he gave currency to the phrase, "Defenestration of Prague," the incident which sparked a rebellion in Bohemia that resulted in the horrendous Thirty-Years War.[6]

During three succeeding decades of conflict, the Habsburgs imposed penalties, executed lords and burghers and confiscated Czech lands. The *Majestät* accords were rescinded and the 1618 ban on the Jesuits lifted so they could triumphantly spearhead re-Catholicization. Among legislative initiatives taken, Habsburg Emperor Ferdinand II reduced the power of the diet, took to himself the right to admit foreigners to permanent residency status (which favored the importation of more German-speaking settlers), and re-instated German to equal status with the Czech language, while forbidding all religions but Catholicism. Non-Catholic nobles were given a choice of converting or emigrating, many of whom chose the latter, moving in droves to German Saxony, a few kilometers to the north.

Peasants did not have the same choice! Many left illegally especially when invading Protestant armies gave them the opportunity. When the Jesuits assumed control of literary and cultural life, to their credit, they recruited Czech speakers, thus providing for the religious needs of the masses in both German and Czech. Nevertheless, German became the accepted language for civil affairs and in that respect the language of class, thus elevating the privileged German speakers above the lower class peasants. Because the official language of the province was their mother tongue, the Germans also got a better chance at commerce and trade. During this period, too, lands vacated by fleeing Protestant lords and peasants were claimed by German-speaking newcomers, some of whom acquired land for services rendered to the dynasty.

During the second half of the 17th century, Leopold I (1657-1705) became distracted from Bohemia by wars against the Turks and the French. Under Charles VI (1711-1740) in the 18th century, money was needed to wage foreign wars and to support the aristocracy – also, to the neglect of Bohemia. Charles' daughter, Maria Theresia (1740-1780) initiated reforms to lighten the burden on Bohemian peasants but was invaded by Bavaria and Prussia – wars fought on Bohemian territory at the expense of the local population, resulting in the surrender of Silesia to Frederick II (the Great) of Prussia. Maria Theresia's son Joseph II, an enlightened despot, issued decrees in 1781 to

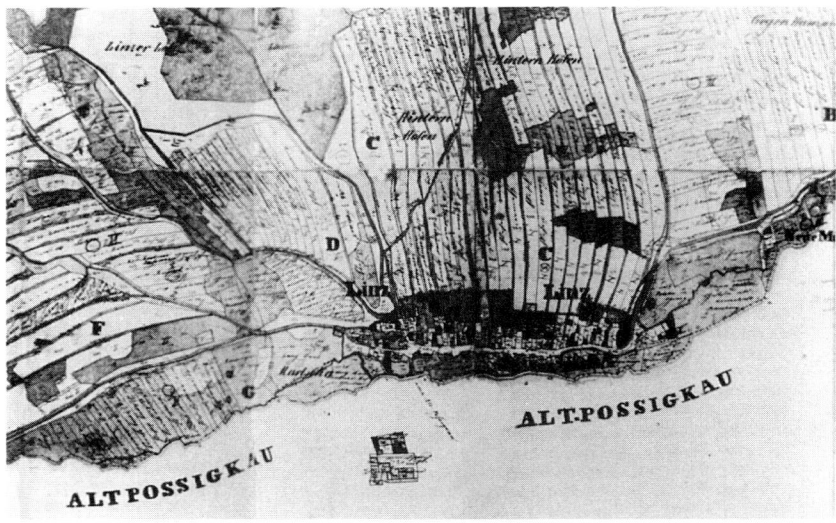

Field maps showing the complicated breakdown of 1838 farm fields in the Linz [Bohemia] region with the village of Alt-Possigkau. A farmer might own two or three acre pieces in all four directions from his farm yard inside the village, thus rendering farming, pasturing, and harvesting difficult if not sometimes uneconomical. LB

improve the lot of the masses, abolish restrictions on the peasants and grant sweeping religious toleration. His initiatives were accepted by his successors, Francis I (1792-1835) and Ferdinand V (1835-1848) who promoted the transition from a manorial to direct peasant ownership of the land.[7] All of these rulers contributed in one way or another to the conditions that made Bohemia ripe for emigration in the latter half of the 19th century. While oppression and neglect generated the "need" to leave, tolerance in religious and land questions eventually "enabled" the peasantry to depart. Economic factors following 1848 likewise encouraged emigration.

Prior to the 1848 liberation of the peasants [about which more a few paragraphs farther on], Bohemian serfs operated at the pleasure of their lords – renting land for cash or in kind payments and performing labor service, known as *robota* in Czech and *Frondienst* in German. Actually the lords preferred cash income from their lands. Ready cash in place of the "in kind" consignment of grain and animals enabled them to live in towns and at royal courts where they enjoyed cultural and political advantage. However, there were periods when agricultural demands arose, and when the wants of the lords increased, thus making the demand of *robota* a fluctuating phenomenon. Always the burden for *robota* had to be honored before a serf was free to devote labor to his own crops.

An understanding of this complicated economic arrangement for the Bohemian peasants explains why in the latter half of the 19th century so many emigrated. There were two categories of peasant land holders, the rusticals and the dominicals, the former on registered peasant-occupied land and the latter on acreage capriciously rented to serfs on a temporary basis. Most peasants in Bohemia were rusticals. They were *Eingekäufter*, peasants who had bought into the land. The dominical servant merely occupied *Hofland*, strictly the property of the lord, for which a peasant contracted three to six years at a time. Also, there were subcategories for the peasant, *Ganzbauer* (full peasant), *Häusler* (cottage industries) and *Tagelöhner* (day laborers). Serfs were bound to the land and none enjoyed much status or many rights before the law. Neighboring countries had reciprocity laws which forbad fugitive serfs refuge in their territory. Thus, until the enlightenment brought relief, the serf in the crown lands of Bohemia did not enjoy much freedom. His rights were few, his tax burden high, and while he could not be bought and sold like a slave, his obligations to the lord were not substantially less than for a man with slave status.

Robota would cease altogether according to a plan advanced by Franz Anton von Raab and put into effect on an experimental basis in 1775 on two estates which had been acquired by the government from the Jesuits when they were disbanded in Austria two years earlier. A clandestine intent of the Raab plan was to restock the population of Bohemia with German immigrants, which had been decimated by the Thirty Years War. Both Saxons and Prussians arrived in large numbers, intensifying the age-old problem of mixing German-speakers into the Bohemian society.

The Raab experiment called for the elimination of *Leibeigenschaft* (the equivalent of American slavery) according to which a serf was attached by heredity and chattel laws to a specific land owner without compensation. The peasant would now become an *Erbpächter*, a leaseholder of the land with the right to mortgage, bequeath, or sell it. The lord, on the other hand, continued to pay the taxes out of rental fees and retained the authority to force the peasant to till his land. Peasants received title to the buildings, animals and other improvements but had to make installment payments over a maximum period of ten years. *Robota* all but disappeared except as required by local governments that levied taxes on peasants for the rural infrastructure: roads, bridges and ponds. Serfs now could marry without their lord's approval, could transfer their domicile from one estate to another, were permitted to learn trades and could seek employment as their talents allowed. On the one hand, this improvement now made it more possible for peasants to emigrate to North America. However, the net result was not total freedom because without satisfying obligations to seigniorial authorities, peasants were not granted "passport" certificates without which a freed serf could not obtain a new residence permit anywhere in the realm.

Ten years and more into the plan, there were still hundreds of disputes, including petitions from peasants who doubted whether they were really any better off under the Raab plan than they had been under *robota*. Their incomes hardly improved, while their responsibility increased considerably. They quibbled over receiving tracts of land that were too small, occasioned sometimes by poor surveying systems rather than outright bad will, or having to pay fees and rents they felt were too high. Sometimes complaints arose because soldiers were quartered locally and because the military requisitioned horses or supplies without paying for them. Fees based on the quality of land, some hilly, some level, some rich, some exhausted, were not adequately differentiated. Sometimes newly imported settlers (often Germans) got three to five years of farming *gratis* before needing to pay rent. Naturally, indigenous Czech peasants resented favors to Germans. Despite difficulties encountered in the introduction of the new system, it was a success.[8]

As always, Austria was at war with the Turks whereas Prussia made friendly overtures to these perennial invaders. In Bohemia, the Napoleonic era [1800-1815] was in many respects not the destructive burden that raged elsewhere, nor was it a force for great liberation. Joseph II's successors [Leopold II 1790-92, Francis I 1792-1835 and Ferdinand V 1835-1848] retained the centralized administrative system they inherited from Maria Theresia and Joseph II, continuing the transition from manorial to peasant ownership of the land. This meant the emperors managed to come to terms with the landowning nobility who, to their credit, preserved in their roles as patrons of learning, art, theater, music and better methods in agriculture.

Although these institutions operated bilingually in both German and in Czech, the Germans always seemed to dominate, a phenomenon that gave rise to jealousies and to Czech nationalism which in turn nourished feelings of Czech kinship to other Slavic peoples. German-speakers in Bohemia continued to hold the advantage over the Czechs in terms not only of ownership of property, ability and success in the trades, but also by way of connections to the government, access to education and a host of related fields of enterprise. Making matters worse during the repressive Metternich era [1815 to 1848], the crown severely limited political activity on the part of Czech speakers. The repression had the effect of awakening vibrant stirrings of Czech nationalism – yearnings for freedom from kings and from German upper classmen. Led by educated Czech writers and cultural leaders, the mostly-spoken Czech language from about 1840 onward, developed into a literary tool which gradually evolved into a rallying device for the youthful Czech spirit. All of this in its own often-misunderstood way contributed to creating an atmosphere that "pushed" emigrants from the realm.

In the years leading up to the revolutionary year of 1848, the German intelligentsia in Bohemia, believing they had common cause with the Slavic Czechs (liberation from Metternich),wrote histories of the Bohemian nationalistic past and promoted it as a device to free both ethnic groups from imperial authority. Published in German, the histories had the unanticipated effect of heightening Bohemian pride in their anti-German past: White Mountain, the Hussite wars, and the long domination of Bohemia by the Habsburgs. When the 1848 revolutions for democratic rule erupted across Europe, the Germans in Bohemia felt a strong affinity for their brothers at the Frankfurt assembly who dreamed of a united Germany to which all German speakers would belong. The Czechs, however, had other ideas that included liberation from German-speaking Vienna. Building from feelings of triumph generated by what they perceived to be the defeat of Napoleon by the Slavs (the Russians in particular), the Czechs by 1848 sensed that they could excise foreign (German) influence from their territory.

Although Joseph II had granted Bohemian peasants personal freedom, the right to move about, to marry without regard for their lords and to study, he was unable to liberate them totally. In a Parliament meeting in Vienna in mid-1848, a Silesian German named Hans Kudlich demanded the complete emancipation of the peasantry with the result that all Austrian peasants were freed from the vestiges of *robota*.[9] But they still either had to buy the ground in installments that equaled the approximate amounts of the former annual rent, or to give up a portion of the lands they commanded by earlier law in order to meet their debt obligations. This meant that the large landowners were rather well compensated, an outcome that was not positive for peasants. The more established got the chance to own their land but these financially stronger peasants soon behaved like miniature lords. They were now in a position to take advantage of the poorer serfs who under the new policies lost protection from their patriarchal barons. Poorer peasants were accordingly persuaded to leave the land and find work in industry or, just as likely, to emigrate.[10]

Reactionary powers eventually forced Hans Kudlich to flee to America, which fueled Czech nationalism among prosperous farmers with medium sized land holdings. In the meantime, new crops developed, especially sugar-beet cultivation and similar commodities fostered by farm economy associations that preached the use of selective breeding and improved methods for agriculture. On the model of these self-improvement agricultural societies, mutual aid organizations sprang up for Czech craftsmen and small businessmen, often with a pro-Czech and anti-German spirit of nationalism evoked to rid Bohemia of what the Czechs called "alien economic forces." To a degree this meant that the lower class German peasant had a more difficult time than the Czech speaker to leave the rural lands for the cities where industrial jobs were available to former serfs. In this predicament, emigration was an increasingly appealing option for the German-speaking peasant who by going to America could retain his agricultural way of life – if not his native homeland.

German leaders in Bohemia wanted to send delegates to the Frankfurt assembly. The Czechs, however, led by their heroes, Frantisek Palacky, the historian author of *A History of the Czech People*, along with his assistant, along with the journalist, Karel Havlicek Borovsky, and their student political scientist, Frantisek Rieger saw in the Frankfurt assembly not the liberal government that it promised but only a modernized Pan-German (*Grossdeutsch*) replacement in Bohemia for the old pattern of central control epitomized by Austrian Vienna. The Bohemian Germans in turn saw in the Palacky Czech plans the absolutist Pan-Slavism symbolized by the Russian czar. Karel Havlicek Borovsky died early. Palacky lived until 1876, while his disciple and son-in-law, Rieger, held sway among the Czechs until the end of the century. The influence these three pacesetters exerted was strengthened after 1859 when Austria's army did poorly in a war with Sardinia. The battlefield outcome diminished Vienna's power in the Bohemian crown colony and caused an economic depression that swept across all Austrian provinces. Palacky and Rieger meanwhile kept pressing for local Czech domination while the ethnic Germans in Bohemia saw ever more clearly that their fate lay more with the Austrian central government than with the outcome portended by the Czech triumvirate.

When Austria lost the war with Prussia over the duchies of Schleswig-Holstein in 1864, Bismarck quickly orchestrated yet another chance to humiliate the aging Austrian empire. His chance came on July 3, 1866 at Sadova (Königgrätz) when the Prussians resoundingly defeated the Austrian army due to three advantages they enjoyed: by their use of new weapons, by an ingenious use of the railroad to deploy troops and war materiel, and by superior strategy. Within a year, Austria compromised to frame the new constitution of 1867 which established the dual monarchy with Hungary. Bohemia, however, did not gain co-equal status, remaining instead a subject of Austria. Meanwhile in Prussia, Bismarck tried to persuade the Czechs to declare their independence and join Germany, but without success. Rieger wanted to retain Viennese control, declaring in 1866 "We wish to preserve the Empire, for we see in its existence the guarantee of our national existence and that of other small nations which it embraces."[11]

Dispossessed of its Italian provinces, Austria retained its German hegemony over a majority Slavic population. Although Rieger and others sought to reorganize the historic provinces into a loose federation under Vienna, they did so more out of fear of Prussia and Russia than out of a genuine belief that a common state was viable. The Germans in Bohemia naturally perceived their destiny to lie more with the Germans across the borders in Saxony and Bavaria, and less with the weak Austrian monarchy in Vienna. Modest hope for people living in

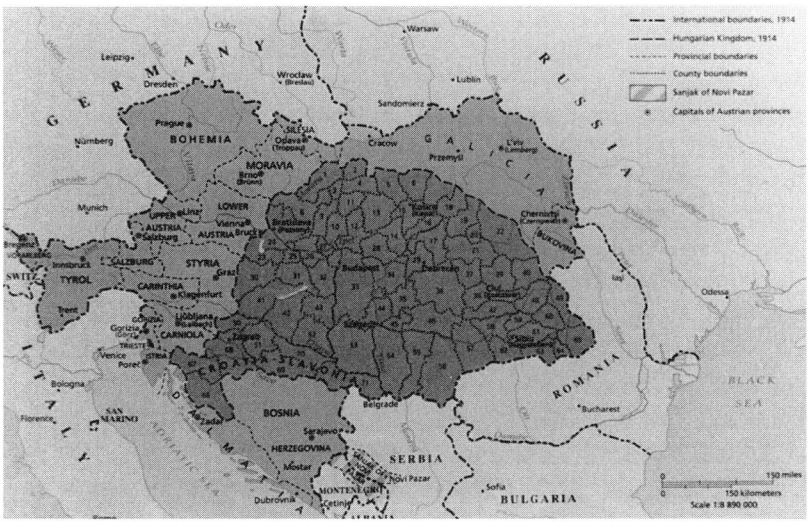

The Austro-Hungarian Empire with its named and numbered subdivisions as it existed from the time of the dual-monarchy compromise of 1867, by which Austria and Hungary unified, and the year 1914 when World War I erupted in Sarajevo, the capital of Bosnia-Herzegovina.

the crown provinces was signalled by the dual monarchy's decentralization from Vienna. Perhaps it was these expectations that enabled the 1867 compromise to last until the 1918 conclusion of World War I, when the emperor abdicated, following which the dual monarchy was parceled up by Versailles treaty makers. To New World immigration authorities, meanwhile, German-speaking Bohemian emigrants often declared themselves "Germans," illustrating the mental transfer about nationality that had already taken place.

Through it all, the lands of Bohemia and Moravia harbored innumerable grounds for discontent. Although the emperor in Vienna was still the King of Bohemia in name, the Czechs vehemently asserted separate national consciousness. Rieger and Palacky traveled to Russia, Poland and France to plead their cause while France's Napoleon III made injudicious overtures to the Czechs. But when Napoleon III was resoundingly humiliated at Sedan in the 1870 war resulting in Prussia crowning King Wilhelm I Kaiser for all of Germany, the Austrians timidly appeased the Bohemians in hopes of detering them from making an alliance with the Kaiser. Viennese concessions included language rights to the Germans in Bohemia, preference for German speakers over Czechs in civil service positions or the army, and concessions to the Czech majority by permitting the use of Czech in court and civil service matters. Rather than abating anti-German sentiment, however, these compromises further ignited feelings of Czech nationalism.[12]

Depleted both by emigration and by industrialization, the German peasant population living on the poorer soils of the Bohemian periphery became less and less successful. Increasingly, these German-speakers shifted either as laborers to the industrial centers of imperial Germany or as immigrant farmers to the United States. In the farming regions of Bohemia where the Germans still were in the majority, Czech craftsmen and shopkeepers moved into the formerly all-German towns to operate the small businesses. However, until the close of the century the impression still held sway that the Germans were in charge and that they were the employers of the Czech working man. Feeling superior and confident about the German language as a prerequisite for commerce, the Germans naturally insisted on schools where German would remain the language which they believed Czechs would be only too grateful to learn.

All through the latter half of the nineteenth century, Czech speakers struggled to gain the upper hand. In 1881 a national Czech theater opened in Prague. In 1882 the University of Prague separated into German and Czech branches when the philosopher-politician Thomas Masaryk returned as a professor from Vienna to Prague. In music, distinctly Czech styles grew to maturity in the works of Bedrich Smetana and Antonin Dvorak. Both composers gained world renown for their ability to identify and incorporate Czech folklore and folksongs into operatic and symphonic compositions.[13] Both composers embodied in their music what a contemporary Czech novelist exemplifies in his novel:

> All nations have their popular art. But for the most part it can be distinguished from their culture without much difficulty. Every western European nation has had an unbroken cultural development, at least since the Middle Ages. Whereas in the 17th and 18th centuries the

Czech nation almost ceased to exist, in the 19th century it was virtually reborn. Among the older European nations it was a child. It had its past, and rich culture too, but these were separated from it by an abyss of 200 years during which neither nobleman nor burgher had spoken Czech. The Czech language retreated from the towns to the country-side and became the exclusive property of the illiterate. Among them, however, it never ceased to continue creating its own culture – a humble culture, completely hidden from the eyes of Europe. A culture of songs, fairy tales, ancient rites and customs, proverbs and sayings. And this was the only narrow bridge which spanned the 200 year gulf. The only bridge, the only crossing point. And so the men who at the turn of the 19th century began to create a new Czech literature and music grafted it upon this existing culture. That was why the first Czech poets and musicians spent so much time collecting fairy tales and songs. That's why their early poetic and musical efforts were often only a paraphrase of folk poetry and folk melodies.[14]

What Kundera articulates in his novel, Dvorak exemplifies in his music. At Spillville, Iowa he worked American folksongs into his "New World Symphony" for the rest of posterity to contemplate, reminding us that youthful America, like Bohemia, relied on the power of the folk in the formation of a culture for the new nation. Building on national pride in folk culture, the Czech language in a wellspring of Czech nationalism forced its way through the German upper-class.

On the opposite side of this Czech coin raged the likes of Georg von Schönerer, a *Waldviertel* Pan-Germanist who in the post-1871 period wanted all Austrian German-speakers to free themselves from Habsburg emperors and unite with the glorious empire of the Hohenzollerns in Berlin.[15] In his proposal for *Anschluss* with imperial Germany, Schönerer included all lands formerly held in the German Confederation, which encompassed all of Bohemia and Moravia. Openly condemning the Habsburgs, Schönerer denounced the Jewish Rothschild, vituperated the Holy See as an ally of the Slavs, glorified the Protestant Kaiser in Berlin and would have fully Germanized the Czechs and the Moravians.

Because there were too few German candidates for the priesthood in Habsburg Austria in the latter half of the 19th century, the Austrian clergy was constituted largely of Slavic clerics who, in Schönerer's

Alexander Berghold, author of a volume The Indians' Revenge *(San Francisco, 1891), about the Sioux uprising in New Ulm, and for twenty years pastor of Holy Trinity parish in New Ulm, from its beginning until the 1890s. BC*

opinion, de-Germanized members of their parishes. In fact, quite the opposite was true. In both the Old World and the New, Slavic pastors curried the loyalty of German Catholics.[16] The Schönerer master plan suggested that Slavs (whether German-speaking or not) would have no place in a Germanic Europe. Conveniently Schönerer triumphed with the 1879 alliance between the dual monarchy and imperial Germany, which left to Hungarian influence the provinces of Dalmatia, Bosnia, Hercegovina, Galicia and Bukovina. To the Austrian sphere of influence belonged the German-speaking territory between Germany and the Adriatic Sea as well as Bohemia and Moravia. This bloc Schönerer sought to incorporate into a Middle European customs union in which the German language would hold sway under the slogan "durch Reinheit zur Einheit" (through purity to unity), which Schönerer's enemies quickly twisted into "durch Reinheit zur Kleinheit" (through purity to pettiness).[17]

Many Germans in Bohemia responded to the calls of Schönerer, especially the vigorous Egerländer, who became champions of Pan-Germanism. For a time, Schönerer even served as a deputy from the Eger region of Bohemia to the Berlin government. By 1890, however, the Germans gave way on the minority schools question, allowing the Czech tongue in school if there were at least forty children requesting instruction in Czech and if their families had lived in that school district for at least five years. The German-Czech rivalry reached a climax in 1897 when Count Kazimierz Badeni offered a compromise providing for wider use of Czech in Bohemian civil affairs and in the courts.[18] These proposals, however, met with student riots in the streets of Vienna followed by demonstrations in the German-speaking towns of Bohemia, and the eventual pillage of German and German-Jewish schools, theaters, businesses and dozens of residences in Prague. Faced with sending in the military Badeni abdicated with the result that his dream of a cooperative bilingual nation of Bohemia had vanished.

German and Czech parties continued their annual discontent until the year 1906 when it was hoped that universal manhood suffrage would solve the problem. But even with suffrage, the situation became ever more hopeless until Austrian emperor Franz Joseph was himself called upon to decide awkward ethnic questions. In the process, the Austrian empire with its impossible-to-govern territory of Bohemia slipped backward, blundering hopelessly toward the First World War, a calamity that would end the for all time the precarious German-Bohemian arrangement. The First World War also concluded nearly a half century of German-speaking emigration from Bohemia to Brown county, Minnesota, the story of the succeeding chapters.

Notes

1. The *Brittannica Macropedia* 1987, Vol. 16 pp. 955 ff. gives a fine historical overview plus a full page of bibliography, from which comes the information here and below.

2. Among many sources, see Dr. Fritz Machatschek, *Landeskunde der Sudeten- und West Karpatenländer* (Stuttgart: J. Engelhorns, 1927) and Rudolf Urban, *Die Sudeten-Deutschen Gebiete nach 1945* (Frankfurt & Berlin: Alfred Metzner, 1964), with a packet of maps. Concerning the period under German control from the occupier's perspective, see Friedrich Heiss, *Das Böhmen and Mähren-Buch. Volkskampf und Reichsraum* (Berlin: Volk und Reich Verlag Prag, 1943).

3. Samuel Harrison Thomson, *Czechoslovakia in European History* (Hamden, CT:

Archon Books, 1965) supplies good general information on the period. Excellent maps of Bohemia's historical development are available in Robert Magocsi, *Historical Atlas of East Central Europe* (Seattle: University of Washington Press, 1994).

4. Litomysl has deep significance for Czechs in the United States and in Minnesota, as exemplified by the several parishes (and communities) that bear this name. See in general Milan W. Jerabeck, "Czechs in Minnesota," M.A. Thesis University of Minnesota, 1939 and C. Winston Chrislock, "The Czechs," in *They Chose Minnesota*, ed. June Drenning Holmquist (St. Paul: Minnesota Historical Society, 1981), pp. 335-351. Both have extensive bibliographies.

5. Here and below see the useful books Adam Wandruszka, *The House of Habsburg. Six Hundred Years of European Dynasty* (New York: Doubleday, 1964), Robert A. Kann, *A History of the Habsburg Empire 1526-1918* (Berkeley: University of California Press, 1974) with its fine bibliographical essay and index, H.G. Koenigsberger, *The Habsburgs and Europe 1516-1660* (Ithaca: Cornell University Press, 1971) and especially Victor L. Tapie, *The Rise and Fall of the Habsburg Monarchy*, tr. Stephen Hardman (New York: Praeger, 1971).

6. The situation was complicated from the outset because an elector from the Rhine Palatinate in western Germany was appointed king of Bohemia, who however, was a son-in-law of King James I of England. Named Frederick V, he received financial help from the Netherlands but otherwise the German Protestant potentates resisted becoming involved because both Lutheran Saxony and Catholic Bavaria were allied to the Habsburgs in Austria, who claimed the right to the Bohemian throne. Maximilian I of Bavaria, therefore, led the Catholic forces at the gates of Prague in the famous Battle of White Mountain (November 8, 1620), deposing Frederick and installing Ferdinand II of Habsburg who together with his successor Ferdinand III ruled until 1657.

7. This process is described in detail by William E. Wright, *Serf, Seigneur, and Sovereign. Agrarian Reform in Eighteenth-century Bohemia* (Minneapolis: University of Minnesota Press,1966). Ample bibliography. See also Jerome Blum, *Noble Landowners and Agriculture in Austria, 1815-1848. A Study in the Origins of the Peasant Emancipation of 1848* (Baltimore: The Johns Hopkins Press, 1948), esp. pp. 68 ff. 145 ff. and 171 ff.

8. Wright, ibid., p. 128. The transition was successful, especially if one looks at the increases in livestock as reported in the annual censuses for Bohemia from 1778-1793. Total horses stayed about the same at an average of 150,000 but cows increased in numbers from 560,000 to 805,000 and oxen (presumably including steers) multiplied from 262,000 to 376,000. For a discussion of the applicable wage rates in the various provinces of the Austrian empire, see Blum, ibid., pp. 188 ff.

9. Among many sources see Elizabeth Wiskemann, *Czechs and Germans. A Study of the Struggle in the Historic Provinces of Bohemia and Moravia* (New York: Oxford University Press, 1938), p. 20. See also Gary B. Cohen, *The Politics of Ethnic Survival:Germans in Prague, 1861-1914* (Princeton: Princeton University Press, 1981), and in general Cynthia H. Enloe, *Ethnic Conflict and Political Development* (Boston: Little, Brown, 1973); Suzanne G. Konirsch, "Constitutional Aspects of the Struggle Between Germans and Czechs in the Austro-Hungarian Monarch," *Journal of Modern History*, 27 (1955), 231-261; Stanley Z. Pech, *The Czech Revolution of 1848* (Chapel Hill: University of North Carolina, 1969); and Harrison S. Thompson, "Czech and German: Action, Reaction, and Interaction," *Journal of Central European Affairs*, 1 (1941), 306-323.

10. Cohen, pp. 39 ff. See also Edward Peterson, "Cherma's Origins in the Old Country," *Pierce County's (Wisconsin) Heritage*, 7 (1980), 29 ff. Most of the volume's 157 pages are dedicated to the Czech Bohemians in Pierce county.

11. Victor L. Tapie, *The Rise and Fall of the Habsburg Monarchy*, trans. Stephen Hardman (New York: Praeger, 1971), p. 305 ff.

12. Wiskemann, p. 38 ff.

13. See Brian Large, *Smetana* (New York: Praeger, 1970), Hans-Hubert Schonzeler, *Dvorak* (New York: Scribners, 1984) and Patricia Hampl, *Spillville* (Minneapolis: Milkweed editions, 1987).

14. Milan Kundera, *The Joke*, quoted in Patricia Hampl, *A Romantic Education* (Boston: Houghton Mifflin, 1981), pp. 229-230.

15. Tapie, p. 338.

16. In New Ulm and other parishes in the greater Archdiocese of St. Paul, it was well known that Archbishop John Ireland recruited Slavic (rather than German-born) priests to administer to the German-speaking members of his fold. Early in its program the St. Paul diocese was served by Father Francis Pierz who recruited many Slavic German-speaking priests for Minnesota, among them Father Alexander Berghold who served New Ulm and its German-speaking Bohemian immigrants for over twenty years. See Sister Grace McDonald, "Father Francis Pierz, Missionary, *Minnesota History*, 10 (1919), 107-125 and LaVern J. Rippley, "Alexander Berghold, Pioneer Priest and Prairie Poet," *The Report:* A Journal of German-American History, Society for the History of the Germans in Maryland, 37 (1978), 43-56; ibid., "Archbishop Ireland and the School Language Controversy," *U.S. Catholic Historian,* 1 (1980), 1-16.

17. Wiskeman, *Czechs and Germans,* p. 41 ff.

18. Cohen, *The Politics of Ethnic Survival*, p. 238 ff.

Two

German-Bohemians Settle in Brown County

THE GERMANS IN BOHEMIA, like their Slavic ethnic neighbors the Czechs, did not join the emigrant stream from the European heartland until after the 1848 revolutions.[1] By the year 1910, however, the United States Census counted almost 540,000 foreign-born and second-generation Czechs in America. Of these over 33,000 lived in Minnesota, which ranked seventh from the top among the states with Czech populations, behind Illinois, Nebraska, Ohio, New York, Wisconsin and Texas.[2] Although there is no way to confirm the percentage, many of these "statistical" Czechs were German-speaking. Writers who treat the Czechs usually separate out the Slovaks, but tend to assume that all immigrants listed in the census reports as coming from the geographic region of Bohemia were Czech-speaking and thus they ignore the Germans. By the converse, authors who focus on German-speakers tend to concentrate on emigrants who were German by nationality. That is, if the time focus is on pre-World War I immigration, then the presumption is that the people speaking German came from within the geographic boundaries of the Pre-World War I German Reich. But if the time frame is post-World War II, then only the boundaries of divided and after 1990 the reunited Germany become the target of investigation for contemporary German-Americans.[3] For example, the German Interest Group of the Minnesota Genealogical Society, following the unification of Germany in 1991, debated in its publications what its new logo should be and settled on a map of the new Federal Republic of Germany. The re-united Germany with its newly acquired five states captures the imagination to the disregard of any reference to the many trans-border lands in which German-speaking Americans in the late 20th century would need to seek for their genealogies.[4]

Scholars and genealogists in North America have a tendency to forget that the "melting pot" was never quite as successful on the European side of the Atlantic as it was in the United States. Often in Europe, however, there was voluntary assimilation. Frequently also there was forced Germanicization, Polonization, Magyarization or other measures for the incorporation of one ethnic group by another. The question of who absorbed whom was often decided by which was the majority. Frequently as well, what mattered was which economic power determined the social status of one group over another. Or perhaps a more sophisticated culture was what determined the final outcome. Sometimes, therefore, it was easier for a higher-status minority [like the Germans in Bohemia] to persist while the lower-status minority or even majority, as discussed in the previous chapter, languished.

When the opportunity to emigrate from Bohemia came, however, there was little German-Czech hostility based on ethnicity between the emigrants themselves. Czechs who arrived in America almost simultaneously with Germans often settled close to them. Routinely they were economically involved with the Germans, much as they had lived and worked side-by-side in the old homeland.[5] In the early 1850s, emigration from the western region of Bohemia still amounted to a trickle because various factors inhibited a rapid exodus. Passports were costly and difficult to obtain, and unlike in Germany, the borders were patrolled. Austria did not automatically permit emigration the way Germany did. Only after the *Ausgleich* [the Austro-Hungary compromise union of 1867] was emigration officially conceded. As a matter of fact, not until near the end of the 19th century was the right to emigrate universally accepted in Europe as a whole, and even then restraints continued in Russia and Turkey.[6]

Even though conditions varied from province to province, it was especially the breakup of feudal laws, which transformed the peasant into a free proprietor, that caused emigration. Once emancipated peasants acquired the right to subdivide their land, they slivered it up into agricultural parcels that soon became incapable of supporting the families who depended on them. Emigration became the best escape. Once it got under way, it was sustained by the common fever that "everyone was leaving," and was intensified by return letters from relatives who had already crossed the Atlantic. Sustained by these trusted letters of information about economic prospects in the New World, Czech- and German-speaking emigrants during the 1850s began settling first in Wisconsin, in Milwaukee, Sheboygan, Kewaunee and later Pierce counties.[7]

Soon they were coming also to Minnesota. Then usually called Bohemians, Czechs [the preferred term only since the formation of the Czechoslovak Republic in 1919] arrived soon after the opening of settlement to whites in Minnesota, made possible treaties with the Indians in 1852. By the mid-1850s, Czech settlements had appeared in four basic areas – the Lake Minnetonka-Hopkins region of western Hennepin county, the Steele county rural area south of Owatonna, a large pocket spread over many acres in LeSueur, Scott and Rice counties stretching from New Prague in the north to Veseli and Montgomery farther east and south, and lastly near Chatfield in Filmore county. Czech settlements developed later in McLeod county at Silver Lake, Hutchinson and Glencoe. Soon they also appeared in Freeborn and Wright counties. Within a decade they had also settled in Winona, St. Paul, and Minneapolis. Eventually they extended their communities to Douglas county near Alexandria (1868), then Yellow Medicine county near Canby and Wilkin (1874), to Polk (1880), and then to Jackson (1882) counties. Due to job opportunities in logging and finally farm lands on the cutover, settlements followed by 1915 in Mahnomen and St. Louis counties.[8]

Presented below is a table of Bohemians and Czechoslovakians in Minnesota by highest numbers per county, as derived from the manuscript census and reported in *They Chose Minnesota*.[9] The designations "fb" and "fm" mean "foreign born" and "foreign mixed." The latter designation is for the native born of either foreign or mixed parentage as given in published state or federal censuses from 1890 to 1970. Data missing in the Minnesota book for the year 1910 are supplied from the federal census because they reported town and country of birth as well as languages spoken and are therefore valuable to the continuity of this study.[10]

County	1860		1880		1895		1905		1930	
	fb	fm	fb	fm	fb	fm	fb	fm	fb	fm
Brown	67	6	575	357	617		7	11	241	606
Douglas			24	26		141	164	397	129	334
Freeborn	10	3	267		85	252	207	562	137	406
Hennepin	40	7	407		257	815	834	1,826	2,868	6,614
Le Sueur	131	13	1,220		968	1,226	1,019	3,016	524	1,647
McLeod		26	6	869	407	974	534	1,414	470	1,238
Nicollet				244	154	85	7	26	26	48
Pine				19	12	2	359	949	499	1,08
Ramsey		14	2	643	422	1,245	1,071	2,741	1,576	3,675
Redwood			17	11	78		106	302	87	288
Rice		2		648	503	847	617	2,004	301	1,310
Scott		74	3	644	391	537	420	1,140	286	814
Steele		48	20	764	740	772	772	1,733	478	1,529
Todd				21	18	104	113	258	133	451
Wilkin				51	32	71	98	253	74	24
Winona		3	2	362	135	300	57	170	73	237
Wright		28	4	89	110	138	124	301	75	249

Since these census figures only report legal nationality, they do not distinguish between the German and the Czech-speaking individuals from the Bohemian nation as constituted after 1919. Also, naturalization papers in the various counties reveal that Slovakian immigration to Minnesota was minimal.[11] The highest concentration of rural Czech-speaking immigrants to Minnesota overlaps three counties south of the Twin Cities – Le Sueur, Scott and Rice – with communities clustered around and in the towns of New Prague, Veseli, Lonsdale, and Montgomery . Over time they have expanded to Northfield and Faribault. Another rural Czech-speaking settlement is in Steele county south of Owatonna at the junction of County Roads 14 and 27 around the rural Catholic church called Litomysl. Finally, there is a large rural Czech-speaking settlement is at Silver Lake in McLeod county.

Since 1900, the largest concentration of both Czech- and German-speaking Bohemians (Czechoslovakians) in Minnesota is no longer in rural counties, but in Hennepin (Minneapolis) with 2,868 foreign born, and Ramsey (St. Paul) with 1,576. But the metropolitan urban area is not the subject of our investigation. Attracted to, and scattered among, several Twin Cities concentrations, are German-speaking and Czech-speaking immigrants from diverse regions in the old homeland who in the new homeland seldom live in close proximity to their ethnic neighbors.[12] Thus, the Bohemian population reported by the censuses for the Twin Cities is diluted by various cultures and thus more assimilated.

This brings us to the large concentration of Bohemians in Brown and in the western fringe of Nicollet counties. Beginning with the first census taken in Minnesota in 1860 there were already 67 foreign-born Bohemians in Brown county and, as shown in the table above, they increased substantially to 575 by 1880. Just as Scott, Le Sueur and Rice counties comprise a single community of Czech speakers, so the counties of Brown and Nicollet [around the villages especially of St. George in West Newton township but including also Klossner in Lafayette township] constitute a community of German-speaking Bohemians. There are a few daughter settlements of this primary community, e. g. in Redwood county around Wanda between Lamberton and Wabasso.

In looking at the table above a few additional observations need to be made. First that the state census of 1905, which reports only seven foreign born Bohemians for each Brown and Nicollet counties, is grossly in error. A count of those born in Bohemia as reported in the 1900 Federal manuscript census amounts to 172 for Brown. In a mere five years the total could not have dropped to seven. In addition, many individuals still living in 1900 who in 1880 (the 1890 Federal census is not available) had reported Bohemia as their place of birth, in 1900 said either "Germany" or "Austria."

Technically Austria is correct! Reporting place of birth as "Germany" for the German-speaking Bohemians is of course *not* correct but it was a common occurrence. The immigrant often made the mental transfer according to the language spoken in the family, and the practice certainly was not confined to Brown county and New Ulm. However the mental shift of national identity was indeed frequent among the German-Bohemians in Brown county. It was even more widespread in 1910. By 1910 the designation *Austria* became especially ubiquitous for children reporting the birth place of their father and mother. Also in the 1910 census, it was ordinary for individuals to report as birth place combinations of "German Austria," "Austria, German," and similar geopolitical confusions.[13]

The 1910 manuscript census adds the column "Whether able to speak English; or if not, give language spoken." Although most Bohemian born adults in Brown county by 1910 could speak English, a sizable number reported as their "language spoken" German. Others listed "Austrian" or a combination of the two such as "Austrian German." Importantly for our study, not a single individual in 1910 reported Czech, Bohemian, or any other Slavic language in this column. The point, then, is that all of the people of Bohemian background or birth in the Brown, Nicollet, and Redwood county region, were of German-language ancestry.

At the outset of this investigation, it was virtually impossible to determine from where in Bohemia the local residents originated. Gradually, by studying the naturalization papers that are sufficiently late as to be detailed, along with some applications for marriages and the like, towns and villages began to emerge, often badly misspelled. Eventually it became apparent that the search could be narrowed to the Pilsen district because oral tradition frequently reported the name of that city.

Upon pursuing this site as the presumed origin, it became clear that none of the immigrants actually came from Pilsen. In the first place it would have been a-typical for residents of such a large city to settle almost exclusively on rural land in southwestern Minnesota. In the second place, none of the early arrivals demonstrated any crafts or trades which would have pointed to urban residence in Europe. All were farmers! And farmers come from tiny rural European villages, not from cities, nor even from small towns. Enough village names eventually came to light to pinpoint the county (*Kreis*) of Bischofteinitz with lesser numbers of immigrants from the neighboring counties of Tachau to the north, Mies to the northeast in the direction of Pilsen, and Taus, Markt Eisenstein, Bergreichenstein and Prachatitz to the southeast. A smattering may have come from undetermined counties to the north, or from the former Silesian districts of northern Moravia but none of these could be documented. By and large, the immigrants came from the German border areas of Bischofteinitz and Tachau in the Bohemian forest (*Böhmerwald*). This is the territory opposite the Bavarian Forest (*Bayerischerwald*) on the German side of the border.

In the table below are listed the names of individuals whose natu-

The citizenship document for Wenzel Helget who arrive in America May 1, 1870 and on November 2, 1880 acted to become a citizen. Note that he renounces allegiance erroneously not to Austria but to the Empire of Germany, a common occurrence because immigrants often confused the language they spoke with the nation they left. BC

ralization papers have been microfilmed, and which provide sufficient detail to pinpoint exact place of origin. To be sure this is but a small percentage of the people who actually came. But the family names indicate that those listed here are representative of the many families who reached Brown county over a period of five decades. Often new immigrants joined family representatives already in the area, thus confirming the likely origins of the predecessors to be the same as the later arrivals listed here.[14] The papers show various, not always consistent, information and are presented here in alphabetical order. The roster supplies a profile of Bohemian family names, Bohemian place names, date of arrival, time of citizenship, place of residence, and occupation. Further commentary follows the listing. Frequent misspellings of the place names have been rectified.

Name	Bohemian date and place of birth	Year Immigrated	Year Naturalized	Current Residence	Occupation
Baier, Frank	July 18, 1886 Unterhütten, Austria	April 20, 1903	May 7, 1917 (intent)	Courtland	farming
Baier, Anton	June 14, 1872 Neid, Austria	May 9, 1890	Feb. 17, 1908 (intent)	New Ulm	laborer
Bauer, George	April 9, 1892 Neugramatin, Austria	July 29, 1911		New Ulm	laborer
Bauer, John	November 22, 1871 Oberhütten, Austri	May 7, 1888		Cottonwood Twp	farming
Baumann, John	January 1, 1881 Muttersdorf, Austria	July 6, 1900	Feb. 3, 1911	Springfield	laborer
Bäumel, John	February 14, 1876 Zemschen, Austria	October 9, 1895	May 6, 1910 (petition)	New Ulm	laborer
Biebl, Frank (Muehs)	October 30, 1864 Mies, Bohemia, Austria	August 1, 1867		New Ulm	farming
Bosdech, George	May 11, 1866 Lusenitz, Austria	May 15, 1881	April 9, 1908	329 Front, New Ulm	laborer
Dietrich, Anna Marie	April 21, 1913 Unterhütten, Czechoslovakia	uly 15, 1914	1942	RR 5, New Ulm	
Dietz, Lorenz	January 13, 1958 Fuchsberg, Austria	May 8, 1894	Feb. 15, 1908	Sigel Twp.	farming
(wife Barbara)	Althütten, Austria				

Name	Bohemian date and place of birth	Year Immigrated	Year Naturalized	Current Residence	Occupation
Dietz, Joseph	September 10, 1883 Althütten, Austria	May 15, 1894	May 25, 1909	Sigel Twp.	farming
Dietz, Augustin	Austria	July 15, 1858	Feb. 25, 1870		
Dietz, Georg	Austria	Nov. 18, 1858	March 1, 1870		
Dusik, Franz (wife Bertha same)	June 4, 1878 Oberlentensdorf, Austria	Oct. 30, 1903	Jan. 2, 1909	132 Central, Sleepy Eye	laborer
Dusl, John	Feb. 5, 1889 Berg, Bohemia, Austria	July 22, 1910	Jan. 28, 1920	Springfield	common laborer
Dussel, George	Oct. 1, 1890 Berg, Bohemia, Austria	July 4, 1909	June 26, 1920	Springfield	laborer
Ebenhoch, Joseph	Oct. 31, 1887 Pössigkau, Austria	May 25, 1901		Sleepy Eye	blacksmith
Fischer, Joseph	Aug. 24, 1883 Trohatin, Austria	March 1, 1900		Stark Twp.	farming
Fischer, John	March 5, 1866 Grammatin, Austria	Feb. 18, 1882	Jan. 3, 1910	New Ulm	farming
Fischer, Frank	Sept. 5, 1889 Trohatin, Austria	May 26, 1901	Jan. 11, 1920	Stark Twp. Brown	farming
Fisher, Wenzel (wife Franziska same)	July 30, 1856 Trohatin, Austria	May 26, 1901	Feb. 13, 1911	Stark Twp.	farming
Floetl, Frank	July 28, 1890 Muttersdorf, Austria	March 12, 1905		New Ulm	butcher

Name	Bohemian date and place of birth	Year Immigrated	Year Naturalized	Current Residence	Occupation
Gassner, Joseph	Dec. 6, 1876 Maxberg, Markt Eisenstein	March 10, 1906		New Ulm	laborer
Gimpl, George	May 22, 1894 Chernahora, Bohemia	May 18, 1907	Dec. 30, 1915	North Star, (Springfield)	laborer at Brownlee
Goblirsch, Joseph	Jan. 21, 1872 Zemschen, Austria	Oct. 30, 1903		Center Street, New Ulm	laborer
(wife Julie) (children)	Oberleutensdorf				
Grau, Frank E.	July 15, 1886 Waldorf, Bohemia	Sept. 13, 1897		New Ulm	farming
Greyser, Johann	Feb. 9, 1849 Sirb, Bohemia (resided at Ronsberg)	Feb. 23, 1901		New Ulm	laborer
Gröbner, Josef	April 9, 1886 Muttersdorf	June 6, 1901		Springfield	laborer Burnstown
Groebner, Frank	Jan. 12, 1885 Wasserau, Austria	May 20, 1903		Springfield	laborer
Haala, John Paul	Feb. 28, 1878 Bohemia	June 26, 1879	Feb. 5, 1909	Mulligan, Brown Co.	laborer/ farming
Haas, Peter	Jan. 2, 1894 Trohatin, Austria	Oct. 17, 1908	Sept. 9, 1916	New Ulm	laborer

38

Name	Bohemian date and place of birth	Year Immigrated	Year Naturalized	Current Residence	Occupation
Haas, Josef	June 6, 1881 Trohatin, Austria	Sept. 11, 1901	Feb. 4, 1908	Sleepy Eye	baker
Haas, Peter	Dec. 24, 1878 Trohatin, Austria	April 14, 1894	Feb. 4, 1908	Sleepy Eye	baker
Haefs, Georg	Austria	Oct. 15, 1857	Feb. 21, 1870		
Hartmann, Johan	Austria	Dec. 15, 1854	Feb. 21, 1870		
Hauser, Josef	Austria	Jan. 13, 1859	March 1, 1870		
Helget, Lorenz	Sept. 7, 1885 Althüten, Austria	July 28, 1903		Stark Twp., Brown Co.	laborer
Helget, George	Nov. 23, 1846 Schilligkau, Austria	Oct. 6, 1880	Feb. 6, 1908	520 Franklin, New Ulm	laborer
Helget, Andrew	June 27, 1876 Trohatin, Austria	April 28, 1891	Sept. 1, 1914	New Ulm	laborer
Herbeck, John	June 16, 1873 Berg, Austria	April 28, 1884	Sept. 24, 1909	22 Front St., New Ulm	carpenter
Hochhaus, Anton	Austria	Oct. 10, 1856	Feb. 18, 1870		
Hoecherl, Joseph	March 18, 1881 Unterhütten, Austria	April 17, 1902		New Ulm	laborer
Hoffmann, Joseph Hermann*	Oct. 20, 1882 Zemschen, Germany (??)	Aug. 28, 1884	Sept. 4, 1909	Stark Twp.	farming

Name	Bohemian date and place of birth	Year Immigrated	Year Naturalized	Current Residence	Occupation
Hofmeister, Ludwig Karl	June 10, 1889 Neuern, Austria	April 30, 1903		New Ulm	student
Holm, Johann	Austria	Jan. 13, 1859	March 1, 1870		
Holm, Josef	Austria	Nov. 15, 1858	Feb. 28, 1870		
Holubek, John	Dec. 27, 1877 Deutsch Moliken, Austria	May 12, 1905 (Rotterdam to Quebec)	Feb. 9, 1911	New Ulm	carpenter
Jenischek, Anton	April 17, 1867 Chrudim, Austria	Jan. 26, 1904	Aug. 3, 1910 Sleepy Eye	132 No. Center,	laborer
Kachelmeier, Josef	Austria	Jan. 2, 1857	Feb. 21, 1870		
Kirsch, Joseph	March 3, 1890 Unterhütten, Austria	April 17, 1902	Feb. 14, 1920	New Ulm	laborer
Kirsch, Andreas	May 19, 1859 Unterhütten, Austria	April 17, 1902	March 4, 1910	Front St., New Ulm	laborer
Koenig, Wenzel	July 20, 1886 Schilligkau, Austria	from Trohatin May 10, 1901	Aug. 30, 1940 (?)	Springfield	laborer
Kosek, Frank William	(1988) Neustadt	1890	1917 (affidavit)	New Ulm (city)	
Kraus, Karl	Jan. 26, 1876 Neu Grammatin, Austria	June 5, 1894	Aug. 18, 1915	Sigel Twp.	farming

Name	Bohemian date and place of birth	Year Immigrated	Year Naturalized	Current Residence	Occupation
Krzmarzich, John	June 15, 1855 Dejenitz, Bohemia	July 2, 1864		Home Twp.	farming
Lang, Josef	Sept. 18, 1880 Zemschen, Austria	May 22, 1905	Sept. 6, 1913	Sleepy Eye	laborer
Leiminer, Martin	Austria	Oct. 15, 1857	Feb. 21, 1870		
Liebl, Johann	Austria	Sept. 13, 1858	March 3, 1870		
Macho, Jacob	July 25, 1860 Neuhaus, Budweis Kreis, Austria	June 10, 1880		New Ulm	farming
März, Georg (wife Barbara)	March 8, 1846 Unterhütten, Austria Grosgorschin	July 15, 1903	Aug. 20, 1908	New Ulm	laborer
März, Frank	Oct. 4, 1887 Unterhütten, Austria	July 30, 1903	Aug. 26, 1919	Springfield	laborer
Mather, Lorenz	Austria	May 1, 1856	Feb. 23, 1870		
Meidl, Anton	Oct. 29, 1880 Stalling, Austria	Sept. 19, 1901	Sept. 13, 1909	1st North & Garden, New Ulm	engineer
Meidl, Michel	Oct. 28, 1860 Kaltenbrunn, Austria	March 7, 1880	Dec. 9, 1908	Stark Twp.	farming

Name	Bohemian date and place of birth	Year Immigrated	Year Naturalized	Current Residence	Occupation
Neid, Andreas	Nov. 8, 1879 Wonischen, Austria	Nov. 3, 1908		Cottonwood Twp.	farming
Oschowitzer, John	Oct. 8, 1873 Pössigkau	April 7, 1902	July 18, 1910	Sleepy Eye	laborer
Paa, Vincent (wife Barbara)	July 29, 1879 Unterhütten, Czechoslovakia (married in Waier)	July 16, 1914	Jan. 15, 1942	321 Valley St., New Ulm	laborer
Paa, Joseph George	Oct. 17, 1884 Oberhütten, Austria	June 8, 1900		New Ulm	butcher
Pechtl, Andreas	May 26, 1851 Wasserau, Austria	May 17, 1902	Feb. 18, 1908	113 Lake St., Sleepy Eye	
Pechtl, Gregor	May 12, 1866 Wasserau, Austria	April 3, 1891	Feb. 15, 1908	926 No. Franklin, New Ulm	laborer
Pleniger, John	Sept. 7, 1867 Hostau, Austria	Nov. 14, 1896	July 22, 1918	New Ulm	farm worker
Pleniger, Joseph	Sept. 26, 1899 Ronsperg, Czechoslovakia	Sept. 5, 1922		New Ulm	laborer
Pregler, Karl	Feb. 2, 1857 Schwarzach, Bohemia	June 26, 1891		New Ulm	laborer
Reimer, Heinrich	Dec. 10, 1883 Vollman, Bohemia	Aug. 25, 1903		New Ulm	brewer

42

Name	Bohemian date and place of birth	Year Immigrated	Year Naturalized	Current Residence	Occupation
Rein, Karl Theodor	Austria	April 15, 1858	Feb. 25, 1870		
Rewitzer, Georg (wife Franciska)	Dec. 11, 1851 Neubäu, Austria Muttersdorf	June 10, 1869	May 19, 1908	Sleepy Eye	retired farmer
Reznick, John	Oct. 15, 1879 Alt Pössigkau	Feb. 28, 1907		New Ulm	laborer
Rezni, John	Oct. 15, 1879 Alt Pössigkau	Feb. 18, 1907		New Ulm	laborer
Rieger, George	Jan. 15, 1887 Neid, Austria	June 15, 1893	Dec. 7, 1912	New Ulm	laborer
Ries, Georg	May 21, 1875 Mirschikau, Austria	July 12, 1902	Feb. 14, 1910	New Ulm	laborer
Rothmeier, Josef	(1856) Austria	1891	1894		
Rothmeier, George	(1885) Trohatin	1908	1908 (intent) 1912 (petition)	Sleepy Eye	farm
Rubey, Joseph	Sept. 2, 1891 Wasserau, Bohemia, Austria	May 26, 1901	July 12, 1920	New Ulm	laborer
Rubey, Andreas (wife)	July 3, 1869 Feb. 4, 1875 Wasserau, Czechoslovakia	June 27, 1902	July 2, 1935	New Ulm	laborer

Name	Bohemian date and place of birth	Year Immigrated	Year Naturalized	Current Residence	Occupation
Rumel, George	March 12, 1850 Althütten, Austria	April 29, 1901	April 17, 1907	Division St., Springfield	laborer
Rummel, Joseph	Jan. 5, 1879 Althütten, Austria	May 16, 1901	Feb. 2, 1911	Springfield	laborer
Säckl, Franz (wife Margaret)	Feb. 15, 1874 Pössigkau, Austria	1903	Jan. 2, 1909	Central St., Sleepy Eye	laborer
Saffert, Andrew	June 20, 1877 Muttersdorf, Bohemia	June 2, 1892	June 24, 1920	New Ulm	butcher
Saffert, Louis	March 18, 1883 Muttersdorf, Austria	June 5, 1900	Feb. 17, 1910	Front St., New Ulm	butcher
Schmidt, John	Dec. 23, 1867 Waldorf, Bohemia, Austria	May 25, 1883		New Ulm	Clerk in implement store
Schoedl, Wenzel	July 22, 1870 Sankt Johan, Bohemia, Austria	Sept. 15, 1889 (left from Karlsbad)		Comfrey	blacksmith
Schrimpf, Anton	Aug. 24, 1873 Viertl, Bohemia	April 11, 1889	Oct. 12, 1936	Cottonwood Twp.	farming
Schweinfurther, Carl	Jan. 22, 1888 Hirschsteinhäusl, Gibacht	Aug. 20, 1902		Searles	laborer

Name	Bohemian date and place of birth	Year Immigrated	Year Naturalized	Current Residence	Occupation
Sellner, Frank	May 16, 1877 (Schwannenbrückl) Schwannenbruck, Austria	May 4, 1887	May 9, 1932	700 S. Minn. St., New Ulm	park overseer
Sellner, Wenzel Michael	June 22, 1880 Schwanenbrückl, Austria	June 2, 1892	Aug. 29, 1922	Sleepy Eye	laborer
Sieber, Josef	Nov. 4, 1875 (near Weissensulz) Schmolau, Czechoslovakia	June 19, 1899	Oct. 22, 1924	Springfield	laborer
Simon, Joseph	Feb. 1, 1892 Mauthaus, Bohemia	May 24, 1907		New Ulm, Prairieville Twp.	farming
Singer, Joseph	Nov. 11, 1911 Honositz, Czechoslovakia	Mount Clay-vessel July 26, 1921	April 24, 1933	N. Minn. St., New Ulm	farming
Singer, John	Aug. 4, 1908 Honositz, Bohemia	July 25, 1921 Mount Clay-vessel	Dec. 5, 1928	West Newton Twp Newton Co.	
Sperl, Charles	June 19, 1884 Pabelsdorf, Bohemia, Austria	June 25, 1901	Feb. 8, 1919	New Ulm	laborer
Steinbach, Martin	Aug. 28, 1868 Waldorf, Austria	May 10, 1891	Jan. 25, 1922	New Ulm	laborer
Stuiber, Christ (wife)	June 5, 1860 Rindel, Bohemia	June 15, 1873	Feb. 20, 1907	Milford Twp.	farming

Name	Bohemian date and place of birth	Year Immigrated	Year Naturalized	Current Residence	Occupation
Tauer, George Wenzel	Oct. 24, 1862 Schilligkau, Austria	April 1, 1899	Aug. 20, 1908	Springfield	section worker
Tietl, Joseph	April 24, 1883 Eich, Bohemia	March 5, 1914		New Ulm	brick layer
Trost, Karl	Oct. 20, 1883 Albern, Neubestritz, Bohemia	June 5, 1911	March 11, 1918	Sleepy Eye	teamster
Ubl, Andreas	Aug. 10, 1860 Wottowa, Austria	April 28, 1882	Feb. 14, 1910	Sigel Twp., Brown Co.	farming
Ubl, Andreas	June 29, 1875 Wottowa, Austria	Nov. 22, 1906	Sept. 10, 1912	Sleepy Eye	laborer
Ubl, Joseph	Sept. 4, 1868 Raschnitz, Austria	May 1, 1902	Feb. 18, 1908	108 Main, Sleepy Eye	laborer
Ubl, Frank	Aug. 3, 1876 Aglasterhausen, Bohemia, Austria	Aug. 27, 1902		Sleepy Eye	laborer
Vogal, Simon	Austria	May 10, 1857	Feb. 19, 1870		
Vogel, Simon	Austria	Nov. 13, 1856	Feb. 18, 1870		
Weninger, Mike	Oct. 7, 1881 Kaltenbrunn, Austria	June 13, 1901	Feb. 13, 1911	New Ulm	laborer
Weninger, Anton	Aug. 11, 1892 Kaltenbrunn, Austria	May 1, 1906		New Ulm	laborer

Name	Bohemian date and place of birth	Year Immigrated	Year Naturalized	Current Residence	Occupation
Wild, John Mick	Jan. 3, 1886 Utterhütten, Austria	May 27, 1905		New Ulm	laborer
Wild, Wenzel	Feb. 16, 1884 Utterhütten, Austria	April 18, 1902		New Ulm	laborer
Wollinger, Frank	May 20, 1907 Neumark, Czechoslovakia	June 1, 1910		Comfrey, Brown Co.	farming
Wraneschitz, Phillip	March 5, 1872 Neu Preran (Neuparisau ?)	July 5, 1904	Sept. 3, 1914	Sleepy Eye	laborer
Zangl, Michael	Aug. 10, 1866 Waier, Bohemia, Austria		Feb. 19, 1907	1101 Franklin, New Ulm	laborer
Zangl, Johan Baptist	March 8, 1863 Amatal-Waier, Austria	June 1, 1900	Sept. 2, 1908	New Ulm	laborer
Zeig, Franz	Austria	Sept. 23, 1858	March 1, 1870		
Zupfer, Anton	Nov. 6, 1873 Waldorf, Bohemia, Austria	May 1, 1882		New Ulm	laborer

47

The foregoing listing of individuals is offered to demonstrate several things. First it should be noted that prior to the 20th century none of those being naturalized was obligated to mention a home village, nor place of birth, and sometimes not even a nationality. Only late in the 19th century were place names entered on naturalization papers. In the case of the Bohemian Germans this is confusing because their nationality was technically Austrian, but many chose instead to mention the crown colony of Bohemia. Occasionally immigrants mentioned their nationality as "German," apparently because of the language they spoke. Because earlier naturalization papers lack specific information, the federal censuses are often a better source about the number of German-speaking Bohemian persons in Brown county.

Presented below, therefore, are tables of the population taken by the federal census each decade, showing Bohemian family names, overall numbers, and percentages of people living in Brown county who came from Bohemia. If a family originated in Bohemia and had children born in Minnesota after arrival, these offspring are nevertheless considered with their parents to be Bohemian families. For the 1860 and 1870 census of population, there was as yet no full component of townships so the reported populations for these two decades are not broken down in that way.

In 1860 there was a total of 2,193 people in Brown county, which included much unsettled land to its west. In 1870 there were 5,917 in the county, which then included some additional land as well. In 1860 there were only 94 declared Bohemians. Family names in the City of New Ulm were limited to Hartmann, Schmitz, and Sprenger. In Cottonwood, family names from Bohemia are as follows: Wagner, Siebenbrunner, Dietz, Beck, Leminger, Hochhauer, Vogel, Haas, Kretsch (sometimes rendered Gretsch), Gag, Seifert, Holm, Hauser, Zeug and repetitions of these. In 1860, therefore, only about 4% of the people in the county were of Bohemian-German origin.

In the expanded total 1870 population of 5,917 the Bohemians had grown to a count of 549, or about 9.3%. Family names in the 1870 count listed alphabetically include:

Arbes	Keck	Schlägel
Arbes	Knoedel	Schleicher
Balbon	Kober	Schluck

Otto Dietz family taken about 1895. Children in the 1st row: Catherine and Henry Dietz. In the second row, George Dietz, son Frank Dietz, and Dorothy Beek Dietz. Back row, Grandfather George Dietz, Joe Dietz (an uncle) and John Dietz, father of the family. BC

Becan	Koreis	Schneider
Benkelt	Korwel	Schroepfer
Bier	Kowarsh	Schubert
Bouskbauer	Kral	Schulzko
Brann	Krau	Schwebach
Bro	Kretsch	Seifert
Dietz	Krippner	Serbus
Dreschsler	Lang	Siebenbrenner
Ebenhh	Lang	Siefert
Eckstein	Lano	Sitauer
Emrich	Lehmann	Soellner
Epple	Liebl	Sprenger
Felber	Marihart	Sprenger
Forster	Maresch	Stade
Giebisch	Mathiowitz	Staeffel
Grau	Merkle	Staffel
Grbner	Müller	Stelzner
Groll	Ochs	Sukopf
Grossmann	Pelzl	Tauer
Guchna	Peschker	Vogel
Haller	Peuser	Wagner
Hammerschmidt	Praukraz	Wartha
Hauser	Prokosch	Wettsch
Henle	Prokosch	Wildscheck
Hilsmasik	Prokosch	Wildscher
Hoffmann	Reimke	Wurscher
Holm	Richter	Wissner
Holm	Roebt	Zeig
Huberl	Schiffert	Zeug

In the above list, there were many repeats of the same family name, here listed only once each. By 1880, the population of the county had risen to 12,695 and of these the Bohemian representation amounted to 1,294 or 10.2%. To this total, for considerations of the tightly knit German-Bohemian community in and around New Ulm, should be added the 465 Bohemians living just north of Brown county (and north of the city of New Ulm) in Lafayette Township, with a few extending into Courtland township, both in Nicollet county.

Family names of the Bohemian-born and repetitions thereof included in the 1880 census follow, presented alphabetically, and now broken down by township and city.

For the City of New Ulm 1880:

Arbes	Hoffmann	Merkle
Baar	Keckstein	Meyer
Baschie	Keller	Polta
Bender	Kokenz	Polta
Biebel	Kretsch	Rewitzer
Dauer	Kubitzka	Schaefer
Eckstein	Kunz	Schellhorn
Eichman	Lang	Schneider
Fiddler	Lauten	Simon
Forster	Leiminger	Stelzner
Gender	Lindmeyer	Tomaska
Gira	Lockway	Valentin
Grausam	Loesch	Vogel
Helget	Macho	Wagner
Helmor	Maresch	Wissner
Herian	Mathiowitz	

For Cottonwood Township 1880:

Ambroth	Hochhaus	Schwendinger
Arbes	Kistner	Seifert
Arendt	Kopp	Seifert
Beck	Kowarsch	Sperl
Billstein	Macho	Springer
Bulden	Macke	Springer
Dauer	Macko	Suger
Dauer	Martin	Sukas
Dietz	Mohr	Supher
Drexler	Pecktl	Trach
Eckstein	Raen	Ubl
Fritsche*	Rebitzer	Vogel
Gag	Rechal	Wagner
Grebner	Saundstine	Wagner
Grebner	Scheifert	Warter
Grossman	Schiffert	Weibel
Grossmann	Schneider	Wisner
Haas	Schnobrick	Wokach
Heers	Schubert	

* A German name from Saxony, but married into and living among Bohemian Germans in Sigel Township.

For Lake Hanska Township 1880:

Helget	Tauer
Lieb	Weltsch
Scheiffert	

For Sigel Township 1880:

Bechtall	Hoffmann	Ries
Bier	Hoken	Roesier
Boetner	Holm	Schnieder
Bottger	Janni	Schroepfer
Dietz	Klckl	Seifert
Dittrick	Knebel	Sellner
Domeier	Knedl	Siebenbrunner
Drach	Knedle	Soukup
Eckstein	Koeck	Stadik
Flor	Kral	Stueber
Forster	Kretsch	Tauer
Genk	Neudecker	Ubel
George	Pechelt	Vogel
Gerk	Prokosch	Wilfahrt
Grau	Reinhard	Wiltscheck
Hammersmith	Rewitzer	Wurzberger
Hauser	Riechter	Zeug

For Home Township 1880:

Allec	Halla	Reibel
Brenner	Kowarsch	Schaffler
Dobias	Kryzmarzich	Serbus
Drexler	Losleben	Steffl
Emmar	Pour	Strohmer

For the Village of Loreno 1880:

Buscheck	Krausen
Fiebiger	Schneider
Frodal	

For Albin Township 1880:

Goblish	Reminger
Groebner	Welsch

For Stark Township 1880:

Brown	Kroi	Saffert
Bruckbauer	Mathiowetz	Schafer
Falber	Merrihart	Schaffer
Helget	Proksch	Schuller
Hillesheim	Raschka	Schwab
Kober	Reminger	Termer

For Levenworth Township 1880:

Garosch	Holm
Haala	Pascher

For Mulligan Township 1880:

Holer	Tauer
Mathiowetz	Zeroska

For Burnstown Township 1880:

Artas	Schatscho
Lang	Wurscher
Rubie	

For the Village of Springfield 1880:

Penkert	Schotsok

For West Newton Township, Nicollet County 1880:

Anton	Gabriel	Preckner
Barden	Garber	Satter
Beyer	Green	Schwab
Biebl	Johanna	Sehr
Depholder	Kokesch	Stadtherr
Dosie	Koreis	Stratt
Famdale	Kories	Walenter
Frandon	Kripman	Wendinger
Frank	Mettes	Zimbra
Frank	Monde	

For Ridgeley Township Nicollet County 1880:

Arbes	Leidel
Bashal	Vete
Faultine	

For Lafayette Township Nicollet County 1880:

Altmann	Jungbauer	Schenk
Bartl	Kackelmeier	Schleicker
Baumann	Kass	Schluck
Baumann	Kitzberger	Schmaus
Bauml	Klenent	Schuler
Brey	Koepl	Schuller
Brix	Koreis	Simmet
Buschl	Lackner	Singer
Ebenhoh	Maitl	Smasal
Forster	Martinka	Sporer
Gabriel	Miller	Staderl
Giesley	Minch	Stadick
Goblirsch	Preising	Stafel
Gruber	Reichert	Tauer
Hacker	Ropert	Wagner
Hacker	Ruby	Weber
Hanslick	Saitz	Woratschka
Hegert	Sauckl	Zischka
Henian	Schattenbauer	

The manuscript census records for 1890 were destroyed.

For the year 1900 Bohemian names appear in the various Brown county townships as follows:

For the City of New Ulm 1900:

Alex	Eckstein	Guldan
Ambrosch	Eibner	Guldan
Arbes	Fischer	Hammerschmidt
Baas	Flick	Hauser
Baier	Flor	Held
Bartl	Forster	Helget
Bartl	Forstner	Helget
Bauer	Gabriel	Helget
Baumann	Gag	Hengel
Bender	Genlach	Herbeck
Braun	Gobart	Heursch
Brix	Grau	Hofmann
Dauer	Groebner	Hofmeister
Deutsch	Groebner	Hogen
Dietz	Groener	Holm
Domeier	Grunert	Kachelmeier

Karl	Meidl	Sellner
Kloeckl	Miler	Serhase
Klutschka	Motzert	Soukoup
Kobarsch	Neidecker	Soukup
Koeck	Neidecker	Springer
Korbel	Neuwirth	Stadich
Kowarsch	Paa	Stuiber
Kral	Portner	Tauer
Kraus	Postel	Tauer
Kraus	Prokosch	Tauer
Kretsch	Reinarts	Theurer
Krippner	Reinartz	Ubl
Kruses	Reininger	Vogel
Lampl	Reuter	Waibel
Lang	Rewitzer	Wartha
Lang	Sach	Wiedl
Lemberger	Sandhoefner	Wiesner
Lilla	Schloegel	Wildt
Lindmeyer	Schmidt	Wilfahrt
Lockway	Schroepfer	Windschidel
Lutschuh	Schroepfer	Witcheck
Macho	Schubert	Zangl
Macho	Schubert	Zeig
Martinka	Seifert	Zeug
Mayer	Seifert	

For Albin Township 1900:

Baar	Kostner	Schroepfer
Dietz	Pechtel	Sellner
Goblirsch	Peihl	Sperl
Gottern	Relget	Suess
Haala	Reminger	Suess
Helles	Rewitzer	Weltsch
Herr	Schiller	
Keim	Schlaegl	

For Bashaw Township 1900:

(all the following Bohemian names were reported as having nativity in Germany, even though earlier censuses gave them as Bohemia.)

Fischer	Roiger
Richter	Schumacher

55

For Stately Township 1900:

Fecker	Newmann	Schroepfer
Haas	Ruby	Tadewaldtz
Knadle	Saffert	
Neubauer	Schnobrich	

For Burnstown Township 1900:

Carrick	Lang	Ruby
Forster	Mugan	Sturm
Heitzer		

For Cottonwood Township 1900:

Bartel	Haas	Schmelz
Biebel	Helget	Schmidt
Diettrich	Holm	Schneider
Dietz	Kamm	Sprenger
Drexler	Linomer	Sprenger
Eckstein	Lohmer	Tauer
Fesenmeier	Mack	Ubl
Flohr	Maier	Wagner
Fortwengler	Mathawitz	Wartha
Gag	Mier	Wiesner
Griebel	Planinger	Willinger
Groebner	Portner	Workasch
Grossman	Posl	
Grunet	Saffert	

For Eden Township 1900:

Helget	Aigler	Hofmann
Arbes	Ott	Neubauer
Mathiowitz	Wanders	Schroeder

For Home Township 1900:

Goebner	Kryzmarcick	Steffl
Hillesheim	Lange	Volten
Hoffman	Losleben	Witt

For Lake Hanska Township 1900:

Helget	Uble	Zeig
Schnobrick	Tauer	

For Leavenworth Township 1900:

Arbes	Holm	Soutschka
Forster	Schneider	Stangle
Hartmann	Schumacher	
Hegler	Sellner	

For Leavenworth Village 1900:

Fischer	Kopp	Sperl
Grossmann	Rewitzer	Zupfer

For Linden Township:

Hesse	Koester

For Milford Township 1900:

Ambrosch	Landsteiner	Tomaschke
Arbes	Lehman	Veit
Gebhard	Maresch	Weir
Groebner	Pregel	Wild
Kuehn	Seifert	

For Mulligan Township 1900:

Bauer	Mathiowitz	Syess
Dauber	Mathiowitz	Tauer
Dauber	Molday	Wersel
Dietz	Molilau	Windschitl
Haala	Raschka	Zwaschka
Hockert	Saffert	
Laux	Sellner	

It should be noted here that by 1900 the names appear in ever larger multiples which account for the growing population but the intent is only to follow the names and not the individuals or their family genealogies. From this point forward, however, the spotlight is on a few select specific families who are thought to be typical. The objective is to show what occurred to a small cross section of families in the course of about four generations in the belief that they were characteristic of many others.

Since the German-Bohemians were not very conscious of their history or their origins before World War I, it is explainable why they did

Wanda Gag. Wanda's father was Anton Gag who, according to the New Ulm Review *of May 27, 1908 announcing his death, was born in Neustadtl, Bohemia June 13, 1859 and an 1873 immigrant to the New Ulm area where the family first farmed in the Iberia area but then moved to New Ulm where Anton exercised his talent as a painter of considerable ability, and became the father of the famous author and sketch artist, Wanda. BC*

not generally find their way into the biographical section of Fritsche's *History of Brown County*.[15] Still, quite a number are included, a few – as in the case of Schnobrich and Schroepfer – with their nationality stated erroneously as Germany. Mentioned correctly with biographies giving their Bohemian origins are: Henry Seifert, Albert Flor, Andrew Saffert, Christian Sprenger, John Seifert, John H. Forster, Frank Schnobrich, John M. Schroepfer, Andrew Goblirsch, Joseph J. Sperl, Joseph C. Hofmeister, Frank Holm, and Joseph M. Vogel. Among these are two of New Ulm's prominent physician families, John Seifert and Joseph M. Vogel. None of the Gag families gained a biographical entry, even though they were prominent artists, especially later when fame arrived on the coattails of artist-writer, Wanda Gag.[16]

The Bohemian German family name of Vogel originated with Simon and Joseph Vogel who were born in Bernstein, a village near the Bavarian border just west of Ronsperg. They settled already in the

Simon and Barbara Vogel were born in Bohemia but immigrated in 1856 to farm in Sigel township before retiring in New Ulm. BC

mid-1850s in Cottonwood Township (*Volksblatt* Dec. 6, 1893, *Journal* Apr. 13, 1918). Joseph served in the Civil War and in due course the family converted to the Lutheran faith. Alfred Vogel, son of Joseph, later owned the Lampert Lumber Yard in New Ulm and fathered Dr. Howard Vogel who became New Ulm's personal physician and "take-charge" promoter. He received numerous accolades and in 1965 was named one of the 100 outstanding Minnesotans. His daughter Dr. Ann Vogel, also a physician, describes him as a Yellowstone Park type of geyser who would burst with activity and then enjoy periods of rest. Howard is considered one of New Ulm's big three in medicine – Fritsche, Seifert, and Vogel (*Journal*, Oct. 30, 1979).

The Seifert medical doctor family originated with Johann Seifert, born 1830 in Gibian (Jivjany on Czech maps) in the district of Mies north of the county line with Bischofteinitz. The family of Johann Seifert arrived in the United States in 1855, having sold their property to the Remiger family (members of which eventually also came later to America). Married to Katharina Eschta, also of Gibian, the Seiferts arrived first at Dubuque in 1855 and in 1856 came to Cottonwood

59

Joseph P. Vogel, the son of Simon and Barbara came with his parents to the UnitedStates and farmed on the Sigel homestead. He in turn sired the well-known New Ulm physician, Dr. Joseph H.Vogel who practiced for decades in his home town, following his 1903 graduation from medical study in Chicago. BC

Township. Among Johann Seifert's children was Henry (born July 16, 1864) who married Anna Forster (*Journal* May 7, 1937).

On their Cottonwood Township farm on February 5, 1888 the Henry Seiferts became the parents of oldest son Dr. Otto John Seifert. Otto attended New Ulm's Holy Trinity parochial schools, St. Thomas Academy in St. Paul, and the University of Minnesota. Following additional study in Berlin, Seifert joined with the aforementioned Joseph Vogel to open a clinic in New Ulm. The Seifert family was exceptionally blessed with success. Henry's daughter Elsie became a nurse and married a doctor, Ohmer Warner, with whom she lived in Canby, Minnesota until her death in a 1916 gasoline explosion. Son Arthur V. Seifert was a well-known dentist in New Ulm, while another son, Leo J. Seifert, was a partner in a prominent law firm in St. Paul. In turn, Otto J. Seifert's son, James (born Apr. 16, 1923), became a dentist and practiced in New Ulm.

More typical than the few doctors and dentists were the numerous farmers and farm laborers. An example was Wenzel Helget, born at Natschetin west of Ronsperg in 1843, the son of George Helget and Margaretha Schroepfer, two common German-Bohemian family

Mr. and Mrs. John Seifert. According to the New Ulm Review June 31, 1906 when Mrs. Seifert died, and the October 25, 1911 Review when John died, the couple were married in Bohemia before immigrating to Minnesota after a brief 1856 interlude in Dubuque, Iowa. They farmed in Cottonwood township, he participated in the 1862 defense of New Ulm, and in later life was a member of the Second Regiment Band. BC

names in Brown county. Wenzel had immigrated in 1870 to New Ulm, where he began as a farm laborer, marrying Barbara Kiefner from the neighboring village of Trohatin in 1871. In Bohemia both previously worshiped in the same Berg village church. In 1873 Wenzel and Barbara bought a home in the Goosetown section of New Ulm where Wenzel worked as a laborer at the mill. By 1874, Wenzel's 60-year old widower father joined him in New Ulm, followed in 1900 by his brother Joseph, sister Madgalena, and a niece Anna, all of whom at first lived together at Sixth and South Front Street in Goosetown. Subsequently Joseph moved to St. Paul to become a tailor, while Magdalena married Joseph Tauer and farmed in Nicollet county's Lafayette township. Anna became a domestic, also in St. Paul, but later returned to New Ulm and married. To Wenzel and Barbara were born three children, two lost in infancy. Only one son, Joseph, survived to become an adult. By 1881 Wenzel had saved $1,900, enough

George Rewitzer Farm, Sigel Township, Section 25. seated: son-Alfred Rewitzer, father-George Rewitzer, mother-Franziska Rewitzer born Grossmann, her father, Joseph Grossmann. standing: daughters, Bertha and Sophie Rewitzer and Barbara Grossman, wife of Joseph Grossmann. RP

to buy an 80-acre farm in Cottonwood Township but it had only 40 acres under cultivation.

The paterfamilias, George Helget, died in 1893 at age 93. Meanwhile 33-year John Pleniger, the son of Wenzel's eldest sister Anna came to America where, in order to pay back his passage, he worked for Wenzel whose land holdings had by now grown to 400 acres. Eventually, son Joseph Helget married Mathilda Rewitzer (her parents were both born in Bohemia) at Holy Trinity in 1898. For the next 10 years both families lived together in the small Cottonwood farm house as five children were born to young Joseph and his new wife "Tillie." Only three children reached adulthood: Minnie, Josephine and Rosa. In 1908 Joseph bought an additional 120 acres from George Rewitzer (his father-in-law) in Sigel township, bringing the Helget farm to 520

*Joseph Helget and
Mathilda Rewitzer, wed-
ding photo of May 31,
1898. Second generation
German-Bohemians kept
the tradition of a dark
wedding dress. They are
the grandparents of Robert
Paulson. RP*

acres. The joint family were in diversified farming operations, growing wheat, oats and corn, and herding milk cows, hogs, chickens and geese. In the winter they cut firewood from their 10-acre woodlot along the Cottonwood River to earn extra income.

In 1909 surviving son Joseph died of typhoid fever, leaving behind three daughters and elderly parents along with his widow Tillie. Tillie now rented out the farm land and moved into New Ulm where she lived on Washington Street to be near the Catholic church. Here Barbara Helget died of asthma at 78 in 1916 while Wenzel died a year later in 1917 at age 73.[17] The Helgets thus typify families who arrived poor, struggled successfully with the farm economy that Brown county offered, and within a generation or two, again more or less vanished from the scene of their ephemeral prominence.

The above mentioned George Rewitzer left Bohemia via Bremen to

New York in 1869 together with his sister Katherine and her husband Frank Wagner and their two children. First they went to Wheaton, Illinois where the Wagner family lived before moving on to Nebraska. The 17-year-old George continued on to New Ulm where he worked as a hired hand on the Michael Grubel farm to earn back his passage to the United States, which he owed to the Wagners in Illinois. In 1872 George married Franziska Grossmann, who had been born in Muttersdorf, directly east of Neubäu, a little village (since destroyed) adjacent to the Bavarian border. Franziska and her sister Barbara had come to New Ulm in 1868 with their father Joseph and his second wife. Being millers in the market center of Muttersdorf, the Grossmanns were more well-to-do and better educated than the Rewitzers, making it unlikely that George Rewitzer would have received young Franziska's hand in marriage if the Grossmann family had remained in Bohemia. While the Rewitzers first farmed in Cottonwood, in 1877 they moved to Sigel and by 1886 had 320 acres of land, not to mention eight children, among them Mathilda, born in 1877 who married the above mentioned Joseph Helget.

But just when all seemed to be going very well for this immigrant family, George Rewitzer in 1902 suffered a severe heart attack at the age of 51 and had to give up farming. Shortly thereafter the family moved to North 15th Street in Sleepy Eye so as to reside directly across from St. Mary's Catholic Church. In 1909 George sold the farm to his son-in-law Joseph Helget. A devout Catholic family, George Rewitzer and his sister in 1913 sent several thousand dollars back to his native village of Neubäu in the Böhmerwald for the construction of a small church dedicated to his namesake St. George (since torn down by the post-World War II communist Czech government). Villagers in that part of Bohemia previously had to walk to Heiligenkreuz to worship. Here again, a family achieved major success as immigrants in the Brown county, exhibited significant financial prowess accompanied by philanthropy, and yet by the middle of the 20th century had virtually disappeared.

The Mathiowetz family illustrates a similar outcome. Simon Mathiowetz derives from Bartl and Margaretha Mathiowetz at Preheischen in Bohemia where he was born on January 2, 1838 and arrived in the United States late in 1868, together with his parents, and lived in Eden township. Simon married Kathrina Hirschmann at West Newton in

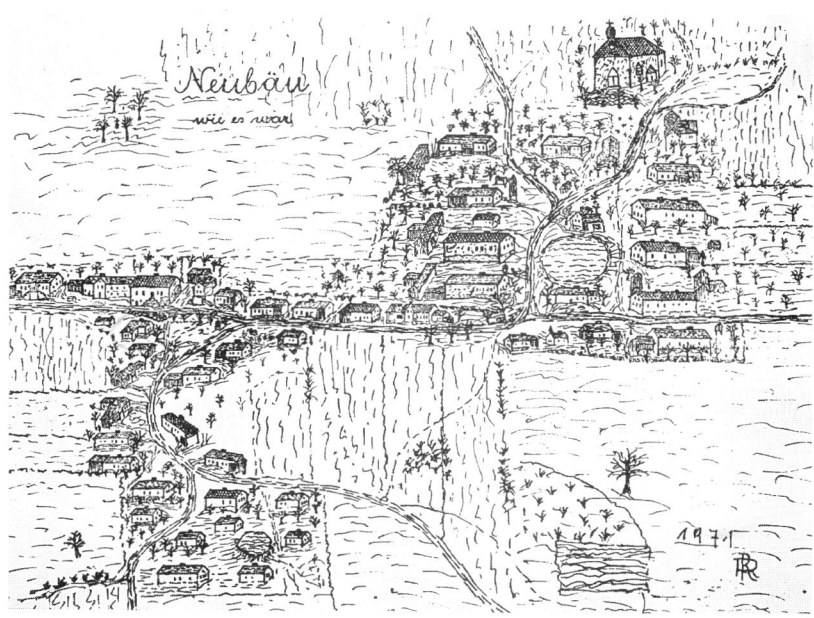

Artist's sketch of Neubäu, which was destroyed by the Communist regime following World War II to create a no man's border land to Germany. Note the small church for which Rewitzer donated money in the upper right hand section. RP

Nicollet county with Father Alexander Berghold officiating. Born at Hemitzach on August 11, 1848 she lived with her husband until his death on April 8, 1928 at the home of his daughter Elizabeth, then Mrs. Joseph Treml, in Redwood county. They farmed a quarter of land on Section 13 of Eden Township, a family farm that today belongs to John D. Mathiowetz, a fourth generation removed from the Old Homeland. Bartl and Margaretha with their offspring were charter members of the St. Mary's Catholic Church in Sleepy Eye which was organized in 1876. Simon and Kathrina moved to New Ulm about 1910 and lived at 823 North Broadway. Today the Old Homeland village bears the name Přehysŏv.

Typical too was Johann Woratschka who was born August 28, 1848 at Weshorsch (Czech Zhoř) in Mies county south of the monastery at Kladrau. His cousin, Simon Woratschka, born the same year, accompanied him to New Ulm from Bohemia in 1867. Johann worked and

65

George Rewitzer family. Seated: George Rewitzer, Albert Rewitzer and Franziska Grossmann Rewitzer. Standing: Bertha Rewitzer Hutton, Elizabeth Rewitzer Hillesheim, Willhelmina Rewitzer Wagner, Alois Rewitzer, Mathilda Rewitzer Helget, Sofie Rewitzer Lambert, Katrin Rewitzer Hermer. RP

later farmed in Nicollet county's West Newton township, fathering nine children with his wife Barbara Gruber, born in 1846 in Neumark (Vseruby) located south of Taus (Domažlice). Johann's son Joseph (born March 20, 1870) married Margaret Weier who had been born in 1873 in the village of Gibian, whence the Seifert family derived, located a few kilometers south of Weshorsch. The original immigrant, Johann, first farmed but later operated a saloon in New Ulm. Son Joseph also operated a saloon, this time in Klossner, and later farmed east of there. Their son Edward married Louise Hostelka (also from Weshorsch) in New Ulm and farmed, then worked in the mill and later on the highway in Lafayette. Edward's son, Joseph Woratschka, became a male nurse and currently lives on North Broadway in New Ulm (*Woratschka family genealogy*).

The Woratschka family illustrates the tendency of German-Bohemians for endogamy. They married not just within the overall

Catholic Church at St. George, Nicollet County. BC

German-Bohemian community but often selected mates from identical Old World villages. In the current generation, the Woratschka family is married into the Wendinger families of St. George, who also derive from Neumark.

From the village of Ober Sekershan in the Bohemian Forest came the Haala family, the grandparents of Eleanor Haala Kretsch, born on June 28, 1913 to John and Minnie Haala, who farmed in Stark township southeast of Sleepy Eye. Being an older sibling, eight grades sufficed for her education though a 20-years-younger sister became a teacher at St. Mary Help of Christians elementary school, where the European-styled parish church reigns like Chartres over the prairie fields. Eleanor recalls nostalgically caring for horses, assisting with milking, and doing field work with four-horse-pulled harrows and drags. Shocking grain, husking corn by hand, assisting "every aunt and uncle with confinement and new babies," until Sunday when baseball games brought relief and rest. Winters witnessed home butchering, sausage making, smoked-meat preserving, interrupted evenings and weekends by card games and horse drawn sleigh rides with the neighbors.

At the time of Eleanor's marriage with Anton Kretsch on September 12, 1933, the Joseph Neideckers served breakfast in town followed by a ceremony at the Catholic church, dinner and supper back on the farm, succeeded by a dance in the Sleepy Eye Opera House and concluded by another lunch at 11:30 P. M. In the years thereafter, farm work interlarded itself with crocheting, the birth of Earnest, identical twins Patrick and Paul, and followed by Monica (Mrs. Randy Wenninger). Forty-seven years of farming came to an end in 1980 when the couple moved to New Ulm where Anton passed on from bone cancer.

The Warta family originated in Pössigkau which adjoins Zemschen in the northwestern area of Bischofteinitz county (*Warta family genealogy*). Beginning with Johann Wenzl Warta, born December 13, 1800 the generations descend next to Josef (born Aug 19, 1854) who immigrated to Brown county about 1884, to farm. He married Franziska Pankratz. Together they produced six children, of whom three, Joseph Jr., Mary, and Henry married Hoffmann siblings, a family from Rindl. Mother Franziska had been married previously to Franz Pinzka with whom she lived at West Newton where the wedding of Franziska to Josef Warta took place. Mr. Pinzka died in a lightning strike on their farm near Lafayette shortly after their arrival in the United States. Their two young boys had already died of disease en route to America. Maria Warta (Hoffmann), one of the six children, married John Hofmann.[18] Her younger brother, Henry (born April 4, 1900) married Theresa Hoffmann (born March 27, 1896) and sired two sons, Denis and Norman. Denis (born Dec. 20, 1927) married Dorothy Kraus in St. Mary's Church September 26, 1950 and has two surviving children. The elder Henry Warta was a laborer in the Eagle Roller Mill. Son Denis attended St. John's University but before graduating returned to New Ulm to work in a bank and then bought the Lindsay Soft Water business which has been his occupation since. His wife Dorothy Kraus is also a third generation Bischofteinitz immigrant.

Like the Helgets, Rewitzers and the Woratschkas mentioned above, the Warta family illustrates the rustic struggle which Brown county immigrant life exacted, and the modest success that came to most German-Bohemian immigrants who spent their lives in Brown county. These family genealogies are offered to typify the thousands of others who weathered pioneer life in the county, struggled to acquire modest wealth and to achieve peer recognition. While it is difficult to generalize about the success the German-Bohemians experienced on the land in comparison to the non-Bohemians, some observations are warranted.

One source to ascertain a statistical profile of German-Bohemian wealth in Brown county is the R.L. Polk Company's 1900 *Brown County Directory* of farmers.[19] The state agricultural censuses end with 1880 and are inconclusive. In order to manipulate the basic data found in the *Directory*, the information about land and values was entered into a data base. All farmers were categorized by occupation (farmers, whether they owned or rented). Also factored in were the number of sections on which land was situated, as well as the township name. Ownership was reduced to the site of the predominant amount of land owned in order to narrow the choice to just one township. The purpose for this decision was to locate geographically the neighborhoods of the German-Bohemian farmers on maps and to allow for a comparison of family owned economic units. To enhance the significance of land owned in terms of wealth holdings, an additional factor was included, that is, assessed value of the land if owned (as opposed to rented but operated). In order to tie property and its owners to a specific geographical place, a final factor of distinction was used, namely, the reported post office for mail delivery.

In any compilation of this nature, there are bound to be approximations. Occasionally a farmer is listed as both an owner and a tenant, presumably because he rented additional land, or perhaps because of a typographical error. Other errors complicate the situation. Sometimes the directory reports no acres at all but a sizable valuation of the "acreage owned." Tenant farmers on occasion are reported to own no acres, but they do have "assessed valuation of the same" which appears contradictory. Still, it seems worthwhile to compare the German-Bohemians to the non-Bohemians in Brown county using the available data from the year 1900. This date seems appropriate because it offers the widest range of data, is late enough to show at least several generations, and yet is prior to the homogenization process that occurred following World War I. In Brown county in 1900 there were 407 Bohemian German farmers out of a total of 2,716 farmers of all ethnic backgrounds, including Reich-born Germans.

First threshing crew on the William Seifert farm in Milford township west of New Ulm when treadmill horse power was conspicuous. BC

The Bohemians accounted for about 17% of the total. In this breakdown, the farmers are gathered into township clusters of rural ethnic communities.

Listed in order of concentration of German-Bohemian farmers, Sigel township had by far the most with 87. Only in Sigel did the Bohemians outnumber all other ethnic groups (four non-Germans among the total of 79 non-Bohemians), all of whom, it should be noted, were German speaking. Cottonwood had the next largest concentration of Bohemian farmers with 62, however the numerical strength in Cottonwood is radically diminished by the presence of 128 (twice the number in Sigel) non-Bohemians in the township. Thus the Cottonwood Bohemians amount to only 48% of all the township's farmers. Stark township follows with 47 Bohemians, only 31% of the total, with 147 non-Bohemians in residence. Mulligan township to the southwest of Stark had 32 Bohemians vs. 101 non-Bohemians giving them a 31% share of the whole, the same as in Stark township. In Milford township to the immediate west of the city of New Ulm the Bohemians tallied 30 vs. 189, giving the Bohemians just 15%. Next

Peter Domeier and wife Barbara (Neidecker) in Sigel township, preparing ducks for butchering.
BC

down the scale comes Albin township with 26 vs. 151, or 17% of the total. Home township lying directly west of Milford had 19 Bohemians (vs. 144) giving the Bohemians just 13%, followed by Bashaw with 17 (vs. 122), yielding only 14%. The remaining townships with their numbers are Leavenworth (11), Eden (11), Burnstown (9), Hanska (8), Prairieville and North Star (5 each), and Lind (4). Stately township in the far southwest corner of the county had no Bohemian farmers at all.

As noted above, 17% of the farmers in Brown county in 1900 were of Bohemian-German origins. Of the 407 Bohemian farmers only 87 held farms ranging in sizes of 240 or more acres. That is to say, 21% of the Bohemians owned "large" farms (defined as 240 or more acres). There were 361 non-Bohemians with 240 or more acres, out of a total of 2,520 non-Bohemians, with the result that only 14% of non-Bohemians vs. 21% of the Bohemians owned large farms as defined above. Owning over 400 acres were 25 Bohemians vs. 93 non-Bohemians (6% of the Bohemians, vs. 3.5% of the non-Bohemians).

In terms of valuation of those acres, the Bohemians who owned more than $3,000 worth of land in 1900 totaled 38, or 9% vs. 56 non-Bohemians or 2.2% of all such farmers. One non-Bohemian by the name of David L. Keyes in Stately township held in excess of 1,000 acres and had a valuation above $10,000. Also one Bohemian by the name of Joseph Sellner in Stark township owned more than 1,000 acres and held value in excess of $10,000. On the lower end of the wealth scale, there were 126 Bohemians who owned less than $1,000 in valuation (or 30%) while there were 1,317 non-Bohemians with less than $1,000 worth of valuation (or 52%). While this evidence does not definitively show that the Bohemians in 1900 owned proportionally more of the wealth and/or land than was properly theirs on a percentage basis, still on a broad scale the suggestion is left that as farmers the Bohemians in Brown county were on the average somewhat better off than their non-Bohemian farmer neighbors.

Because farms often tended to be about 160 acres, especially after the Homestead act of 1862 permitted this amount to be acquired free, we would do well to compare valuation with acres operated by farmers owning between 160 and 240 acres. In this median range of land ownership there were 94 Bohemians (23% of all Bohemians) and 561 non-Bohemians (22% of all non- Bohemians). Using the category of farm size from 100-160 acres, there were 49 such Bohemian farmers (12%) and 309 non-Bohemians (also 12%). Thus in the mid categories of farm size ownership, the Bohemians and their neighbors seemed to be on an equal footing.

Looking at the comparative valuation of farm land defined as an owner worth from $1,000-1,999 we find a similar outcome. This valuation category in 1900 equated well with farm size from 100-200 acres, and hence is a good average representation. Falling into this valuation range in 1900 were 121 Bohemians (30% of all the Bohemians) vs. 764 non-Bohemians (also 30% of non-Bohemians). The conclusion to be drawn from this comparison of German-Bohemians and other ethnic groups on the farm is that there were far fewer poor German-Bohemians than non-Bohemians in Brown county, and that on a percentage basis there were far more wealthy German-Bohemian farmers than non-Bohemians. In the middle ranges, however, there was almost an identical status in farm size and wealth held by both groups.

Listed on a descending scale below on the left are the 12 wealthiest

Bohemians and on the right the 12 wealthiest non-Bohemians with their townships.

Bohemians	Township	Non-Bohemians	Township
Joseph Sellner	Stark	David L. Keyes	Stately
Mathias Hoffmann	Stark	Peter Turbis	Stark
Andrew Lang	Burnstown	Knud E. Mo	Stately
Joseph Prokosch	Stark	John Reinhart	Cottonwood
John B. Sellner	Mulligan	Julius Krueger	Prairieville
Joseph Gag	Sigel	Dominic Bertrand heirs	Eden
Simon Mathiowitz	Eden	George Wooldrich	Prairieville
Andrew Sellner	Leavenworth	George Potter	Burnstown
Joseph Schnobrich	Cottonwood	Charles Schultz	Stark
Thomas Stadick	Sigel	Judas Newhart	Stark
Joseph Mathiowitz	Mulligan	Carl Hammermeister	Eden
Michael Sturm	Mulligan	John J. Penning	Stark

The wealthiest Bohemians were located in the more centralized townships in Brown county where they were more concentrated, while the non-Bohemians were more scattered on the peripheries with the major exception of Stark township which had roughly equal representation of both groups with respect to wealthiest farmers.

In concluding this section on wealth holdings, it should be noted that the Bohemians on a statistical or family history basis are not totally different from their neighbors. Perhaps the comparisons which have been offered can be explained by factors such as quality of soils, location, access to transportation and a host of similar catalysts. However, there seems to have existed a consciousness of difference in social rank based on background and origins that induced the Bohemians to keep their distance from big business and sophisticated commercial activities in the city. After all, the Bohemians were peasant types that liked to perpetuate their Old World styles on the farm. In the process they seem to have perpetuated their family heritage longer. In the Bohemian neighborhoods, the German language seems to have been preserved while non-Bohemians, especially Reich Germans in New Ulm, found it more convenient to eschew the German tongue. As a result, the "Germanness" of German-Bohemians seems more sustained than is characteristic of the *Reichsdeutsche* within the county. At any rate it is not the intention here to show superiority or inferiority, only to illustrate nuances that heritage confers on a people in a region.

Notes

1. Concerning the overall migration out of the territories of Bohemia and Moravia, here and below, see Thomas Capek, *The Cechs (Bohemians) in America: A Study of Their National, Cultural, Political, Social, Economic and Religious Life* (Boston and New York: Arno Press, 1969, reprint of 1920), pp. 1-5, 9-19, 29 ff., 123.

2. C. Winston Chrislock, "The Czechs" in June Drenning Holmquist, ed., *They Chose Minnesota. A Survey of the State's Ethnic Groups* (St. Paul: Minnesota Historical Society, 1981), p. 335.

3. As the tables in Chrislock, "The Czechs" clearly show, geographical place of birth overrides the importance of ethnicity for the census taker. Tables, ibid., pp. 337 ff. See also United States, Census, 1910, *Population*, p. 981. Studies of the Czechs in neighboring states likewise give the impression that all the immigrants coming from a geographic region belong to the same ethnic group, e. g. Karl D. Bicha, "The Czechs in Wisconsin History," *Wisconsin Magazine of History*, 53 (1970), 194-203.

4. Mary Bellingham, Dr. Edward R. Brandt, et al., *Research Guide to German-American Genealogy* (St. Paul: German Interest Group, 1991). See Chapter VI on the geography and history of German-speaking people in Europe, pp. 32 ff. In other words, despite an all-inclusive treatment of sources about German-speaking immigrants, the logo and seeming focus of the book is on the geographic boundaries of today, not on those existing at the time of emigration from a specific place. See. esp. pp. 46-47.

5. See for example the discussion in Karel D. Bicha, "Karel Jonas of Racine: First Czech in America," *Wisconsin Magazine of History*, 63 (1979-80), 122-140.

6. Maldwyn Allen Jones, *American Immigration* (Chicago: University of Chicago Press, 1960), p. 197-8.

7. See in general, Glen L. Taggert, "Czechs of Wisconsin as a Culture Type," Ph. D. dissertation, University of Wisconsin, 1965.

8. Chrislock, "The Czechs," p. 337.

9. Ibid. pp. 337-338.

10. See the comments about "Tables and Their Sources," by Jon A. Gjerde in *They Chose Minnesota*, p. 595.

11. Naturalization papers are available on microfilm at the Minnesota Historical Society.

12. The evidence comes from screening the manuscript censuses of the years 1880 and 1910 on microfilm at the Minnesota State Historical Society.

13. Manuscript U. S. Census 1910, microfilms for Brown County.

14. Found originally among the court records of Brown county, the naturalization papers have been microfilmed and are held by the Minnesota Historical Society.

15. L. A. Fritsche, *History of Brown County Minnesota*, II (Indianapolis: B. F. Bowen, 1916). In subsequent portions of this chapter, citation is given in the text to either Fritsche, or to the various New Ulm newspapers.

16. Alma Scott, *Wanda Gag. The Story of an Artist* (Minneapolis: University of Minnesota Press, 1949), p. 4 mentions that Wanda's grandfather Georg came from Neustadt bei Heid but this village can not be documented. Probably Scott means Neustadtl, a village of some 200 homes and 1400 inhabitants in 1850, which is in Tachau county, the one immediately north of Bischofteinitz. See *Haid und das Haider Land* (Langerwehe: Arbeitskreis Haider Buch, 1985), p. 263.

17. Rose V. Helget married Hugo Paulson at New Ulm in 1932 and in 1936 became the mother of Robert J. Paulson. See unpublished genealogy Brown County Historical Museum.

18. See the chapter on "the music of the German Bohemians."

19. R. L. Polk & Co., *Brown County Directory* (St. Paul: National German American Bank Building), 1901 and 1911-12.

Three
Departing from the Old Homeland, Establishing the New One

ROM THE ACCOMPANYING maps and the census data in the previous chapter, the "old homeland" is the region at the most western tip of present-day Czech Republic. The principle legal districts are Tachau in the north, Mies in the northeast stretching toward the city of Pilsen, Taus, Markt Eisenstein, Bergreichenstein and Prachatitz to the southeast and Bischofteinitz in the center.

The primary or central civic unit from which Bohemian immigrants to Brown county arrived, Bischofteinitz, is the county in which are situated the villages most often represented by the immigrants in the New Ulm market area: Muttersdorf, Trohatin, Natchetin, Neubäu, Schilligkau, Zemschin, Possigkau, Wasserau, Rindl, Amplatz, Hostau, Ronsperg, Schüttwa, Heiligenkreuz, Weissensulz and others. The most recent comprehensive publication about this county is the 1,000 page tome, *Unser Heimatkreis Bischofteinitz*, put out by the Heimatkreis (the homeland region) Bischofteinitz, now situated in its sister city of West Germany, Furth im Wald.[1] The county of Bischofteinitz is bounded on the west by mountains with special names of significance to the local people, all in the range of 800 meters above sea level, the highest being the Hirschstein which peaks out at 876 meters.

The principal river in the county is the *Radbusa* which flows generally from the northwest around Heiligenkreuz toward the east through the city of Bischofteinitz and on eastward into the Bohemian heartland. It has at least 25 tributaries which, together with the main artery,

77

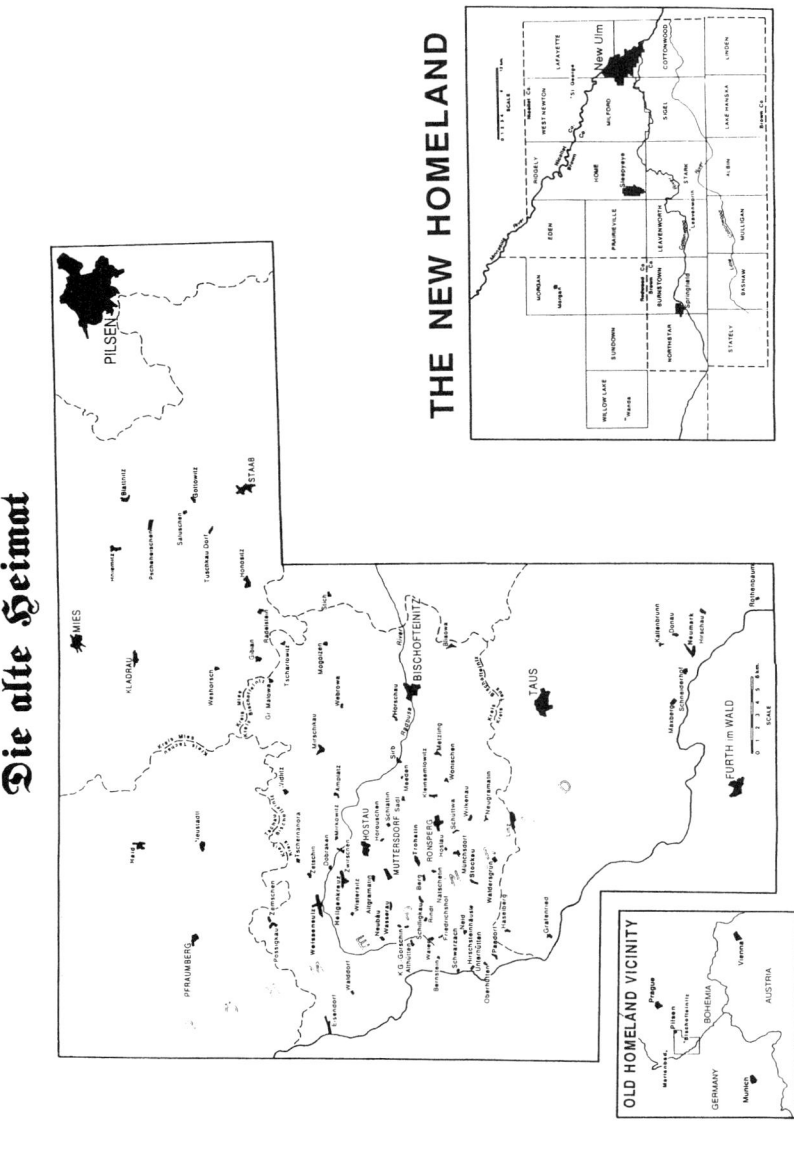

Map inset into base of monument holding the bronze immigrant statue in German Park, New Ulm. Note German homeland district oriented to the cities of Munich, Prague and Vienna with detail map of the emigrant district in Western Bohemia and primary settlement region in the New Ulm area.

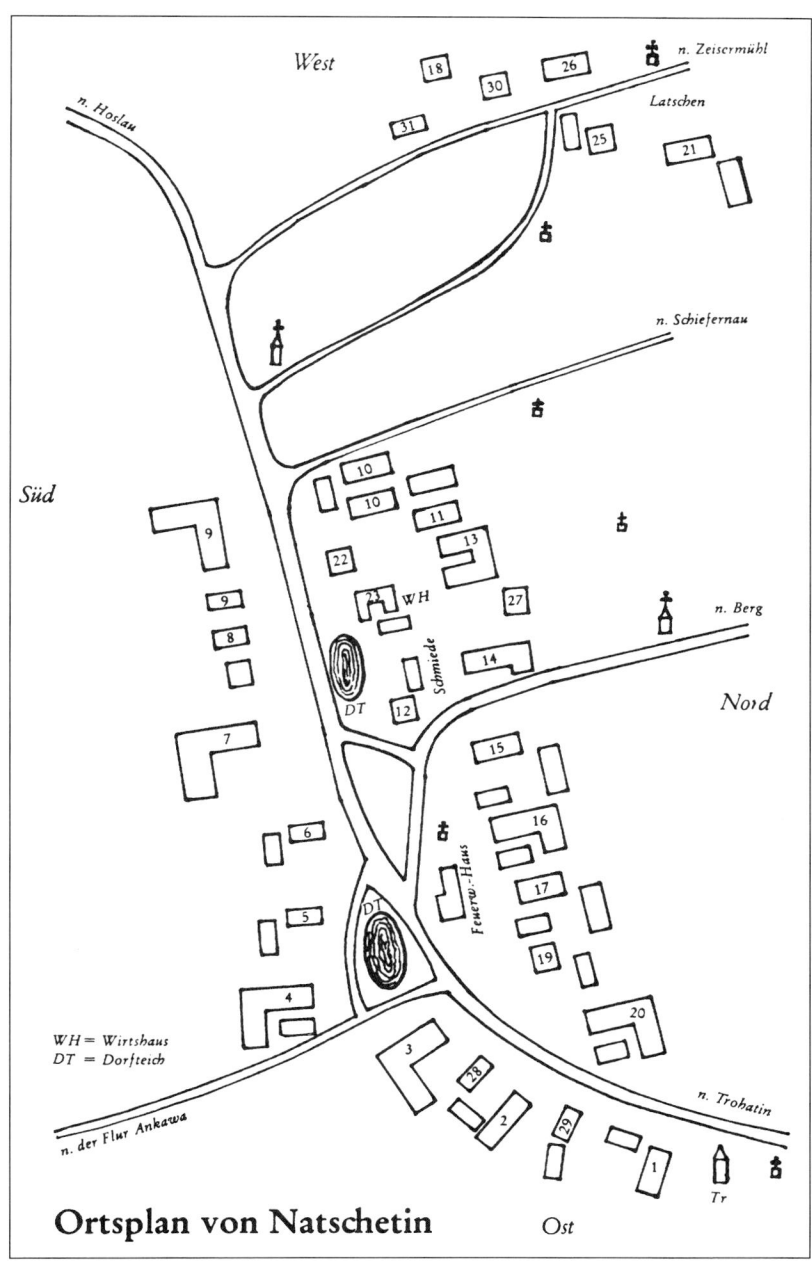

West

n. Zeisermühl

Latschen

n. Hoslau

n. Schiefernau

Süd

n. Berg

Nord

Schmiede

WH

DT

Feuerw.-Haus

WH = Wirtshaus
DT = Dorfteich

n. der Flur Ankawa

n. Trohatin

Tr

Ortsplan von Natschetin

Ost

Village of Natschetin map with house numbers. Note the location of two ponds iden-
tified as Dorf Teich in German, plus the designation WH for Wirtshaus or restaurant-
tavern. PB

powered nearly 100 water wheel or turbine mills which propelled the grinding of grain as well as sawmills, small tools for emery work, hammering, glass and paper production. Such streams and their water-delivered horsepower have been replaced in the 20th century by electrical substitutes. In many villages there were also freshwater ponds, mostly used to raise fish but also to store water during periods of low demand in order to power the mills during heavy daytime use. Most of the water flow into the *Radbusa* ends in the Elbe and the North Sea at Hamburg, Germany, although the *Warme Bastritz* flows into Bavaria near Furth im Wald and eventually into the Danube before emptying into the Black Sea. Thus Bischofteinitz encompasses within its boundaries a major watershed within Europe. A long and melodious poem, *Das Lied der Radbusa*, sings the virtues of this main river and the towns through which it flows.[2]

Directly north of Bischofteinitz between Pilsen and Marienbad is the county [Landkreis] Mies, from which scores of families in Brown county also immigrated. Prior to World War II Mies had 137 organized communities with 43 additional smaller settlements and market places, then the largest rural district in the Egerland region.[3] The 1936 census reported 79,000 inhabitants of whom 54,000 were German and 24,000 Czech, although by 1939 out-migration reduced the total by 10,000. Typical of its medieval origins, were the dozens of fortresses and castles with which the German population had been associated since the 13th century. Illustrative of all the villages was Gibian [Jivjany] from among whose 1849 population of 350 the following Brown county names derive: Beranek, Berdan, Baier, Bier, Neubauer, Steinbach, Guldan, Kraus, Schiller, Sprenger, Remiger, Woratschka, Schleicher, Schmid, Liebl, Mahal, Krippner, Müller, Schlögl, Moldan, Felber, Haala, Wolf, Lutz and Heller. On the list of feudal labor [*robot*] for the noble landholder in the area in the 1860s were Wenzel Remiger and his two brothers Johann and Martin all three of whom immigrated to Stark township in 1868. Organizationally Gibian belonged to the once-elegant monastery at Kladrau which during communist rule fell into serious disrepair.

Just north of Gibian lies another Mies county Kladrau-dominated village, Weshorsch [Zhoř], with a population in 1849 of 322, from which came the Brown county names [many repeats of Gibian]:

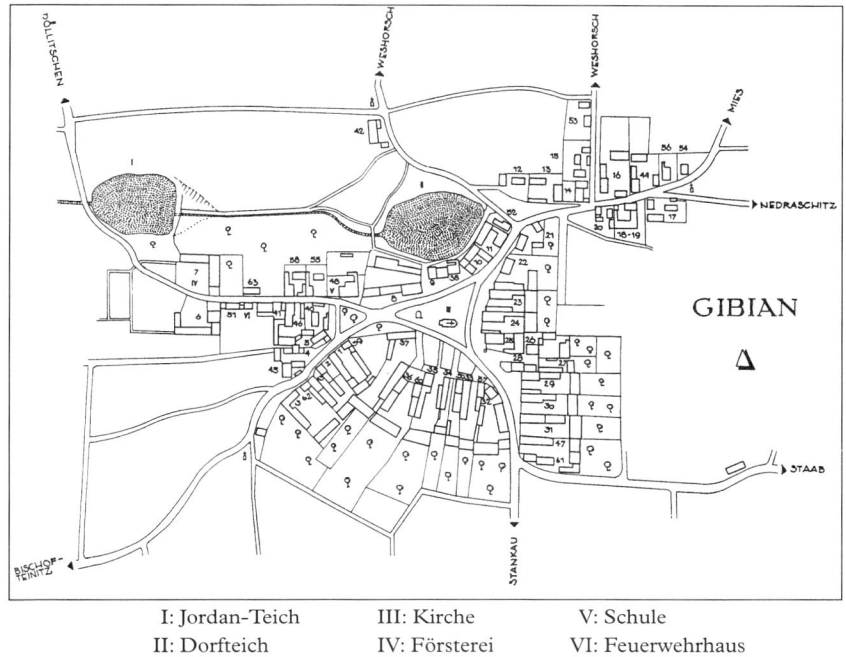

| I: Jordan-Teich | III: Kirche | V: Schule |
| II: Dorfteich | IV: Försterei | VI: Feuerwehrhaus |

Village layout of Gibian, home of Seifert and other New Ulm German-Bohemian families.

Beranek, Kraus, Bier, Dobner, Eckstein, Woratschka, Willinger, Fröhler, Kramer, Krippner, Gareis, Wenisch, Mahal, Remiger, Steinbach, Hammerschmidt, Haala, Smasal, Lang, Schnurer, Berdan and Schwab. From Lochutzen [Lochousice] village a few kilometers to the east came the names: Franta, Schwan, Kral, Lippert, Wurm, Beranek, Müller, Guldan, Haala, Remiger, Steffl, Steiner, Weber, Walter, Schiller, Schleicher, Schmidt, Fröhlich, Glöckl, Ott and Turnwald. The smaller village of Müllhöfen [Milevo] north of Gibian and Weshorsch in 1849 had just 165 residents but supplied the Brown county names of Berdan, Beranek, Krippner, Jung, Klöckl, Simon, Haala, Polta, Reiter, Schwab, Steiner, Mayer and Christl. Kostelzen [Kostelec] a bit to the east gave the names of Arbes, Ernst, Guldan, Keckstein, König, Kastner, Dobner, Beranek, Zischka, Krippner, Schiller, Schwarz, Steinbach, Wurmstein, Franta and Steiner.

81

In general Mies and Bischofteinitz counties were agricultural in nature. Though small, their farms produced cattle, sheep, pigs, and chickens. Field crops included oats, wheat, barley and flax, a commodity needed throughout the centuries to keep spinning wheels humming. These crop rotations persisted in the New World after the promise of a better life in Minnesota uprooted them from their homeland. In both Mies and in Bischofteinitz counties, the climate is mild. But if we judge it against the prevailing moderate weather patterns of central Europe, extremes have at times been tortuous to the residents. In 1845, for example, and again in 1857 the July temperature reached 37 degrees Celsius. By contrast in 1864 ice a centimeter thick was recorded on ponds, also in July. Again, in August 1892 temperatures climbed to nearly 40 degrees Celsius followed by January 1893 when temperatures plunged to as low as -29 degrees Celsius. The winter of 1928-29 was equally severe with temperatures in February dipping to –35 degrees Celsius, during which time there was much lament about the fruit trees and other vegetation that froze out. In spite of the extremes, wild animals and a wide variety of flora covered the landscape.[4]

Ever since about the year 1,000 the Bischofteinitz region grouped itself politically with the counties of Mies, Taus and Klattau under the city of Pilsen. However, the area was commercially integrated through the Cham valley into Bavaria, and from there westward to the general marketing district of Regensburg. In 805 Charlemagne led a campaign through the region against the Slavic peoples, in 817 when the empire of Charlemagne was split up it was allotted to Louis the German, and in 845 fourteen dukes from Bohemia were led as a group to Regensburg to be baptized. By the year 1,000, however, the Bohemian political Premyslid family ruled Bischofteinitz.[5]

Soon the city of Taus developed as a commercial and military stronghold while the fortress of Pfraumberg dominated the area settled by Slavic farmers who were known as the Choden. Gradually Christianity from Germany made its presence felt in the area and secured it for the West by establishing three monasteries: at Kladrau, Chotieschau and Stockau. These cultural magnets stabilized both the Roman church and the German political system within the area. With a Germanic cultural imprint established in the region, settlers from

Bavaria soon followed. Within a few decades the cities of Bischof-einitz, Taus, Tachau, Mies and Pilsen were Germanized.[6]

At that time, the city of Bischofteinitz bore the Czech name *Horsuv Tyn*, which is close to its current post World War II designation of *Horsovsky Tyn*. In the decades after Prague became a bishopric in 973, it organized an archdiaconate in the region, which linguistically led to the name which in German incorporates the bishopric's significance (*Bischof* = Bishop or Bishofteinitz). Although early church history of the region around Bischofteinitz is sketchy, by 1384 there were at least 52 parishes subordinate to this administrative center.[7]

Practically all names of places in the county of Bischofteinitz are derivatives from the Slavic. For example the village of Wasserau today is known as Bezverov. Once it was called Ostrov which in the local Czech dialect sounds like Wostrow. Suffixes for German names like *–ingen* equate with the Czech *-ice* or *-ovice* and then re-equate with the German *-itz*, for instance, the village of Tasnovice in Czech, becomes Taschlowitz in German. German origin names in the area have quite recent beginnings, for example, the many villages that have the suffix *–hütte* or *dorf*, come from the German words for hut or village and are common in the border area near Bavaria. Thus, names like Eisendorf or Walddorf (iron village and forest village) imply an activity or situation as do place names like Glasshütte and Unterhütte (glass blowing village and lower village).

Czech names were sometimes translated into German by retaining the main syllable of the place name but giving it a German suffix, for instance, the town of Mutenin of today was Muttersdorf in German. Mnichov now, during German times, was Münchhof. Other situations illustrate re-naming, for instance Poběžovice in 1502 was given a new coat of arms with a leaping ram. Hence the German name of Rams-berg in the local dialect it becomes Ronsperg. Kramolin in Czech yields Alt- or Neu- Gramatin in German. The Czech name of Hos-toun becomes German Hostau. Others like Drohatin and Trohatin in Czech were easily picked up in German as Natschetin and Trohatin. Additional name origins are perhaps not as clear but still can be ascribed to sounded similarities, for instance, Czech Sitbor in German is rendered Schüttwa.

The Bischofteinitz county economy can be described only circumstantially. The first records from which information can be gleaned derive from 1654 in the form of a tax rolls. This date follows closely on the conclusion of the Thirty Years War (1618-1648) which began and ended in Bohemia and which likely caused significant local destruction. Still, there is not much indication of war-related reductions in the rural economy. Farmers raised both winter and summer wheat, and tended cows, young stock, sheep and pigs. Cows were kept more typically than sheep, goats and the like while pork raising was also important. The tax rosters also reveal that there were a few but not many Jews living in the region, about a dozen each in Ronsperg and Muttersdorf and lesser numbers in other small towns.

Typical first names for males at the time were German traditionals – Georg, Hans, Mathias, Andreas, Simon, Jakob, Nikolaus, Wenzel and others. Common names for females were Anna, Margarete, Dorothea, and Katharina. Characteristic family names listed for 1654 are some that appear in the New Ulm area today, many with slightly varying spellings ([own name first, followed by family name]: Muttersdorf-Sperl, Neubäu-Liebl, Ronsperg-Mattheowicz, Schüttwa-Saffert and Schrepfer, Trohatin-Tauer, Haselberg-Rebiczer, Schilligkau-Pechtl, Heiligenkreuz-Hoffmeister, Kleingorschin-Saffert, Neugramatin-Losleben, Linz-Schröppfer, and many others. As early as 1654 therefore, the names of the 19th century immigrants were represented in the tax rolls of the towns from which they eventually emigrated to the United States.[8]

Court chronicles from the 1700s mention early emigrations from the district, though none give any reference to a departure for Brown county Minnesota. In 1727 some 20 families expatriated from the western region of Bischofteinitz into the interior where they founded Deutsch-Nepomuk. In 1827, due to failing economic conditions, 56 families departed for the Banat in Hungary. Again in 1873, records show that a contingent left for Brasil where they lived in a German colony, preserving their language and customs for generations. But no record of the numerous departures to Minnesota is known to exist.[9]

The question arises often whether warlike conditions or the military draft were reasons why the immigrants from western Bohemia came to southern Minnesota. Always, of course, there is a hint of evidence here and an oral tradition there. But one searches in vain for hard confirmation of military experience as a cause for emigration. The only military engagement during the second half of the 19th century that might have affected the region was the Prussian-Austrian war of 1866 which essentially began and ended at Königgrätz (printed on Czech maps as Hradec Kralove). Here, in northeastern Bohemia where the Adler River meets the Elbe, the Prussians solidly defeated the Austrians on July 3, 1866. The consequence of their victory was a treaty in Prague where Prussia, in addition to some reparation, succeeded in gaining permission to annex several provinces in greater Germany, but acquired no territory allocated legally to Austria. The Battle of Königgrätz (also known as the Battle of Sadowa, the Seven Weeks War, and the Austro-Prussian War) was but a blip on the minds of western Bohemians, for it lay at least 200 kilometers distant.[10]

A few reports in the local newspaper, *Bohemia* (Sept. 11, Sept. 20, 1866) make reference to the war. Regiments Nr. 35 and 73 were expanded to full strength with soldiers from western Bohemia, and these participated in the battle. Men with the last names Killian, Koch, Lang, Mayer, Sperl, Steinbach, Süss, Kraus and Plass were from the local villages. Both Sperl and Süss are familiar family names in Brown county, Minnesota. Since apparently no local men lost their lives, were captured, or otherwise suffered the spoils of war, community residents were troubled only about their possible obligation for reparations and the arrival of Prussian soldiers to collect them.

Rumors abounded that the army was on its way westward to Pilsen and that the feared Prussians would arrive in Bischofteinitz by the seventh of July. But they did not even reach Pilsen until July 27. They bore no military intent whatsoever except to levy reparations for the Pilsen district, in the amount of 150,000 Guilders. Bischofteinitz had to pay 8,000, Hostau and Ronsperg each 3,000, Taus 7,000. On July 28 a tremor crackled through the villages as the people awoke to the cry "The Prussians are here." In panic, the police chief and his troop fled the city of Bischofteinitz. What arrived in reality were four quite easy-going Prussian soldiers one of whom stayed, the others dispersing to neighboring towns. Word went out that the assessed sums had to be in Pilsen by eight o'clock on July 29. Once the messages had been distributed, the four soldiers gathered in the Gasthaus "Zum weissen Löwen" where they made themselves comfortable (höchst gemütlich), played cards and narrated that they too were the fathers of "families who were living in the Danzig area." They enjoyed the Austrian cigars which the people of Bischofteinitz gave them, gradually collected their payments or pledges by villagers that they would relay to Pilsen, and departed having left the region poorer but otherwise in good spirits. The feared invasion was over.

Other news aroused villagers' attention far more than did matters of war. In 1873 there was a new steam-driven sawmill that delivered 60 horsepower in the village of Walddorf near the German border (west of Weissensulz). In 1874 came the news through the villages that two of the Brasil emigrant families had returned, the victims of Brasilian immigration agents who had induced 67 persons to come, of whom (surely exaggerated) most were said to have died at sea before their arrival. Because the emigration to America went along smoothly, apparently, it never made the news!

Fires plagued the region in 1876 when four houses burned down in Schmolau, five in Dingkowitz, and six along with seven barns in Hostau. In the crowded villages of central Europe fire was always a threat, which resulted in codes requiring most human dwellings and many barns to be built of masonry materials. The following 1877, fires again swept through Hostau destroying 47 dwellings and 32 business- es. Victims of the flames included the church, school, city hall, post office and most local records and tax forms. Even though Bischoft- einitz, Heiligenkreuz, Neustadtl and Weissensulz had sent their fire departments to assist, Hostau still lost a half million guilders in the conflagration.

In 1879 the problems included severe flooding. On August 22 with- in fifteen minutes after a cloud burst, the low-lying south side of Ronsperg lay under water, in which 84 buildings were severely dam- aged, three lives lost, and 40,000 guilders wrought in damage. Two men lost their lives up the road in Trohatin where four homes floated away. Pastures were lost to heavy sand deposits and the wet earth ren- dered the potato harvest useless. Ten years later in 1889 villages were buzzing with the tragedy of crown Prince Rudolf of Habsburg. Unhappy in his marriage to Stephanie of Belbium, he died apparently of his own hand, together with his seventeen year old beloved Mary Vetsera on January 30, 1889 at Mayerling castle near Vienna. This was the tragic, romantic stuff which fanned the flames of interest among the common villagers. The emperor ordered black banners of mourn- ing hung not only from churches and public buildings but also from all private dwellings. Despite a current-day oral tradition in New Ulm, wars, the draft, and resistance to military service, just were not matters of concern during the late 18th century emigration.

As the century wore to a close, matters other than military continued to dominate the news. When Archduke Albrecht died, a funeral mass was said in Bischofteinitz on February 25, 1895 at which an officers' corps and members of the 50th national guard battalion joined the fire department and veterans units to form an honorary color guard. What military activity there was, it turns out, called for ceremonial participation only. The village of Stankau in 1896 observed the opening of a newly constructed German school building. During the same year on June 7 Bischofteinitz celebrated in honor of the German farmers of Western Bohemia, at which some 3,000 guests were present to lay wreaths at a memorial to Austria's Kaiser Josef II. They also witnessed cannon firings at the fort and otherwise enjoyed themselves in a festival tent at the Radbusa River. On the 10th of December the same year, the Austrian empire mourned the assassination of its Empress Elisabeth with black flags and streamers once again hung from public buildings. In 1899, in the village of Schwarzach on the Bavarian border, all but the customs house burned to the ground. In all, 21 families (106 people) were homeless. But wars and the rumors of wars did not haunt the local population.

When the new century dawned in 1901, floods overwhelmed Weissensulz, currents driving entire trees down the streets wreaking destruction to ten buildings and severe damage to 220 more. Untold animal carcasses, sand and mud polluted the pastures. Ruined bridges and washed-out roads compounded the recovery period.

By 1909 the headlines heralded a new catastrophe for the German population! On August 22 in the Bischofteinitz Gasthaus "Zum weissen Löwen" once again people gathered, this time not to ogle carefree Prussian corporals but to listen to a local Czech court recorder vent his nationalistic feelings with the words, "The Germans have to get out of Bohemia, all of them have to get out of Bischofteinitz, or a lot of blood is going to flow!" The same year Bischofteinitz commemorated the opening of a newly constructed distillery. Two years later in 1911 the newest regional sensation was completion of the telephone network for Bischofteinitz, Ronsperg, Hostau and Taus which linked the Bohemian Forest region to all the major cities of Europe. Within months the lines reached Weissensulz and other Bohemian communities.

Chapel of St. George in Neubäu, funds toward the construction of which were donated by the Rewitzer family of Sleepy Eye/ New Ulm. The chapel was the first building in the village destroyed in 1949 by the Communists. RP

June 15, 1913 was the occasion for a special celebration in the mountain village of Neubäu where a small new church had been built at the instigation of the Heiligenkreuz pastor. A large number of worshipers took part because not only had the Kaiser personally sent 400 Kroners for the construction, a Baron Kotz donated the wood, and more significantly for our purposes, contributions came from emigrants abroad, notably from Johan George Rewitzer of New Ulm, Minnesota.

In 1914 it was time once again to mourn a death, this time the murder of the Austrian successor to the throne. On June 28 in the Balkan city of Sarajevo both the crown prince Franz Ferdinand and princess Sophie Chotek were shot. On July 3rd in Bischofteinitz with black flags and streamers bulging in the breezes, the bells of the churches peeled for five hours – the entire afternoon. On July 4th all national guard units and most members of the nobility and common faithful attended a mass in a suburban church – a catafalque in the main aisle – for the repose of their royal souls. Black cloth draped the walls. At the beginning of August, as mobilization was ordered, this time also in Bischofteinitz, the reality of war had finally come home. On August 7 the Dragoons (heavily armed cavalrymen) decked out in their military best posed before the major church in Bischofteinitz for pictures while crowds as far as the eye could see waved goodbyes to their soldiers. The blessed sacrament was born to an altar arranged ahead of the church where the pastor preached. He then gave the departing soldiers general absolution and waved goodbye as the horsemen headed out of town in the direction of Taus. They would never return to their garrison.

The following years were dominated by the news of soldiers falling in battle, dying a heroic death, having been decorated previously or posthumously. The war also interrupted further emigration to the United States and, in many respects, interdicted correspondence from the departed German-Bohemians living in southern Minnesota. Arrested contacts often were restored after the war, but there never was a genuine recovery from the shock that destroyed the pre-war Minnesota relationship with the homeland. What is remarkable, actually, is how smoothly the 1860-1914 emigration had happened – without any public attention, without any news stories, without any world-shaking causes. The economic push and pull on two sides of the Atlantic ocean, nourished by a constant flow of written correspondence between concerned families, were the instigators that kept a steady stream of German speakers exiting from the Bohemian villages and arriving in southern Minnesota, New Ulm in particular, a fine example of "chain migration."

If one looks in vain for German-Bohemian newspaper references to the departure of the emigrants from Bischofteinitz and the surrounding counties, the picture on the Minnesota documentary landscape is not much clearer. The City of New Ulm itself was founded as a home for elite Germans of a liberal, educated background. These city dwellers were not the Germans from Bohemia. Thus, the *New Ulm Pionier,* the first newspaper published in the county, is virtually silent about the more tongue-tied immigrants from Bohemia. In its founding agreement, the journalists L. Koehne, A. H. Wagner, H. Kattmann, and W. Pfaender stated in English that their paper's mission was "to work for radical progress, independently of any party or clique; to bring the special conditions of our territory to the attention of readers;

Dragoons in Bischofteinitz prepare to depart for military service during World War I. BS

Founders of New Ulm, taken in 1890 by Anton Gag. Rear. L-R. David Haeberle, Anton Henle, Joseph Dambach, Louis Meyer, Peter Mack. Front. L to R. Elizabeth [Mrs. Athanasius] Henle, Athanasius Henle, Christian Ludwig Meyer, and Alois Palmer. BC

and especially, to act as an intermediary between the members of the Turner Settlers society living in New Ulm and elsewhere."[11]

Clearly the community about which the *Pionier* was careful to report was not aware of newcomers from Bohemia. At any rate, there were only a few German-Bohemians present, and none of them was within the city. What is noteworthy about these early days of settlement is that there was no English-language publication in the county. Throughout the first years, however, and especially in 1859, at least to today's peruser, the large number and frequent publication of delinquent taxes raises doubts about the viability of the local economy. Likewise, the weekly listing of sheriff's sales was voluminous. In other words, when the first Bohemians were arriving on the scene, the financial picture was in disarray, the result of the depression unleashed nationally by the panic of 1857. Early histories of the county depict the awful conditions for those who, for instance, had planted their last potatoes only to be obliged to re-dig them to feed their starving children.[12]

Within the city of New Ulm itself the powerful Turnverein (the gymnastic club) determined most of the social and some of the financial destinies of the residents. There were also other organizations, such as the *Ansiedlungs-Verein* (the settlement society) which, like the Turnverein, was headed by William Pfaender and seems to have promoted Turner causes rather than the concerns of immigrants generally. That the *Ansiedlungs-Verein* may not have been entirely a local society is indicated by the fact that dues were payable at the major German bank in Minnesota, Meyer & Willius, in St. Paul, a German bank that advertised for clients continuously in the youthful New Ulm German newspaper. Youthful or not, the fledgling German city founded by the national athletic club, already during the spring of 1858 and following, presented the history of the founding of New Ulm.[13]

In early settlement days there seem to have existed links to Dubuque, Iowa, both in the mention of obituaries that settlers lived briefly in that area before coming to New Ulm, and by the fact that Gelpcke, Winslow and Co. of Dubuque steadily ran advertisements in the local paper claiming to be the primary agency for ship tickets on all European lines. It seemed not to matter that the Deutsche Bank of Meyer and Willius in St. Paul also advertised a few columns away that they too could supply prepaid tickets through their agency Lüddering

& Co. in Bremen for travel from Germany via Bremen to any U.S. port, be it New York, Baltimore or New Orleans. From the advertisements can be gleaned just how normal it must have been to purchase a prepaid ticket for the trip from the old homeland to Minnesota.

According to claims made by Lüddering Co., prepaid tickets were superior to those offered by others because their tickets could *not* be sold in Europe to other individuals, nor used except by the person mentioned specifically on the ticket. If relatives and friends in New Ulm bought a ticket for one of their own who then had a change of heart about departing, then the money for the prepaid ticket would be refunded promptly to the purchaser in Minnesota, less a small commission.[14] It can be extrapolated from these insertions that the prepaid ticket was, under other circumstances, subject to resale abroad in which case the relative or friend in Europe would have betrayed the trust of the American purchaser. From samples of German-language letter exchanges found in Brown county, it can be concluded that some effort was made on the part of Germans in Bohemia to get relatives in New Ulm to feel a certain obligation to send prepaid tickets to those remaining in Europe.

Although there are few documented examples of how the prepaid ticket was used, the letters from the Meidl family of Taus, Bohemia to the Brown county Meidls supply many clues. Born October 28, 1857 at Kaltenbrunn, Michael Meidl had immigrated via Bremen to rural New Ulm in 1880 where he worked at first in West Newton as a mason. After marrying Crescentia Stelzer he farmed in Stark township near Sleepy Eye until his death on September 21, 1940. Illustrating the contact maintained with the homeland are the letters written by Meidl's sister, Franziska, his brother Anton, and another sister Theresia who usually signed her letters as "die Resi." These three siblings lived in villages near Taus to the north of Kaltenbrunn and corresponded regularly between 1910 and 1924.[15] Anton Meidl's youngest daughter, Theresia, strongly considered emigrating to the United States in 1921 but changed her mind in 1922 and then regretted it considerably in 1923. In the correspondence there is mention frequently of others from the local region who depart, planning either to visit or stay with the Meidl family. Theresia writes: "Dear uncle, if you would be so kind as to send me a ship ticket . . . I would like to leave here in the spring of this coming year, let's say by April or May. . . . one needs a lot of papers

William Pfänder, an 1848er immigrant and co-founding father of New Ulm, taken late in life. BC

Michael and Crescentia Meidl, the parents of Mary, John, Max, Sophie, Henry, Mathilda, Edward, Rose, and Albert Meidl. The Meidls trace their ancestry to Haus No. 6 in Kaltenbrunn, southeast of the Bohemian Forest. Crescentia derives from Zenting, across the Czech border, north of Passau, Bavaria. AP

today if one wants to travel. Dear uncle, what do you think? would it be better for me in America than in Europe? I continually hear that women do not have to work as hard there as here and so I would be delighted if I could come over to you."[16]

Complications in Theresia's decision to emigrate came from her family in the old homeland. Midway through her next letter she pleads "Now dear uncle, I ask you if you would be so good, to please send the ship ticket or the money whichever is preferable, but you must also send along an entry permit and everything that goes with such a permit. It would be best if you would talk with Franz Weniger, the guy who recently arrived there from here, for he would know all about current conditions. . . . You write that I should not bring along a lot of things. But I would certainly like to bring along my bed."[17] In January, 1922 Theresia wrote that she had received the papers from her uncle Michael. But in the physical examination now required before an immigration permit to the U. S. would be issued, a heart murmur was discovered which Theresia seems to use to dissuade herself from emigrating, which is reinforced strongly by her father. "I have a great deal of anxiety that I would not be able to withstand the journey. Furthermore, my father has told me I should follow his advice and not undertake such a trip. He would not be able to bear it if something should happen to me on such a journey."[18] Now Theresia offers to return the money.

A year and a half later having received no confirmation from her uncle about receipt of the reimbursement from the ship company, she writes that she wishes she had indeed **not** followed the urging of her father, regretting subsequent events even more. "If I had your ticket here today I would be delighted to come. I have been forced by my father to marry a man whom I do not love. And this man has made me very unhappy. Best of all would be if I could be freed from this man. If things do not improve, I will be getting a divorce from him. . . . . One should not always obey one's parents. If I could be freed from this man, dear uncle, then I would certainly come to America, and even if I had to do so with my own money. . . . If only one did not need all those papers, then I would definitely run away from here immediately and join you in America. We'll see how the situation turns out but I would really be happy if I could be liberated from this man because I do not love him at all. His name is Josef Singer from Springenberg. He

Anna Maria Meidl, nee Rauscher in Kaltenbrunn, great grandmother of Angeline Portner of New Ulm, taken in the city of Taus. AP

has a beautiful farm with 16 head of cattle and one horse, but what good is that if I experience no satisfaction with this man. . . . We would also be very happy if you would pay us a visit from America. Every summer a lot of the people from our village are coming back from America for a visit to their former homeland. If it weren't so far, my father – even at his advanced age – would like to pay you a visit. . . ."[19]

Whether this was a cause for the rupture of correspondence or whether some other matter intervened cannot be ascertained. At any rate, six months later at the end of 1923 Michael Meidl's niece, Theresia, with her father (who is Michael's brother Anton), writes the last letter:

We have written several letters to you and you never write back. Or have you perhaps not been receiving our letters? If you do receive this letter, then please be so good, dear uncle, and brother, to write us once more. It is sad when one has brothers and sisters and other relatives in a distant land who never let us hear from them. . . . If it would be possible, you could come for a visit next summer. What a joy that would be for all of us. It has now been so many years since you have been gone from home and have not been back even once for a visit! Every summer people come back from America for a visit to their former

95

homes here. If you are well, dear uncle and brother, please do undertake the trip for a visit to us next summer. . . . I have already written
you about my sad fate. A half year ago I got married to a man whom I
did not want to marry but my father, brothers, and sisters forced it on
me, and now my divorce is final. I am at last free from this man. There
was ample reason, for he was not able to fulfill his male duty in marriage. If only I had come to America back when you sent me the ship
ticket, then this misfortune would not have befallen me. I regret it very
much and think about it often but I believe I will still some day come
to America even if I do not receive a gift ticket, because I will pay for it
with my own money. But I would still need the immigration visa for
America. . . . I do not want to remain in Europe because I am now a
divorced woman. I am 24 years old and there is little left for me to do.
Josef Bruner who left for America from Kaltenbrunn two years ago is
already married. He had his girl friend sent from Europe to join him.[20]

While the Meidl letters do not address the situation that faced the
first immigrants of a half century earlier, they undoubtedly document
a range of emotions and feelings about the immigrant experience back
then as well as in the 1920s. Unfortunately we do not have the
responses that Michael wrote back to his family in Bohemia, but a flavor of Michael Meidl's willingness to help and a sense of the trust the
family back in Bohemia felt toward him permeates the letters which
arrived from Bohemia. It is obvious that many other families in the
neighborhood also had relatives in Brown county, Minnesota.[21] Likewise, the letters demonstrate some of the isolated reasons for emigrating. Usually they were personal and economic, seldom the result of
world or national events in one country or the other. That Michael
sent the ship ticket for Theresia indicates that he could afford it and,
that he sent it for a niece, probably indicates that he was not trying to
acquire a male hired hand for his farm. Also clear from the correspondence is that members of the German-Bohemian community in Minnesota often visited the old homeland, probably more frequently after
the turn of the century than before, but at any rate more commonly
than is known among the descendants of these families today.

From time to time, there was discussion in the local paper about
the relative importance or the disadvantages of further immigration to
the United States and Minnesota. In terse, general entries newspaper
editors acknowledged that new immigrants had arrived in New Ulm

Michael Meidl home in Stark Township, Section 20 in front of which are mother Crescentia Meidl holding Edward; standing are Matilda, father Michael, and, Mary, Sophie, John, Henry, and Max. AP

and that they were invited to subscribe to the paper.[22] The coming and going of the riverboat steamer "Franklin Steele" usually piqued the interest of on-site editors, probably because this was the ship which the original Cincinnati Colonization Society of North America had chartered in 1857 under William Pfaender to convey them the distance from the Ohio river city to New Ulm. Sometimes the "Franklin Steele" was praised for its speed, sometimes for the fact that it carried 350 passengers, among them, presumably the arriving immigrants, and that it stopped regularly in New Ulm, usually on a Friday or Saturday, in a run between New Ulm and St. Paul. Eventually the "Franklin Steele" was taken out of service in southern Minnesota and moved via the Minnesota river to its new home on the Red River of the North. Repeatedly the young community of New Ulm was pleased to be receiving newcomers, for instance with reference to a new German word "Mover" becoming a German word from Pennsylvania Dutch. Thus the German-language *Pionier* was delighted that newcomers were arriving on *Moverwägen* that rolled through the streets en route to their quarter section farms in the region.[23] Unfortunately the place of origin of the new immigrants is never reported.

The instability of the financial situation in the southwestern Minnesota is exemplified by recurring page-long newspaper lists of foreclosures, sheriff's sales and defaults on property. Obviously many of the "Movers" came, stayed a few months or years, and pulled out for stations farther west. A review of the published defaulting parties reveals that none of these early arrivals bore German-Bohemian-names. More than likely there were no Bohemians with the original settlement company. And when they did reach the county, they seldom made first claims on the land. Rather, they became a stabilizing element in the form of rather poor, but tenacious peasant stock that was willing to abide the soil and wait more patiently for its rewards. Nor did the in-town default situation correct itself soon. For example in 1859 an article highlights the fact that there were over 400 building sites available for purchase within the city of New Ulm.[24]

Politically, the Brown County community was active mostly through the Republican party which invited (though not always received) important speakers the likes of Wisconsin's Karl Schurz to address them. Democrats were small in number in New Ulm at first, which was consistent with the wave of Republican popularity among the Germans during that pre-Lincoln period. At times community leaders vigorously denied false accusations for instance that New Ulm was founded for and by Turners alone. In reply to such an allegation by the *Minnesota Staats-Zeitung* of St. Paul, the local editor remarked that the Turners had only 40 members at the time while there were over 1200 non-Turner people in the city of New Ulm alone.[25] Nor was it true, as the outside paper had alleged, that the *Pionier* was a Turner newspaper, rather it was founded by and for "people who possessed enough common sense to be independent in thought, supportive of others who were independent and who behaved independently."[26]

In the election results for 1860 no names of winners were of Bohemian origin in any of the townships in which they lived. Nor were there any Bohemians who had won at the state level. Virtually all political offices were captured by non Germans, although from 1860 onwards Turner candidate William Pfaender was in and out of several major political races. On the whole, Germans did not have a chance at major political office. The Germans were lucky if they succeeded in rural township choices such as board of supervisors, constable, assessor and the like. In Cottonwood township the names of John Manderfeld, Peter Lieber and others succeeded, in Milford names like Zeller, Hoffmann, Westphal and Dehn occur in the 1860 results. None was a German-Bohemian.[27]

The big news in 1861 was the announcement that the Winona-St. Peter and Missouri Railroad planned to complete construction for arrival in New Ulm by the first of March, 1866.[28] Other developments were petitions to the Post Office in Washington requesting service to Cottonwood, Linden, Lafayette, West Newton, Fort Ridgley, Redwood and Yellow Medicine. Daily service was to be installed to St. Peter thus providing better contact to the more developed regions of the state and nation. Linden, Cottonwood, Milford and West Newton were to receive post offices. Announcements of teacher openings stipulated that candidates had to be able to offer instruction in the public schools in both English and German.[29] Sometimes local promoters complained about "Runners" in St. Paul who were preventing arriving German-speaking immigrants from continuing on to New Ulm.[30] Naturally they made reference to the beautiful city of New Ulm and the rural opportunities that awaited newcomers if they would just come.[31]

Just before the city suffered its greatest setback and the loss of most of its businesses including the German-language paper, there appeared a summary of the city's history, crediting those who endured the financial hard times of the late 1850s and the farmers who came from Wisconsin with some money and a lot of cattle and implements.[32] As of this date, the city had more than 20 business places, two steam mills, one large windmill, two breweries, a tannery, two brick factories, one pottery and a cement works (*Kalkbrennerei*). In addition there was a watch maker, two barrel makers, three wagoners, and five blacksmiths. The town had the services of two doctors, two schools with 118 pupils between them, and river steamer freight connections up to six months each year. Overland roads led to Sioux Falls, the Sioux Agencies, St. Peter, and Mankato. Little did community leaders realize that a month later everything would be wiped out by the Sioux Uprising. The last issue of the *New Ulm Pionier* appeared on August 16, 1862 without a hint of what was in the offing. Some printed resolutions declared that the citizens of the area were prepared to carry out their duty with respect to the Civil war. There was nothing about the impending Indian war. It broke out on Sunday, August 17 in Acton Township, Meeker County, when Native Americans in a store argued over each other's cowardice to steal a white storekeeper's eggs, which ended with murder of the grocer. Believing they would be severely punished anyway, the Sioux within hours seized the opportunity to settle legitimate complaints against the Whites. In the ensuring war, Chief Little Crow unsuccessfully attacked both Fort Ridgely and the city of New Ulm in pitched battles. The Sioux were no match for the Minnesota militia under Henry Sibley as supported by Lincoln's army commanded by General John Pope.[33]

The history of the Dakota in Minnesota in the decades after 1850 is particularly sad. Attempts to remove them to reservations in 1853-54 met with little success and aid promised by the government failed to arrive. Some returned to their homes in Wabasha, Goodhue and Rice counties, but these lands by this time were occupied by white settlers. In August 1862, driven by hunger and broken promises, the Dakota attacked settlements in the Minnesota River Valley, proving themselves especially aggressive at New Ulm. Although the war lasted only a few weeks, about 700 whites died and there was widespread destruction of property. Calls for the removal of the Dakota, if not their extermination, resulted in 38 of them being hanged at Mankato for their part in the conflict. From a population of perhaps 7,000 before the war, the Dakota population in Minnesota in 1866 had dropped to 364.[34]

There is no evidence that the war scare in any way affected the immigration of German-Bohemians to Brown county. The Civil War at that time was the real impediment to new arrivals from Europe. To be sure the Indian episode caught the fancy of Europeans in general and of the Germans in particular, especially after the voluminous publications about American Indians and the Wild West by ever popular Karl May (1842-1912). May's German-language books began appearing in 1892: *Durch die Wüste* 1892, *Winnetou* 1893, *Old Surehand* 1894 followed by many others. Clearly Father Berghold's 1892 edition of the Sioux Uprising was lifted by May's rising tide of popularity, whose publications rose to at least fifty million copies by 1970. But all of this came too late to effect the arrival of German speakers from Bohemia. If anything, they were frightened off by the early widespread publicity which the event gained in the German-language press of the U.S.[35]

Primary sources of information about Brown county following the

1862 uprising are lacking. There was no newspaper until 1864 when the *New Ulm Post* made its debut on February 5, 1864. It ran advertisements for the German Willius Bank in St. Paul, which offered services on both sides of the Atlantic, including the ticketing of passengers. Reports about immigration took devious turns. Sometimes articles boasted about new coal mines supposedly opening up in Cottonwood township which, it was hoped, would induce more immigrants to come.[36] Also New Ulmers occasionally scolded St. Paul agencies and directors of boarding houses who allegedly talked immigrants out of going to the New Ulm area in favor of other "more desirable" destinations.[37] Responses to inquiries from immigrants in Wisconsin wanting information about conditions for work and settlement in New Ulm show how aggressively the community sought newcomers.[38] Full page lists of hundreds of properties that bore delinquent real estate tax status continue to shed light on the less than thriving economy in the region.[39] Usually in the spring and early summer immigrant wagon trains passed right on through town, with no intention of remaining. The paper carefully reported about a large numbers of Norwegians who arrived at La Crosse by steamer, took 75 wagons with a family in each, headed west into southern Minnesota, but never bothered to stop in New Ulm.[40] In the mid-1860s there was no mention of immigrants coming from Bohemia.

Throughout the spring and summer of 1866, however, there was repeated commentary that newcomers were staying temporarily in the local hotels or with friends, checking out the chances of settlement in the New Ulm area.[41] Moreover, the governor of Minnesota appointed a district immigration committee to assist the state office with the recruitment of immigrants, especially from Germany, for Brown county. Serving on that committee from the city of New Ulm were Anton Zieber and Jonas Lautenschläger; from Milford township came August Westphal, and from Cottonwood, Peter Manderfeld. None who served were of Bohemian background, although a John Manderfeld had married Cecelia Drach who was from Bohemia. Also, Anton Manderfeld's wife, Annie, was from Bohemia. A Peter who would fit the age needed for committee service cannot be found in the censuses.[42]

Transportation to New Ulm during this period was either by steamer on the Minnesota River or by wagon train.[43] For years, therefore, the eyes of the community focused on the river as its primary contact to the outside world. Annually the arrival of the first boat was a major event.[44] Always interested in receiving new immigrants, the editors of the *New Ulm Post* praised St. Paul for constructing a new *"Emigranten Herberge"* (immigration shelter house) which New Ulm leaders believed would help funnel immigrants to its region.[45] There was praise when German-speaking immigrants from Illinois arrived and purchased 500 acres each for about $8,000 in cash. And, of course, the editors cheered when the governor of Minnesota appointed Albert Wolff, editor of the St. Paul *Minnesota Staatszeitung*, to become special agent for immigration from Germany.

Wolff's appointment required that he reside in Bremen and visit the areas with the greatest potential supply of German-speakers. Wolff reported his success in the areas of Bremen, Hannover, Hamburg and described plans for upcoming visits to East Prussia and Southern Germany (which would have included the German-speaking watershed eastward to Bischofteinitz).[46] Repeatedly there were speculative articles about whether Brown county might not be sitting on top of Ruhr district types of deep deposits of anthracite, which in turn might trigger a huge industrial boom in the territory.[47] Time would prove that the only hard assets in the region were the rich "black gold" top soil which in due time would be "mined" by the German-Bohemians.

By the time the first full decade of Brown county's existence had come to a close, the population had grown from 2,193 to 5,917, an increase of 3,724, to almost triple its 1860 size. The largest growth was not, however, in the city of New Ulm, which went from 645 to 1,312, but in the rural townships where farmers had acquired land. During this decade the earliest settlers closest to New Ulm departed, some for states like Oregon and California, but newcomers always arrived to take their place. A casual glance at the annual tax delinquencies exhibits the changes of names over the decade. At mid-decade, for instance, there were almost no German-Bohemian names on the rosters. By 1870, however, there still were none in the city but in the key township of Sigel, the names of delinquents include Kretsch, Tauer, Schnobrich, Stadick, Flor, Eckstein and Seifert. In Cottonwood tax delinquent families had names like Gulden, Schnobrich, Hochhaus, and Dauer, all Bohemian names.

New Ulm did not have an English-language paper until 1870 when the *Plain Dealer* began on November 4, 1870. By December 20, 1872, however, it had already given up. The New Ulm *Herald* started a few months later on March 21, 1873 under the ownership of Captain William H. Sigler. It lasted until November 22, 1878. As indicated by the census results of 1880, the 1870s proved ripe for German-Bohemians to come in large numbers to Brown county. Enough were already in residence by 1870 to provide a "chain migration" basis for many new arrivals, both individuals and families, to the New Ulm region. The increases attracted some attention in the press.

The English language press, however, failed to find the increase of German immigrants to be of much interest. But it did report periodically on events relating to the arrival of immigrants. Access by train existed since 1872 on the Winona and St. Peter, and the St. Paul and Sioux City. However, only the Winona and St. Peter came into the New Ulm station. The Cottonwood station at the southeastern end of the city of New Ulm provided access to passengers in the rural areas south of town. They even offered restaurant services from the homes of adjacent neighbors who prepared "carry-in" meals for hungry travelers.[48]

Also during the 1870s a Catholic community prospered. It took two decades for a Catholic clientele to arrive in the city for, to a significant degree, these Catholics were the German-Bohemians. Earlier Catholic Bohemians worshiped in simple pioneer structures out in the rural areas. One was in West Newton, three miles west of current St. George, where the Bohemians and other Catholics constructed the first Catholic Church in Nicollet county in 1857. In 1859-61, they built another log structure in Cottonwood township, about five miles south of New Ulm, the first Catholic church in Brown county. Its old cemetery now graces a pleasant wayside. Holy Trinity Church in Turner-German New Ulm was founded in 1869 after sufficient need arose for an in-city church. Its first pastor was Father Alexander Berghold who until 1890 served the needs of this and other rural parishes in southwestern Minnesota.[49] Berghold was ideally suited for ministry to the German-Bohemian flock, being an Austro-Hungarian national who identified with the mostly Bohemian population in the parish. Among his many writings, Berghold drafted a "Guide to German Emigrants."[50]

Berghold was most successful in bringing the New Ulm Turners to harmonize with the German-Bohemian Catholics. During 1872, hundreds of farmers and draymen volunteered to deliver 7,000 loads of

Old Winona and St. Peter Depot, about 1890. As early as 1872, many German-Bohemian immigrants began arriving in New Ulm by rail. BC

rock for the parochial school building.[51] Following this inter-faith effort, Berghold invited the public to its grand opening on June 5, 1873, promising education to all denominations, and religious indoctrination only for those requesting it. Festivities in both German and English made all feel welcome. Boarders of any faith were welcome for $6.00 per month. Berghold also attracted the attention of non-denominational Germans when he converted a four acre plot of land on the bluffs into a vineyard to raise grapes for German wine.[52] Although Holy Trinity Church was dedicated in 1870, its altar waited for completion and was not consecrated until November 15, 1874 because Father Berghold imported a Bohemian artist by the name of Mikus to produce the masterpiece.[53] Other Christian denominations had begun their efforts in the city somewhat earlier – the German Methodists in 1862 (church rebuilt in 1864), the German Lutherans in 1865, and the halls built by Turners who were a "religious" group unto themselves. Holy Trinity quickly became the largest parish with 186 families in 1875.[54]

In Brown county as a whole, there seemed to be good relations between the English-speakers and the German-Bohemians. Because the Bohemians had settled most densely in Sigel township immediate-

Holy Trinity parish high school taken in 1904. BC

ly southwest of the city, an exuberant description of this region printed in the *New Ulm Herald* is worthy of attention.

> A visitor to Brown County desiring to form a correct idea of the fer-
> tility and beauty, should visit Sigel town, a locality whose charms well
> deserve a tourist's attention. . . . Providence showered on that locality
> all that adds to the happiness of man. The latter, appreciating its
> beauty, exerted itself to improve the paradise of Sigel town. Trimmer
> fences and better cultivated fields are not to be found in the State, and
> the dwellings of the farmers, often substantial and tasteful brick build-
> ings erected at a cost of six or eight thousand dollars, would adorn a
> handsome city. . . . Need we tell that these good folks are German set-
> tlers? . . . As a body they are orderly, wealthy and respected. They will
> scarcely elect a justice, having no quarrels to settle. They stoutly
> defend their rights to bring a keg of beer now and then from New
> Ulm, but no drunkard or pauper lives among them. They are a credit
> to our community, as their town is the garden of our County.[55]

Immigrants from Bohemia continued to arrive and to take up residence with heir trusted and successful relatives and friends in "Garden

of Eden" Sigel and adjacent townships. New Ulm, their home, their market, their cultural center was at first their "home away from home," one that adequately mirrored their place of origin. Soon it would become their new home and the Old Country would be forgotten.

Notes

1. *Unser Heimatkreis Bischofteinitz mit den deutschen Siedlungen im Bezirk Taus*, compiled and edited by Franz Liebl with Josef Bernklau, Franz Dimter, Willi Gabriel, Johann Gröbner, Rudolf Kiefner, Anton Pauli, Emil Reimer, Rudolf Schieberl, and Dr. Karl Stich, 4th printing, (Furth im Wald: Heimatkreis Bischofteinitz, first published in 1967, 4th printing 1983). This volume, like the others written by the 1945-46 expellees from the Sudetenland of Czechoslovakia, is comprehensive. It contains not only the history of the region but also descriptions of each settlement or village along with chapters on folklore, royal families, church and religious life, schools, hunting and fishing, trades and handicrafts, clubs, cooperatives, transportation, an historical overview, and the spoken German dialect.

2. Ibid., mountains, p. 10, River Radbusa p. 17, River Bastritz and poem, pp. 30-33.

3. See in general Anton Herzig, ed., *Die Geminden des Landkreises Mies: Ihre Geschichte bis 1945 und das Schicksal ihrer deutschen Bevölkerung*, 2nd edition (Dinkelsbühl: 1983).

4. *Heimatkreis Bischofteinitz.*, p. 34.

5. Ibid., pp. 43 ff.

6. Ibid., p. 56.

7. Here and below, ibid., the chapter on place names, pp. 58-62.

8. Ibid., pp. 79-98.

9. Ibid., pp. 104-5.

10. Here and below, ibid., the chapter on events reported in local newspapers pp. 106-16.

11. *New Ulm Pionier.* The document is microfilmed at the head of the reel which contains the newspaper, dated August 1857. The Pionier was published in German from January 1, 1858 - August 16, 1862 when the Indian uprising interrupted publication.

12. A. Fritsche, *History of Brown County Minnesota,* I (Indianapolis: B. F. Bowen, 1916), pp. 137 ff.

13. Cf. *New Ulm Pionier,* April 22, 1858, pp. 3 ff. Concerning the bank and its history, see La Vern J. Rippley, "German-American Banking in Minnesota," in *A German Heritage Fulfilled: German-Americans*, ed. Clarence A. Glasrud (Moorhead, MN: Concordia College Press, 1984), pp. 94-115. In addition to Fritsche, see Alexander Berghold, "Geschichte von New Ulm," *Der deutsche Pionier* [Cincinnati] 4 (June 1872), Leota M. Kellett, *Early Brown County* (New Ulm, 1966); Elroy E. Ubl, trans., *Chronology of New Ulm, Minnesota, 1853-1899* (New Ulm, 1978); Hildegard Binder Johnson, "The Founding of New Ulm, Minnesota," *American-German Review* (June, 1946), 8-12 with illustrations; Fred W. Johnson, "The Acquisition of a Townsite," typescript in Brown County Historical Society, New Ulm. Townsite founder, Ferdinand Beinhorn's account of the founding of New Ulm is translated in the *New Ulm Review*, August 15, 1938, p. 4. See also Alice Felt Tyler, "William Pfaender and the Founding of New Ulm," *Minnesota History*, 30 (March, 1949), 24-35.

14. *New Ulm Pionier,* May 6, 1858, p. 4.

15. The letters were found in the Meidl family and turned over to the author by Michael's granddaughter, Angie Meidl (Mrs. George J. Portner Jr., Route 2, Box 31, New Ulm, MN 56073).

16. Letter from Theresia Meidl to Michael Meidl, dated at Kaltenbrunn, August 1, 1921.

17. Letter dated November 14, 1921

18. Letter from Theresia Meidl, dated January 1, 1922.

19. Letter from Theresia Meidl, June 30, 1923.

20. Letter from Theresia Meidl, December 2, 1923.

21. Excellent examples of such letters are published in two issues of Currents. See La Vern J. Rippley, "The Josefine Pany Letters," Parts I & II in *Currents: A Minnesota River Valley Review*, Vol. 4 No. 4 and Vol. 5 No. 1 (1994-95), 5-10, 38-40.

22. New Ulm Pionier, July 22, 1858, p. 3.

23. *New Ulm Pionier*, May 12, 21, 1859, pages vary but entries occur under the heading of "Neu-Ulm und Umgebung." See also Fritsche, *Brown County*, p. 137. The fate of the "Franklin Steele" is as yet unresearched. For instance the *Pionier*, June 23, 1859 p. 3 reports that it ran aground near Red Wood Falls, having been in New Ulm for three stops already that month. In the same column, we learn that a new bank, the Central Bank has just opened in New Ulm, with a "redeeming office" and notes in denominations of 1, 2, 5, and 10 dollars which will be personally guaranteed by the bank's owners, who were Franklin Steele and John Wesley North (the latter, the founder of Northfield, Minnesota and California, as well as being an early regent of the University of Minnesota). Steele, the man, was therefore involved personally with New Ulm, not just with the shipping business to that site. Furthermore, the statement by Fritsche, *Brown County*, pp. 418 ff. that "at first there was little or no demand for banking houses there," is untrue. The above-mentioned Central Bank did close, however, by July, 1861. (*Pionier*, July 6, 1861, p. 3)

24. *New Ulm Pionier*, July 16, 1859, p. 3. See lists of names during the spring and summer issues.

25. *New Ulm Pionier*, Oct. 22, 1859, p. 2. On the support of the Minnesota Germans for Republicans and Karl Schurz in particular, see Hildegard Binder Johnson, "The Election of 1860 and the Germans in Minnesota," *Minnesota History*, 28 (March, 1947), 20-36, esp. 27-29, 36. If Germans were Catholic, they were likely to be Democrats, if Protestant, Republican and the city of New Ulm at the time was especially non-Catholic, hence quite Republican. The Catholic element was in fact the Bohemian element, which was rural, or had not yet arrived.

26. *New Ulm Pionier*, Oct. 22, 1959, p. 2.

27. *New Ulm Pionier*, April 7, 1860, p. 2 and ibid., Nov. 10,1860, pp. 1-4.

28. *New Ulm Pionier*, March 23, 1891, p. 4.

29. *New Ulm Pionier*, April 6, 1861, p. 6.

30. *New Ulm Pionier*, May 25, 1861, p. 4.

31. *New Ulm Pionier*, June 15, 1861, p. 5.

32. *New Ulm Pionier*, July 26, 1862 p. 3.

33. Duane Schultz, *Over the Earth I Come: The Great Sioux Uprising of* 1862 (New York: S.t Martin's Press, 1992). See also Kenneth Carley, *The Sioux Uprising of* 1862, 2nd ed. (St. Paul: Minnesota State Historical Society, 1976); Father Alexander Berghold of Holy Trinity Parish wrote *Indianer Rache oder die Schreckenstage von New Ulm, zweite verbesserte und vermehrte Auflage mit 7 Abbildungen und einer Kartenskizze*, which was published by the Verlags-Buchhandlung Styria in 1892 in Graz. It was a great

success both in Europe and the U.S. It was also translated into English from the first edition and published by P. J. Thomas in San Francisco in 1891. From this original, Elroy E. Ubl of New Ulm issued a facsimile edition in 1976. See La Vern J. Rippley, "Alexander Berghold, Pioneer Priest and Prairie Poet," *The Report, Society for the History of the Germans in Maryland – A Journal of German- American History*, 27 (1978), 43-56, esp. 50. See also the recently translated personal account by Don Heinrich Tolzmann, ed. & trans. *The Sioux Uprising in Minnesota, 1862: Jacob Nix' Eyewitness History* (Indianapolis: Max Kade German-American Center, 1994).

34. Mitchell E. Rubinstein and Alan R. Woolworth, "The Dakota and Ojibwa" in *They Chose Minnesota*, pp. 21-22.

35. Carl F. Wittke, *The German-Language Press in America* (Lexington: University of Kentucky Press, 1957) surveys the press, which in concept if not in detail has been competently updated by James M. Bergquist, "The German-American Press," in Sally M. Miller, ed., *The Ethnic Press in the United States* (New York: Greenwood Press, 1987), pp. 131-159. An attitude of ambivalence toward the Native American prevails in the columns of the German-language press: On the one hand an image of the "noble savage," on the other, the impracticality of trying to live off the land in a time when reliance on "the commons" had clearly given way to modern views on the importance of row-crop agriculture. The Germans also fought hard for managed American forests and similar European traditions. See also Henry Geitz, ed. *The German-American Press* (Madison: Max Kade Institute, 1992).

36. *New Ulm Post*, April 1, 1864 p. 3.

37. Ibid., Feb. 12, 1864 p. 3.

38. Ibid., Feb. 12, 1864 p. 3.

39. Ibid., April 29, 1864 and weeks following.

40. Ibid., June 24, 1864 p. 3.

41. Ibid., April 27, 1866, p. 3.

42. Ibid., Sept. 29, 1865, p. 3. See also Fritsche, *Brown County*, II, pp. 240 ff. and U.S. Censuses, 1860, 70, 80. There were at least two families by the name Manderfeld and it is impossible to decipher which ones intersect as the generations descend to our time. They intermarried with Bohemians at various generational levels.

43. No railroad reached the area prior to February 22, 1872 when the Winona and St. Peter Company completed its line as far west as New Ulm. Later this company became known as the Winona, St. Peter and Sioux City and as such, together with the former (W & St. P. L. Co.), owned many alternate sections of land in Brown County. Eventually this road merged into the Chicago & Northwestern. The Minneapolis & St. Louis railroad was not completed until 1897. A branch of the Chicago & Northwestern left the mainline west of Sleepy Eye, running to the Northwest – the Redwood Branch. Plats of the late 1800s show the sections owned by the railroads. See also Fritsche, *Brown County*, I, p. 492.

44. *New Ulm Post*, April 28, 1867, p. 2.

45. Here and below *New Ulm Post* May 24, 1867, June 7, 1867, May 12, 1869, p. 4, July 2, 1869, p. 3.

46. The best overall source on immigration recruitment is Theodore C. Blegen, "Minnesota's Campaign for Immigrants," *Yearbook of the Swedish Historical Society*, 11 (1926), 3-83. The St. Paul immigrant home is mentioned not only in the papers but on p. 14 of this article. The legislation to recruit immigrants in foreign countries came from the immigration board and was endorsed by Governor W. R. Marshall in his annual message of 1868, p. 15. The report of Albert Wolff to Governor Horace Austin dated

September 7, 1870 gives many details about Wolff's efforts to secure German-speaking immigrants for Minnesota. He conceived his task as a "humanistic and public minded effort to concentrate German emigration to Minnesota" (p. 31). The entire report appears on pp. 55-64. A lot of emigrants, Wolff discovered, were migrating on the strength of letters from relatives and friends, and thus many were determined to proceed according to letter-arrangements to Michigan or Illinois, rather than to Minnesota where Wolff believed they would be better situated (p. 57). The American letter was always a powerful force in the immigration flow.

47. *New Ulm Post* Feb. 26, 1869 p. 3 and ff.

48. *New Ulm Herald*, April 25, 1873.

49. In 1890 Berghold was removed by Archbishop Ireland for his German ethnicity. See details in La Vern J. Rippley, "Archbishop Ireland and the School Language Controversy," *U.S. Catholic Historian*, I (Fall, 1980), 1-16.

50. Governor Pillsbury in 1876 commended Berghold for his success in recruiting German-speaking immigrants for the New Ulm region. Among many sources, cf. Henry J. Scherer, *The Church of the Holy Trinity of New Ulm,* Diamond jubilee (October 8, 1944) who claims in his preface p. 9 that Berghold brought in "fifty German families from Central Europe" (presumably from Bohemia) who in turn attracted ever greater numbers of immigrants. The state archives lack confirmation of the awarding of such a commendation. Early churches are mentioned pp. 14 ff. See also Elroy Ubl, "Founder of Holy Trinity Parish Wrote Many Books," in *Historical Notes: A Glimpse at New Ulm's Past,* I (New Ulm: The Journal Press, 1982), pp. 91-92, and ibid., II, 157-159.

51. *New Ulm Herald* May 30, June 6, 1873. Scherer, *Holy Trinity,* p. 141. Ubl, I, 137 ff.

52. *Herald*, Nov. 20, 1874.

53. *Herald*, Nov. 13, 1874.

54. *Herald*, Jan. 8, 1875.

55. *Herald*, July 30, 1875 p. 6.

𝕱𝖔𝖚𝖗

The Market and Culture Center of Brown County – New Ulm

A Magnet for Immigrants

URING THE 19TH CENTURY, Brown county enjoyed a typical American agricultural economy. Its county seat, New Ulm, served as a central market for a large and productive rural area. New Ulm was also the religious seat of a rural population, a home to fraternal, social, and secret organizations, the most prominent being the Turners, who in their anti-clerical stance were almost as religious as the Catholics and Lutherans. Because cultural activities were engendered either from the churches or from the social organizations (here again, the Turners), New Ulm in some respects displayed the socioreligious character of a European village.

The Central European village is a phenomenon unto its own. None is laid out on the typical grid which is commonplace in the United States, a product of the National Survey.[1] Most have a circular instead of the checkerboard formation common to Midwest America. A few can be defined as a *Strassendorf*, a clustering of house-barns along a highway, sometimes with a widened area near the center displaying an oblong or squared market region. Often European villages circulate around a hub with roadways radiating spoke-like in all directions from a central axis. At dead center are usually three structures which symbolize the three primary subdivisions of society: religion, civil admin-

PLAN des Marktes MUTTERSDORF

Erklärung: ■ Häuser ▨ Gewesene Häuser ☐ Grundstücke ▭ Wiesen ☐ Äcker ▧ Gewässer ▨ Wege

Village layout of Muttersdorf. Basically a dual German Strassendorf *[street village] with the church and market in the main oblong opening. Farmsteads stretch back from the house-barn structures that front the streets. Note also the pond at the right side and the former much larger pond, now filled, in the same area. At the pond site stood formerly a domicile for the nobility.*

istration, and an economy. In the center of every European village are the church, the town hall, and the market square.[2]

In Europe, a principle of "the commons," according to which land surfaces belonged to, and were used by everyone prevailed into the 20th century. Fields lay in carefree patterns along the meandering spokes of highways extending away from the village center. Never were the owner's land holdings adjacent to each other. Despite disadvantages of access, this distribution of the fields seemed fair because each ended up with some good and some poorer quality soils. Until modern times, grazing fields were used "in common" both by the inhabitants of a village as well as by the landowners. Only after freeing the serfs in 1848 was an effort made to separate plow lands from pastures and to assign them to individual owners. Some lands, notably forests, pastures and village ponds were never removed from usage according to the principle of "the commons." In America, a few pasture lands once were for universal use, for instance, in historic Boston Commons, but in Brown county it had no parallel. Immigrants had to adapt at once to a system of land ownership which implied dwelling directly on the land, not in a village where daily intercourse within the community could be taken for granted.

In the *Böhmerwald*, the prevailing village pattern was not a circular one, yet all villages show the obvious central locus with church, civil structure, and market square approximately at the pivot. Often a *Strassendorf* is in evidence, for example, at Hostau, Weissensulz, Muttersdorf and others.[3] Sometimes not only the three social unities but also a village pond or well, and perhaps a central bake house help define the focus even if the overall layout tended more toward the square than the circle.[4] Muttersdorf is an excellent example of the extended *Strassendorf* with a church prominently in the middle, surrounded by an oblong market. Lots extend back from the main roads in the form of narrow housebarns.

New Ulm is not like these villages. It did not grow up naturally but rather was designed by the founders with the result that structures were positioned on geometrical patterns rather than instinctively according to immediate urge or old tradition. In most respects, the communal founding society followed the grid pattern suggested by the survey, but they also made concessions to the river, ignoring meridians and section lines for their orientation.[5] Originally two plats were on record representing New Ulm, forcing the legislature in 1860 to decide which [the Prignitz] would be the legal record for conveyance. While this plat illustrates the expected grid, it offers a concession to the European pattern by means of its centrally located courthouse, adjacent to the Turner Hall (for them the "church"), and a central high school. The two blocks to the east on Minnesota street exemplify a *Strassendorf*, running parallel to the Minnesota River. Parks grace the river, the northern and the southern ends of the village parallelogram.

The semblance of a Bohemian village occurs in New Ulm primarily by means of the long lots on Front Street and by Valley Street on the lower-level east side of the tracks. To this district of town the German-Bohemians flocked when they began taking up residences within the city limits. For immigrants, New Ulm incorporated the necessities nor-

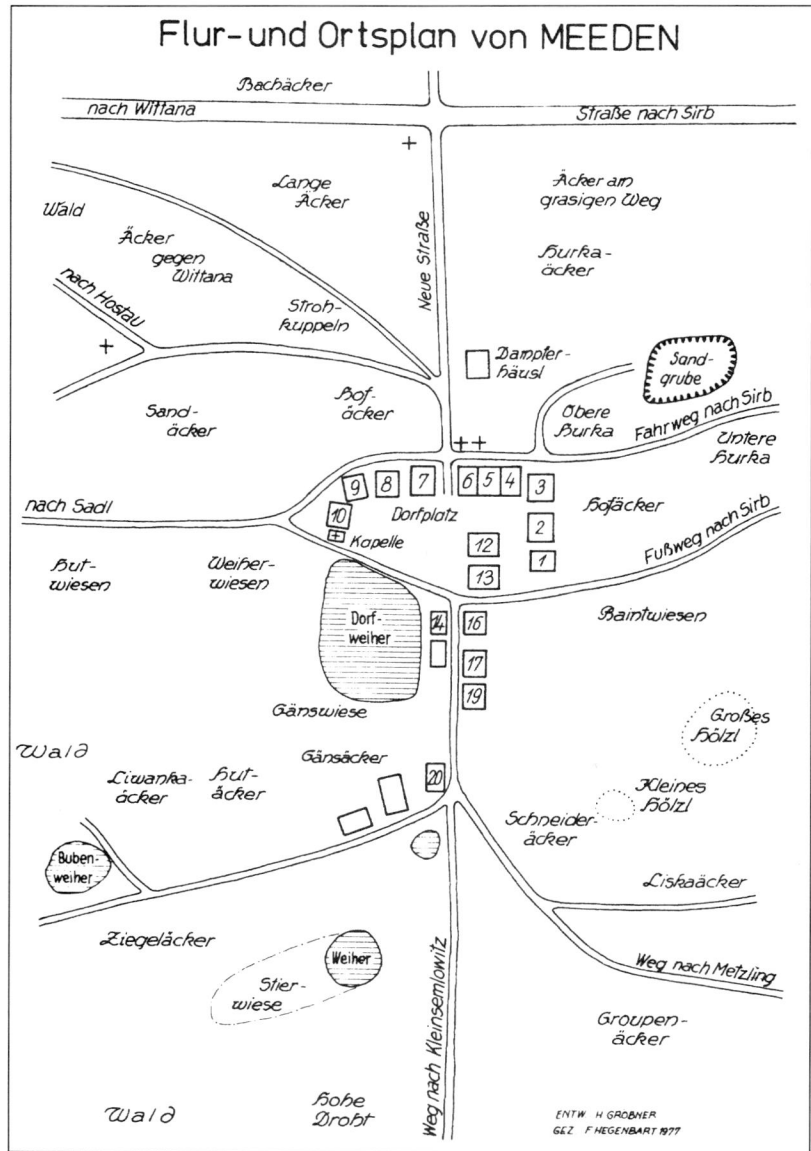

Flur- und Ortsplan von MEEDEN

Sketch of the typically square village of Meeden, including village pond [Dorfwei-her], an open market square with chapel, and a goose pasture around the pond.

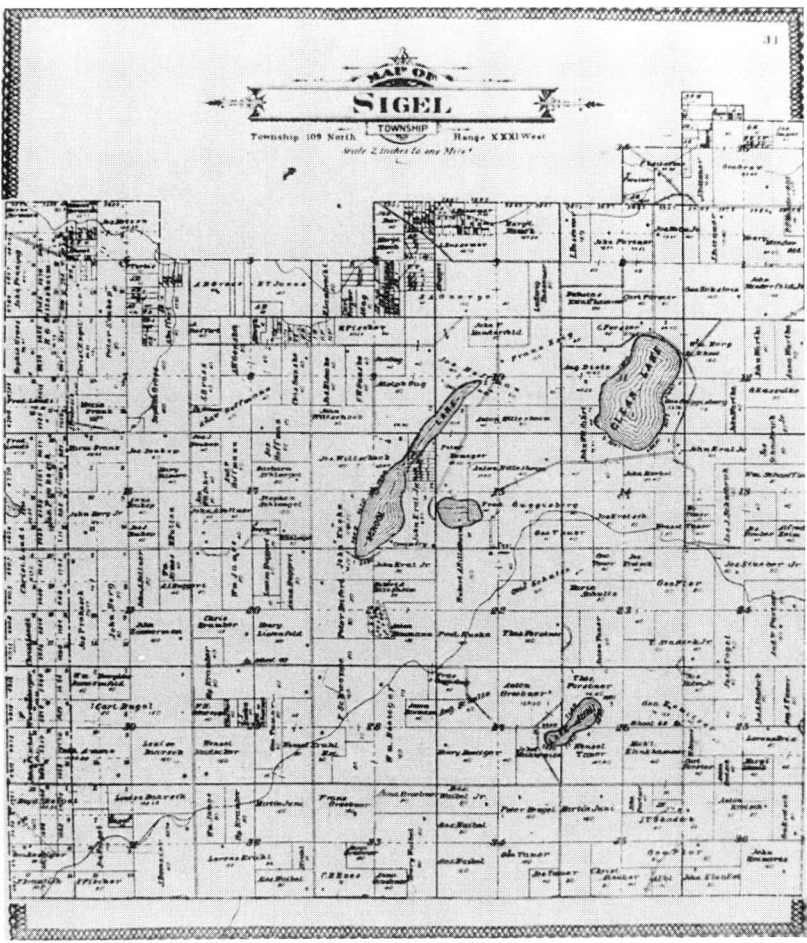

Map of Sigel township from the year 1905.

mally offered by a European village: social, economic, civil and spiritual. Few of the churches command a central position within the city
landscape the way it normally would in a European village, except for
the prominent site of Holy Trinity Cathedral, the primary German-
Bohemian church in the area. The county courthouse occupies a central position to qualify as a symbol which equates to a European civil

Downtown New Ulm, Minnesota Street in the 1880s. BC

unit, the Rathaus, and as noted, the dominant social hall of the Turner Society stands next to the courthouse.

Farmsteads in America had to stand on the acreage itself and therefore no European-style barn-houses line the streets of New Ulm. But hints at a concession to this land-ownership mandate can be seen in the detached barns that line the alley ways in the older sections of the city. In many of these structures, villagers once kept a cow or two, chickens and pigs. Particularly in the Valley-Front Street district below the hill, geese were routinely herded, Bohemian-style. This European tradition soon gave rise to the nickname *Gänseviertel* or "Goosetown" for the area between Minnesota Street and the river.

New Ulm soon had the necessary business institutions like banks, meat markets, groceries, dry goods stores, as well as professionals in medicine and dentistry. "The object of the German Land Company is to procure a home for every German laborer, popish priests and lawyers excepted, in some healthy and productive district, located on some navigable river."[6] However, within a quarter century both priest and lawyer were also welcome! Where Germans settled breweries quickly followed. Two traditional New Ulm breweries were August

Groebner Corner on Minnesota Street. BC

Tending geese in New Ulm. BC

Hauenstein Brewery in New Ulm. BC

Schell, begun in 1861 near caves on the cliffs above the Cottonwood river, and Betz and Hauenstein, completed in 1865 and augmented many times afterwards.

While the breweries were an employment magnet for new immigrants from Bohemia, the real attractions were the consumers of agricultural commodities from the region, namely, the flour milling industries. According to the 1905 state census, Brown county produced more flour than any county in Minnesota except Hennepin [Minneapolis], then the largest in the nation. While mills operated in Springfield, Sleepy Eye and at other smaller locations within Brown county, the Eagle and the Roller mills in New Ulm had the largest capacity.

The decades from 1880 to the end of the century witnessed phenomenal growth in the employment capacity of New Ulm city. For example during 1891, large building projects were undertaken by the Eagle Mill ($46,000), by Hauenstein's Brewery ($21,000), and by the Masonic building ($21,000). In January, 1892 the papers headlined that the year just past brought the city the biggest building boom ever.

New Ulm's Schell's Brewery in an earlier day. BC

All of these industries were agriculturally fueled.[7] For the year 1891, 1,809,000 bushels of wheat yielded 339,213 barrels of flour. The breweries strained to manufacture the 23,000 barrels of beer they sold annually. Creameries, vinegar works and farm machinery dealers all catered to the needs of the agricultural population. In 1891 the Eagle Mill was packing over 1,000 barrels of flour per day, with an additional 450 by the Empire Mill and 390 by the Roller Mill and 50 by the Cottonwood Mill south of town. Many of the common laborers in these mills were German-Bohemians.

The New Ulm creamery annually made 120,000 pounds of butter while it also bought and shipped over 105,000 dozen eggs. From the Vinegar works, 5,000 barrels departed New Ulm annually. The New Ulm brick yard owned by the Aufderheide family also contributed to the local economy by hiring over 40 men to produce nearly three million common along with 70,000 fired bricks each year. Not far away, the Stockert Brickyard annually crafted another 75,000 bricks. An industry now forgotten was cigar making. In 1891, Frank Burg employed 15 men to produce annually 700,000 cigars. Theodore

Empire Mill – the mills provided much needed employment for many German-Bohmian workers until they were able to purchase farms in rural Brown County. BC

Eagle Mill, New Ulm, work site for many German-Bohemians.

Workers at the New Ulm Roller Mill around the turn of the century. At the top of the photo on his knees is John Haeberle, below him seated Christian Lindmeyer and standing to his left John Lang. In the front row L-R: Eric Thordson, the fireman; Jack Kennedy, the engineer; Ernst Wicherski, the bookkeeper; Frank Wennisch, Cole Yunker and Barney Waibel, a railway employee. BC

Mueller needed 10 men to roll 375,000 while the Stelljes Brothers made 140,000. Like the larger firms, smaller cottage cigar making operations apparently used imported tobacco. None was grown locally.[8]

Preoccupied with the city's financial achievements, the *New Ulm Review* on April 27, 1892, p. 5 headlined a section offering the history of each business establishment with the large letters "Prosperous New Ulm." Subheadings boasted: "A city made famous by its mills and breweries – the world their market; the quality of the products unsurpassed; the motto of its manufacturer, 'excelsior'; its natural advantages for a manufacturing and residence city are unexcelled; a beautiful location with delightful homes, possessing all the conveniences of life." Before launching forth with biographies of each business, proudly presented in the April 27 issue, the paper lauded New Ulm:

> We are compelled to state there is no city in Southern Minnesota of equal size containing as many handsome and substantial brick blocks which give the city a truly metropolitan appearance. The retail stores are commodious, light, attractively decorated, and stocked with the latest production of the most reliable manufacturers in their respective lines. The streets are wide, well rounded and lighted by electricity while the sidewalks are principally of flagstone and gravel and kept in fine condition. . . . New Ulm is noted as a city of home owners and many of its residences are models of architectural beauty, while their surroundings and furnishings bespeak the highest degree of culture among its people. . . . Many of them contain a large share of the so-called luxuries of the world, although when these assume the form of books, pictures, musical instruments etc., we are disposed and class them among strictly educational measures. . . . The surrounding farming country is among the richest and most beautiful in the United States. Long driveways extend from the city in every direction through this beautiful country affording much pleasure to lovers of this delightful method of recreation.

Not surprisingly, the business establishments of the city were described with comparably glowing verbiage. Clothed in the flowery descriptions, however, are also economic data which underscore why this was a genuine agricultural market center. The Empire mill owned by Pahl, Koch and Schmidt hired 58 men in production and three in

Nortwestern rail yard and crew. The railroads employed many German-Bohemian workers. BC

sales over the road. The John Hauenstein brewery managed by Fred Behnke used modern equipment to produce annually 15,000 barrels of beer. "The German people especially praise it and in almost every family its use is general." The Eagle mill since taking the Minnesota State Fair competition in 1891 had seen its brands "Gold Coin," "Surprise" and "Eagle's Best" win sales in the eastern United States and in Europe. To assure an adequate supply of wheat, the mill acquired ownership of elevators at Cobden, Evans, Morgan, Redwood Falls, Lamberton, Essig and in South Dakota. August Schell's brewery, owned in 1892 by Otto Schell, was increasing its capacity from 9000 to 11,000 barrels per year.

The Lounhardt Brothers Machine shop offered the services of a general foundry, repairing boilers, engines, and building castings with five men employed. The Joseph Schmucker brewery and malting house, located downtown, was famous over 22 years for the production of lager and malt beer, employing "many men and teams." In 1889 Andrew J. Eckstein (of German-Bohemian origins), after attending the National Institute of Pharmacy in Chicago, took over the drugstore from Dr. W. Weschke. Henry Crone operated both a general merchandise store and employed ten men at his "New Ulm Creamery."

The Dakota House with its forty rooms was a thriving enterprise that offered "neatness, cleanliness, comfort, well cooked and reliable meals" under the management of Albert Seiter. The livery stable was run by Tony Wiesner of the Dakota House hotel. "There the equipment is first class in every particular, special attention being paid to the wants of the patrons. Horses in abundance, stylish roadsters, harness of the latest pattern are kept in first class order. Buggies and carriages in splendid condition and attendants ready to comply with the requirements of the trade however exacting. . . . Horses kept by the day, week or month and at the lowest rates and transients fed and groomed to order are prominent features." The Union Hotel was operated by a German-Bohemian, Wenzel Schotzko, with 26 rooms and tables "abundantly supplied with all the delicacies." In the rural areas there were additional businesses of an agricultural nature that offered job opportunities for newcomer Bohemians. Practically every township had its creamry – Sigel, Cottonwood, and the rest.

In political office during the period from 1870-1900 were the mayors of New Ulm, most of whom were of German origin, Charles Roos, William Pfaender, C. Weschke, John Rudolph, H. B. Contans, Charles Wagner, E. G. Koch, and Charles Silverson. At the state level, several representatives with German-language background came from New Ulm – Emil Munch, William Pfaender, and Tyrolean born Joseph Bobleter who alternately held the office of Treasurer with Pfaender over the period of a dozen years. Pfaender was also a state senator. Bobleter, J. Rudolph, C. Brandt and others also served from the area as state representatives. The evidence seems clear that none of the holders of political office were of German-Bohemian birth or background. Nor were Bohemians among the early professionals – doctors, lawyers, dentists, druggists – Vogel and Eckstein being later exceptions. County offices too – from judges, commissioners, auditors, treasurers to lesser coveted positions – were not filled by the German-Bohemians.

Under the auspices of the Turner society many social functions in the German tradition were held in New Ulm, about which both the German and the English language newspapers reported regularly and profusely. There were frequent dramatic presentations, masquerade

The Dacotah House hotel on Minnesota street in New Ulm. BC

Meyer Tavern on Front Street in Goosetown, a prominent Schell's beer hangout in the 1870s. Its owner, John Meyer, died in 1875.

Sigel township Creamery about the year 1905. The creamery was created in 1868. BC

balls, many parades during the summer season especially on the Fourth of July, and for such fund raising campaigns as that to erect the Hermann Statue. The Hermann monument project, begun before 1880 and culminating in 1888, was orchestrated by the Sons of Hermann lodges under the leadership of the locally prominent Julius Berndt. From time to time, the Caecilia Society of Trinity church gave public choir demonstrations.

Schools quietly went about their business teaching interchangeably in both English and German. Advertisements for teachers often specified that the candidate must be able to offer instruction in both English and German (e.g. *New Ulm Herald*, June 23, 1876, p. 4, and *New Ulm Review*, Sept. 7, 1892, p. 5). Almost simultaneously in the 1890s there was much reporting about, and denunciation of, the Faribault-Stillwater school plan, though not because it was perceived as a threat to local German language education but because it evoked in New Ulm the anti-Catholic ire of the Turners.[9]

Throughout much of recorded New Ulm market life, however, the Germans-Bohemians were silent partners. They worked hard, raised families, worshiped and enjoyed family life. They seem almost conspicuous by their absence from public and economic matters of

St. Mary's parochial school about the year 1893. BC

Rural School Dist. #3 in Cottonwood township. Teacher Domeier is seen with his students. BC

Old timers enjoying Gemütlichkeit in Turner Hall. BC

importance. They seem not to have been named members of the German societies, be they the Turner society, the dramatic units, or the Männerchors. Their names do show up in musical organizations, however, about which there will be discussion in a later chapter. They were, however, members of the Catholic benevolent societies, for example St. Joseph's, St. John's Court, the Knights of Columbus and others.[10] Interestingly, the "Knights in German-Bohemian New Ulm" were under the patronage of St. Patrick even though only a small minority of the members were Irish. Germans-Bohemians were not represented in the many secular societies, such as the Ancient Order of United Workmen, the Odd Fellows, the Masons and similar secret or fraternal organizations having no link to a religion. Festivals connected to the church were always celebrated in grand style. Corpus Christi generally brought all Catholics into the city and offered an occasion for ceremony and celebration (e. g. *New Ulm Herald,* June 23, 1876, p. 4). Visits by a Catholic bishop, be it for purposes of confirmation or other occasions called for a torchlight parade and full partici-

Hermann Monument in the early 20th century. BC

pation by the German-Bohemian Catholic residents (e.g. *New Ulm Herald,* Sept. 21, 1877, p. 4). State-wide and even national conventions of the Turners never aroused interest among the German-Bohemians (e.g. *New Ulm Herald,* Nov. 26, 1875, p. 4, June 2, 1876, p. 4; *New Ulm Review,* Feb. 23, 1887 p. 5, June 13, 27, 1888 p. 5, etc.). Celebrations among the local Bohemians, by contrast, followed old folk and old religious traditions. Church festivals, baptisms, first and solemn Holy Communion days all were of greater importance to these German speakers than were the secular social functions which were orchestrated by Turners and others independently of a church.

The habit of minding the church calendar and its folk traditions was brought to New Ulm from the western Bohemia, about which more will be said in the chapter on folklore, arts, crafts and festivals. Likewise, farm life patterns carried over almost intact from the rural Bischofteinitz countryside. There, as in rural New Ulm, small grains

First communion at Holy Trinity church in 1892. BC

were a common agricultural product. Rather than wheat for flour milling, however, the farmers often raised rye for flour and a great deal of barley for local beer makers. Large breweries operated in Bischofteinitz, in Hostau, Muttersdorf, Weissensulz, Ronsperg and in other towns.[11] Like the Eagle, Roller and Cottonwood mills in New Ulm, there were countless grinding operations, often water driven, all over this western Bohemian county. Their location earlier was universally along streams for water power, but later within the villages where some still operated by water, but later were driven with Steam or diesel fuel.[12] Unlike Brown county, Bischofteinitz yielded a considerable harvest of flax for making cloth not otherwise easily procured because cotton did not mature in the cool European climate and thus had to be imported.

Bohemian farmsteads stood within the village and not directly on the fields as in America. This called for a construction style which was only vaguely reproduced on the American landscape. As a rule, the quadrant layout prevailed. This meant the Bohemian home incorporated a living room up front on the street with a kitchen next in line behind it, followed by attached outbuildings. Many times a line of sheds formed a wall down one side of the farmyard, which was squared off by more sheds or another barn at the rear, and perhaps on a third side by an orchard or garden.[13] Often the human dwelling was made of stone plastered over with stucco material, a style that was partly mandated for reasons of fire control and partly elected because of the European's instinct for the permanence of stone. Outbuildings and the upper superstructure of dwellings, however, were made of wood. The need for these two building materials gave rise to saw mills, positioned along streams, often next to a flour mill.[14] Access to the farmstead was always from the street or main square of a village through a *Hoftor* [entry gate] that was decorated ornately. Usually there was a small personnel door next to it or through one half of the main portal. Inside the farmstead lay the perennial manure pile, pride of the European farmer. Folk sayings abound: "Zeige mir deinen Mist und ich sage dir, was du für ein Bauer bist" (Show me your manure pile and I'll tell you what kind of farmer you are).

In New Ulm before the advent of the ubiquitous automobile following World War I, residents in the cities of New Ulm and Sleepy Eye commonly kept a cow or two, maybe a team of horses for their buggies and some chickens or geese in a small barn at the back of their city lots. Alleys gave handy access. Neighbors sometimes shared the milk of a good cow and rotated their cows' freshening to dovetail with family needs. In the summer, some owners of bovines hired a herdsman to gather cows down the alley and drive them out to a nearby pasture in the morning, then return them toward evening milking time, each instinctively peeling off as she approached her owner's barn. While executed on a minuscule scale, this keeping of domestic animals in town reminded villagers of the Old County, even if town life did not exactly replicate the clustered farmsteads. Nor did manure piles show off these *farmers'* wealth though local gardens the following summer usually did.

Most farm houses were large. Kitchens doubled as living rooms. The parlor was for Sunday dress, and always fronted the public street. Bedrooms were small, sometimes upstairs, but often on the back side of the living quarters. Housed upstairs also was the granary for seed grains and some animal feed. In most kitchens there was a built-in oven for baking bread from coarsely ground flour although earlier the large outdoor, village bake oven was also well known. In the barns

Threshing crew on the Louis Meyer farm. BC

A gathering at the Theodor Rein farm in Cottonwood township. BC

Johann Goblirsch family at their farmstead, House 61 known as Küllagirgl, or the Goblirsch farmstead in Zemschen, South Egerland about 1905. Although all his siblings emigrated to the United States, Johann stayed on the farm which he inherited at age 18. Two of his sons later also emigrated (to Morgan, in Redwood County). L-R: son and daughter of a neighbor; Johann Goblirsch, unknown, Toni Goblirsch, Katherine Goblirsch and her husband Johann.

were a few cows, horses, or oxen, hay wagons and generally a few hogs, a small flock of chickens, some ducks and frequently a gaggle of geese. The latter sometimes roamed the village at will. All of these were housed in the back buildings of the farmyard which surrounded a central well for the farmstead. This was European diversified farming in its traditional form. Understandably much of the farm work was done by hand. Tools were primitive, often made of wood, and all family members participated. Hay was cut with a scythe, raked together with wooden devices, pitched onto a horse-drawn wagon with wooden forks and driven to the village. Rye and wheat were cut by hand and gathered by a rack on the scythe, bound into bundles, and shocked to stand until hauled to the village yard to be threshed by hand-held flails. Surely this was an ordeal from which young people were willing to depart if the opportunity arose for an improved existence in America.[15]

While New Ulm was the chief market hub for Brown county, lesser marketing centers grew up in the form of a township creamery, a rural mill, an elevator, and similar receiving stations. In the Bohemian landscape each village was a miniature marketing center. Cattle raising improved after farmers were freed from the burden of *robota* in 1848 but even then primary advances took place only through the initiatives of royal families. The Trauttmansdorffs in Bischofteinitz since early in the 19th century raised prized breeds, such as the Simmenthal, and readily made them available to local farmers. Gradually during the course of the 19th century, farm organizations, societies with scientific publications, as well as annual auctions and fairs enabled herd improvement. Horse farms evolved from former estates, and on several in the Hostau region the famous Lipizzaner stallions were herded since 1918.

This breed became famous for skilled performances at the Spanish riding school of Vienna. Following their daring rescue in 1945 when American Army Captain Thomas M. Stewart whisked away the breeding stock from Hostau before they could be captured by the advancing Russian armies, the horses acquired prestige in America.[16] Much earlier, regional horse breeding gained prominence when local draft animals were bought by the Austrian military for pulling large cannons. In 1906 Georg Heinl from Trohatin received an honorary degree from the agricultural ministry in Vienna for his contribution to improving local draft horse breeds. In the early 20th century, several other Trohatin citizens received special awards for their success at improved horse breeding, including the introduction of Belgian cross breeds for better field performance.[17]

Hog raising in Bohemia never reached a similar plain of distinction. Still, farmers there did develop a pork-oriented economy. Since not enough piglets were born locally, weekly consignment auctions of stock from elsewhere in the Austrian empire developed every Wednesday in Hostau, Saturdays in Bischofteinitz, and irregularly in Ronsperg. Chicken raising seems to have been mostly for personal consumption, unlike in New Ulm where eggs poured in from local farms by the thousands of dozens. White Leghorns and Rhode Island Reds were commonly raised in the 20th century, both in New Ulm and in the district of Bischofteinitz. Turkeys were seldom raised commercially in Bohemia. Pet birds included peacocks, guinea hens and pheasants. Quite common was the breeding of pigeons, both for pets and for their meat.

Sheep once were numerous in Bohemia but lapsed when industrialization brought yard goods onto the market more cheaply than could be spun from raw wool at home. Goats were a substitute supply of milk for small town families. Small Bohemian farmers raised as many as 50 geese each year, herding them collectively with neighbors along the ponds that dotted nearly every village scape. It was this domestic animal that made Bohemia famous for its featherbeds, and that gave New Ulm from the train depot south on Valley and Front streets the name of *Gnseviertel*, Goosetown.[18]

Commercial enterprises to produce fish did not catch on in Brown county but did reach a sophisticated level of development back in Bischofteinitz. From the point of view of the sportsman, however, both communities held a great deal in common. In the Bohemian Radbusa river, anglers found a paradise naturally stocked with pike, trout, and certain varieties of clean carp. In the Minnesota as well as the Cottonwood rivers there were pike, perch, cat fish and buffalo as well as some bass and bullheads.

Before the days of artificial buttons, clothing manufacturers paid well for clams both in the United States and back in Bohemia. In New Ulm commercial clamming did not develop until the beginning of the 20th century and it was not in the hands of the Bohemians at all. However, German-Bohemians identified with the operation and quite a number found employment in the industry. The venture required a boat equipped with drag hooks and a boiling facility to render the clams (and an occasional pearl) clean, which sold for about $12 per ton. The clamming site in New Ulm was discovered on the Minnesota River bed at the length of about 400 yards off the former steamboat landing near Third South Street below Riverside Park.[19]

In Bohemia the custom of clamming was different. Then as now, fish, buttons, pearls and by-products were not just left to chance. Rather, villagers engineered large ponds that served the double purpose of having adequate water supplies in case of fire, and simultaneously a controlled abundance of fish. Frequently a stream fed the pond and descended across several levels to increase the number of

Clamming in New Ulm. Clam shells were used to make buttons. Another home industry brought from the Old Country. BC

pond units for production. These streams in turn were connected to canals that led the excess water through viaducts to drive flour mills or perhaps blacksmith shop tools. In the halcyon days of Bohemian fish raising in the early part of the 20th century, large trucks gathered at a given pond early on the appointed morning. When the pond gates were opened and the water drained, the fish were harvested for iced-transport to the spas at Marienbad, Karlsbad, Franzensbad and other resorts in the region.[20] No similar commercial venture was ever tried in New Ulm.

Stone and brick works, however, did enjoy a long economic success in the New Ulm region, and offered employment to many immigrants from Bohemia. Quarries located across the river in Nicollet county belonged to New Ulmers, though not to immigrants or their descendants from Bohemia. Employing some thirty to fifty men, the New Ulm Stone company began in 1888 to crush and ship northeastward to the Twin Cities and down into Iowa. The Jasper Granite company also operated near the former company and supplied a variety of materials. Far larger in overall capacity and job opportunities was the New Ulm Brick and Tile Yard begun in 1875 by Frederick Aufderheide, of Westphalia (Längrich) Germany. Since 1879 it has occupied a site just south of New Ulm. Under son Karl Aufderheide the works expanded into the production of brick-related materials, drain tile, culverts, sewer pipe and similar items. The yards continued under the family name until 1982.[21] The German-Bohemian Saffert family built and operated the New Ulm Art Stone business, originally known as the Saffert Cement Construction Company. In 1919, according to the European Bohemian tradition, Saffert designed and executed his own home at 415 North German Street entirely from art stone products.[22]

In German-Bohemian practice, fire laws and a conviction that houses were built for future generations, most residences and outbuildings were constructed of stone. In turn, industries developed to supply it and skilled craftsmen turned the masonry materials into homes, churches, and commercial structures. During the period when emigrants were leaving the Bischofteinitz region for the United States, much of the work in the quarries and in preparing the stone for buildings was done by hand. While exact statistics about the numbers of stone cutters during the late 19th century are hard to find, a table for the year 1939 indicates that there were 375 individual stone cutters who were members of a single stone mason's guild in the Bischofteinitz area. By comparison, in the guild which covered both construction and woodcutting there were 839 men employed. Only the textile industry had more!

Some importance placed on the mason's trade can be gleaned from information that in the district of Ronsperg, thirteen percent of the working population was active in stone work. In the early part of the 20th century, guild masons from the village of Serb held the record for being able to lay an average 1,000 bricks per mason daily. Some of the masons from the area gained fame abroad, and were recruited as far away as the Island of Corfu in Greece.[23] Very popular throughout western Bohemia were also the red roof tile factories which used local brick yard clay. In the communities belonging to the parish church at Berg, inhabitants with the family names of Prokosch, Schröpfer, and Tauer are listed as masons. There were also brick factories located on the south side of Hostau, and scattered across the regional landscape.

Totally unknown in the New Ulm region was a talent common in the Bohemian Forest for glass blowing. Usually this skill was learned in small mountain houses where charcoal was available to produce the hot fires needed for blowing, and gave rise to the many names of vil-

Redstone quarry near New Ulm, where many German-Bohemians found work in the pre-World War I days. BC

New Ulm Brick and Tile Factory in days gone by. BC

Saffert family's New Ulm Artstone factory. BC

lages in the genealogical backgrounds of New Ulmers: Althütten, Strasshütten, Johanneshütten, Goldbrunnhütten and others. Hütte means mountain forest shanty, the kind in which glass blowers established their cottage enterprises. Common family names in Brown county that were connected with the glass blowing tradition include Sellner, Gröbner, Saffert, Schnobrich, Pechtl, Zeug, Kalz, Liebl, Neuwirth and more. While several noble families were responsible for promoting glass blowing as a cottage industry in the Bohemian Forest, the family of Johann Friedrich and Cristoph Wenzel von Wiedersperg of Muttersdorf was especially active in the production of Bohemian glass. Often a successful glass industry depended on an enterprising master who perhaps traveled for a time learning the trade, then settled in a region, acquired wood rights in a forest belonging to a noble family, and finally established a village that housed the variety of workers needed for charcoal production and a thriving glass making venture.[24] Eventually Bohemian glass produced in the region became world famous.

In addition to the glass production, there was in the western Bohemian territory some iron ore mining, copper mining, feldspar, beryl, as well as related minerals and stones. Also associated with the miners were wood workers who made shingles for the roofs of the region. Some also made wooden shoes. For a time such shoes were in great demand for both miners and farmers especially in the period before rubber footwear became common place. Related to these forest products were brooms made of birch twigs crafted by the local inhabitants. Rarely, but on occasion, a more talented wood worker also made furniture, chests, specially carved chairs and the like.[25] In special circumstances around New Ulm, farm folks in the Bohemian tradition also were known to make their own brooms and furniture.

In conclusion, it can be said that New Ulm indeed received the German-Bohemian immigrants who were welcomed in the local market place. Enough European village tradition carried over to make these newcomers feel at home, and to ease them into a workday that was an improvement over the Old Country. Until the end of the 19th century, however, there is little or no evidence to suggest that the Bohemians played more than a traditional European peasant's role in the formation of Brown county's market center. As with patterns that held sway for centuries in the Bohemian villages, the peasants in Brown county were inarticulate. They did not record their feelings, their experiences, or their aspirations. Their lives unfolded in the silence of their family activities, not in the public arena. Nor did their tradition call on them to become captains of the market place or of local industries. They did not find pathways leading into professional success and rapid assimilation. In the next chapter we shall analyze this dichotomy between the activities of the New Ulm Turners and those of the German-Bohemians (the working class) in order to explain how the area today retains a central European culture in the American Midwest.

Notes

1. Hildegard Binder Johnson, *Order Upon the Land. The U.S. Rectangular Land Survey and the Upper Mississippi Country* (New York: Oxford University Press, 1976) and John Fraser Hart, *The Look of the Land* (Englewood Cliffs, NJ: Prentice Hall, 1975).

2. For a discussion of the European village and its focus for life, see e.g. Edit Fel and Tamas Hofer, *Proper Peasants. Traditional Life in a Hungarian Village* (Chicago: Aldine, 1969) and Robert G. Moeller, ed., *Peasants and Lords in Modern Germany. Recent Studies in Agricultural History* (Boston: Allen & Unwin, 1986). See also fine studies like Kathleen Neils Conzen, "Peasant Pioneers: Generational Succession among German Farmers in Frontier Minnesota," in Steven Hahn and Jonathan Prude, eds., *Countryside in the Age of Capitalist Transformation* (Chapel Hill, NC: University of North Carolina, 1985), 259-92.

3. See the village plat drawings in *Bezirk Hostau*, Erich Fischer and Arbeitsausschuss, 3rd ed. (Furth im Wald: Heimatkreis Bischofteinitz, 1979), p. 24-25.

4. Cf. *Hostau*, Mirkowitz, p. 169, Melmitz p. 239, Wasserau p. 236, Plöss p. 312, Taschlowitz p. 360, Weissensulz p. 407, Muttersdorf, p. 278.

5. Concerning the founding of New Ulm, see Hildegard Binder Johnson, "The Founding of New Ulm, Minnesota," *American-German Review*, 12 (June, 1946), 8-12. The centennial edition of the *New Ulm Journal* (Tuesday, June 26, 1962) offers a history of the city with first plat illustrations, while the Brown County Historical Society and Museum holds a variety of city plats. The *Journal* (June 26, 1962) also published the Federal Works Projects Administration report about German immigration, none of it specific to the German-Bohemian situation.

6. Quoted in Fritsche, Brown County, I, p. 466.

7. *New Ulm Review*, Jan. 6, Jan. 18, 1892, p. 1.

8. At the Slim Kalz family reunion in the summer, 1987 family memorabilia on display included the wooden box forms once used in the family business to make cigars. The New Ulm Museum periodically displays cigar forms used by other firms.

9. The controversy is reported in the *New Ulm Review*, August 10, 17, 1892, p. 1. The Faribault-Stillwater plan was devised by Archbishop John Ireland of St. Paul as a scheme to protect Catholic parochial school education firstly, but secondly also to kill the German-language schools in his diocese. Cf. Colman J. Barry, *The Catholic Church and German Americans* (Milwaukee: Bruce, 1953), pp. 186 ff. and Marvin R. O'Connell, *John Ireland and the American Catholic Church* (St. Paul: Minnesota Historical Society, 1988), 322-334.

10. A list of such societies and members appears in *The Church of the Holy Trinity of New Ulm*, Minn., pp. 188-217. See also *New Ulm Review*, Oct. 17, 1894, p. 1 and Fritsche, *Brown County*, p. 417.

11. *Unser Heimatkreis Bischofteinitz*, pp. 660 ff.

12. Ibid., pp. 664 ff.

13. See floor plans and many photographs in *Bischofteinitz*, pp. 543 ff. See also the many village plans exhibiting the quadrant of each building, in *Bezirk Hostau*, e.g. Altgramatin p. 291, Taschlowitz p. 360, and in the book by Johann Gröbner, Rudolf Womes, et. al., eds., *Chronik der Pfarrgemeide Berg* (Furth im Wald: P. Schrott, 1976), village sketches of Natschetin p. 150, Schiefernau p. 172, Trohatin p. 202.

14. *Berg*, village of Seisermühl p. 304. *Bezirk Hostau*, p. 105.

15. *Bischofteinitz*, p. 546 for pictures of farm life, harvesting, and references to young individuals and families that left for America between 1860-1910. Outdoor common bread oven, p. 553. The Bischofteinitz Heimatmuseum in Furth im Wald has typical household rooms on permanent display.

16. *Bezirk Hostau*, pp. 96 ff., *Bischofteinitz*, pp. 572 ff., Brigitte Peter, "Hostau 1945: Die Rettung der Lipizzaner - Wagnis order Wunder," *Zyklus*, 2 (1982), reprint without page numbers, 27 pp.

17. *Bischofteinitz*, p. 560, photographs. *Bezirk Hostau*, pp. 112 ff.

18. *Bischofteinitz*, pp. 562-564.

19. Elroy Ubl, *Historical Notes*, I, pp. 61-62. Many old timers tell how the German Bohemians made a livelihood from the clams. E.g., Herman Mueller interview, March 20, 1986. His father John Mueller had come from Unterhütten.

20. *Bischofteinitz*, pp. 590-596. See also Johann Micko, *Geschichte des Marktes und der Herrschaft Muttersdorf* (Muttersdorf: Selbsverlag, 1922), pp. 22 ff.

21. Fritsche, *Brown County*, I, pp. 472 ff., Ubl, *Historical Notes*, II, p. 185-186.

22. La Vern J. Rippley, "American Artstone-New Ulm," *Currents. A Minnesota River Valley Review,* 3 (1993), 17-27, with photographs.

23. *Bischofteinitz,* pp. 609-611, 658-659; Gröbner, *Chronik der Pfarrgemeinde Berg,* p. 218.

24. *Bischofteinitz,* pp. 612-641.

25. Ibid., pp. 682-685.

Five

The Forty-Eighter Turners vs. the German-Speaking Bohemians

𝕹 OEL IVERSON, WHO SPENT his youth in New Ulm – founded in 1856 by German refugees from the 1848 Revolution – in his book *Germania, U.S.A. Social Change in New Ulm, Minnesota*[1] analyzes four aspects of sociological change in the city – class, status, power and assimilation. Mostly members of the Turnverein, these idealists were nationalistic ideologues for physical fitness. Ludwig *Turnvater* Jahn initiated the movement during the Napoleonic wars, but it was suppressed in Europe and thrived only in the United States where it was re-founded at Cincinnati in 1848.[2] Essentially, Iverson shows that "whenever an ethnic alien is of as high or higher class and status derivation as (than) the group among whom he has settled, he tends to form into status communities rather than into ethnic communities." Community members, if threatened by outside resistance, tend to close ranks against outsiders and form an ethnic or status community. Often their behavior comes in response to a combination of forces. An ethnic community is the product of contradictory forces of acceptance and rejection which originate in the majority society and are directed toward immigrants. A *status* community emerges when members capitalize on the differentiation within their society, and close ranks against outsiders of inferior status (p. 11).

In an *ethnic* community, there is enforced withdrawal. In the formation of a *status* community, internal demands (snobbery, privilege, club or church membership) restrict the entrance of outsiders into the higher or status group. Against the ethnic community, the host society reacts by protecting its way of life from foreign encroachment and subversion. It seeks to isolate aliens socially and psychologically. Foreigners are denied employment in certain fields, are kept out of native clubs, and are restrained from settling in some neighborhoods. Full participation by strangers in the wider community is made difficult.[3] An ethnic community thus might turn more intensely to its traditions, its heritage, its values and may thereby more staunchly resist ultimate assimilation. The German settlements in Russia over the years became more "German" than the Germans. To some extent, the Catholic Germans with their parochial schools in the rural Midwest exemplified a similar tendency.[4] Leaders of some Spanish-speaking communities strive today to prevent assimilation because it amounts to "ethnic" or "cultural" suicide. Thus ethnic community leaders resist assimilation because they perceive any loss of language as but the first step in eliminating traditional values. St. Paul's Archbishop Ireland came to understand this when he tangled with German-speaking priests in his St. Paul diocese during the late 19th century.[5]

The forty-eighter element, Turners for short, formed an elite *status* but not an *ethnic* community in New Ulm.[6] The Turners of New Ulm did not associate with outsiders. Neither with Catholics nor for that matter with Lutherans or with any other religious group at first. They did not find themselves in any sense victimized by the Know-Nothing movement. They did not need or choose whether to associate with Anglo-Americans or even with other German-speaking immigrants in the community. They were not forced to form an *ethnic* bulwark against English-language "outsiders" for there were no non-German-speaking aliens to resist. Unlike most towns which were established on the frontier by New England Yankees, New Ulm from its onset had the opportunity to be virtually all German and elitist.

New Ulm as a Turner city traces its history to both the Turnerbund of North America and to the Chicago Land Verein.[7] Its leader, Ferdinand Beinhorn from Braunschweig arrived in 1852 with plans to establish a utopian German community in the West. In Chicago he founded the Land Verein on August 10, 1853, placed advertisements in German newspapers, and by April 1854 had a dues-paying membership of about 800. In June 1854 scouts for the society arrived in Minnesota Territory, traversed the Minnesota River, encountered un-

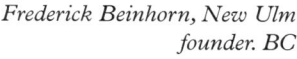

Frederick Beinhorn, New Ulm founder. BC

friendly Indians, but successfully spent the winter on the frontier. The following spring Beinhorn joined his scouts, and on June 26, 1855 at Winona, the nearest land office, the group preempted a town site of 16 quarter sections, about 2,500 acres of land. Each member got 12 town lots and 9 (later reduced to 6) acres outside the village. New Ulm was staked out in plots fronting the river in a pattern that allowed within its grid extra squares for public parks.[8]

One year later when Wilhelm Pfaender reached St. Paul, no lots in New Ulm had yet been assigned. A member of the Cincinnati Turn-verein, Pfaender was seeking land for about 1,300 Turners. Arriving in New Ulm, Pfaender and Beinhorn merged organizations into the "German Land Association of Minnesota" which was incorporated one year later on March 4, 1857 with a capitalization of over $100,000. Pfaender reported back to Cincinnati that not only was there ample wood but that a steam-powered sawmill, a hotel, and a warehouse were already planned. Property would be held in common.

However, the utopian experiment soon fell victim to faulty finances that worsened during the panic of 1857. Four years later the indebted sawmill was sold. Next, the *New Ulm Pionier*, a fiercely anti-clerical Turner newspaper published from January 1858 to August 16, 1862, was cashiered. Nor could the communal store bear the weight of newcomers lacking money to pay for essentials and thus in 1859 the German Land Association began dismembering. By 1862 it had wound up business affairs giving the remaining 24 town lots, $5,594 in cash and 320 peripheral lots to the local school district. Before final annulment, the association supplied four acres of land for a hospital, initiated a fire station, and dedicated several acres of river bottom land for a public beach.

The chief accomplishment of the Land Association was the organization of the New Ulm Turnverein on November 11, 1856 with 13 original members. Immediately they erected their first Turnhalle of wood, a German gable style building surrounded by an entire block of land that still serves this purpose. During the Dakota War in the summer of 1862, this building burned along with about 185 other structures. Rebuilt in 1876 of masonry, the hall served for decades as a community center for town meetings, Sunday classes in morality, and other purposes "of humanity." Religion was strictly taboo in line with the anti-clerical Turner philosophy. Teachers were freethinkers. Gymnastic classes for local residents as well as amateur theater ran year around. Traveling professional drama groups were ruled out to stimulate local talent. Lectures by visiting forty-eighters and nationally known freethinkers were frequent.

In the course of several decades, however, social gatherings were the most repeated events in Turner hall. Traditional disagreements among Turners, such as whether "socialism" or maybe "intellectualism" should hold sway over physical training and related activities, erupted periodically. But by 1881 Wilhelm Pfaender had sounded a note of compromise when he commented on whether the Turnerbund had lost or gained through its New Ulm settlement project: New Ulm "had the reputation of an orderly and pleasant place, where the adherents of religious confessions and freethinkers lived in harmony, and the enforcement of rest on the Sabbath and temperance were unknown."[9]

While New Ulm accommodated the traditional faiths of the

New Ulm's First Turner House completed in 1858 and burned during the Indian uprising of 1862. BC

Fatherland – Lutheranism and Catholicism – it always catered to the freethinker philosophy with anti-clericalism as its linchpin. The most characteristic landmark of New Ulm in terms of its forty-eighter moorings is the Hermann monument on Hermann Heights. Inspired by the erection of the original Hermann the Cherusker monument at Detmold, Germany in 1875, a forty-eighter surveyor and sometimes architect, Julius Berndt, conceived the idea of a replica for New Ulm. Immediately he began to raise money from members of the Sons of Hermann Lodges for the construction of a national German monument in the United States. The first such lodge was established in New York in 1840. The first in Minnesota came years later in 1870 at St. Paul. While German Americans in Eastern cities wanted the statue erected in their region, the Sons of Hermann national meeting at Philadelphia in 1885 determined that it would be built in New Ulm where Julius Berndt resided. Although the cornerstone was laid already in 1888, the statue, which had been modeled after the one in Germany but was not a direct copy, did not arrive in New Ulm until 1890. Final completion and dedication were delayed until 1897.

Whether through symbol, through practice or by means of language, New Ulm remained German if not feethinker in orientation.

Until well past 1900 New Ulm remained a German community though by 1905 some claimed the original forty-eighters were finally outnumbered by other members of the community.[10] New Ulm's Holy Trinity Catholic Church was raised to the dignity of a diocesan cathedral when on December 4, 1957 Alphonse P. Schladweiler, reassigned from the German St. Agnes parish in St. Paul, became the first bishop of New Ulm. Although the freethinker approach to local interaction declined, the German language persisted. For example, as of 1970 only 8.3% of the Minnesota population as a whole spoke German as a mother tongue. But in New Ulm the figure still stood at 41% indicating just how thoroughly German the community once was. To this day, the German flavor persists, however, with a distinct drift to a more Bavarian taste like most German epigones in the United States. Oktoberfest is celebrated on two consecutive weekends in October. A *Glockenspiel* (free standing carillon clock tower) erected in the early 1980's plays programmed pieces at noon, three, and five in the afternoon. The July Heritagefest sustains annual interest. The city's "ambassadors of good will," the Concord Singers, perform their German *Volkslieder* at celebrations across the Midwest and abroad. Schell's Brewery, founded by a forty-eighter in 1860, has regained its former prominence by catering to specialty markets while Schell's 100-year-old mansion and gardens at the brewing site attract many visitors annually.

For about a century until the 1950s, then, New Ulm's founders and their descendants considered themselves a social elite. Rather than a suburban dwelling territory or a capital city power status, this elite used as its rallying point a socio-political institution, the Turnverein. Judging by the heterogeneity exemplified in the community by the 1860 U.S. census, however, it is clear that the group was not unanimous about its German traditions even at the beginning. The myth that most of the early settlers came from the City of Ulm in the German state of Württemberg has scant basis in reality. Of the 635 total 1860 population in the City of New Ulm, only two were possibly of non-German ancestry. Prussia supplied the largest number with 160 followed by Württemberg with 101 and in descending order Bavaria (66), Mecklenburg (58), Baden (37), Saxony (33), Hannover (31), and

Trinity Church with ornate German style baroque "onion-shaped" clock tower. BC

Concord Singers gathered at Schell's Brewery garden site and home adjacent to the Brewery. BC

Hesse (26). Nine each came from Braunschweig, Holstein, Luxemburg and Nassau.[11] Though German in language and tradition, the Turner Germans in the New Ulm community were not homogeneous. They spoke a variety of dialects and practiced an amalgamation of customs. The New Ulm Germans, consequently, did not form the usual *ethnic* community. Rather, the Turners arrogated to themselves from among the other Germans in the community, a superior social and cultural position. Non-Turners did the menial jobs. Turners acquired *status* by doing the rewarding work that gave them prestige. As such, outsiders of lower status were welcome as long as the prestigious and powerful positions remained among the Turners.[12]

Standing in sharp contrast to the elitist Turner Germans in New Ulm were the German-Bohemians. The question arises why so many Germans from Western Bohemia were attracted to settle in the vicinity of Turner-dominated New Ulm. The answer is difficult to pinpoint because German-Bohemians were coming to New Ulm virtually as early as were the sophisticated Turner Germans from Cincinnati and Chicago. Already in 1860 the German-Bohemian roster of names in the vicinity of New Ulm included Siebenbrenner, Dietz, Beck, Leiminger, Hochhauser, Vogel, Haas, Gretsch (Kretsch), Gag, Seifert, Hanser and Zeug. Does this mean that the Bohemians came with Turner Germans or because of them? Or had they settled formerly near the Reich Germans from Chicago, Cincinnati or elsewhere in the United States and then decide to join the elitist founders of New Ulm? Did they arrive independently of the famous members of the utopian community? Or were they already in contact at the time of arrival?

One thing is certain: None of the German-Bohemians in 1860 chose to settle within the city limits of New Ulm! This suggests that they had little affinity to the elitist Turners. Rather, Bohemians stubbornly exhibited their love for the soil. They wanted nothing to do with the urbanized, sophisticated, anti-clerical Turners. Peasants to the very marrow of their bones, the German-Bohemians clung tenaciously to the land. Decades later when Bohemians kept coming to the New Ulm area, the listing of occupations in the 1870 and 1880 censuses often designates them as farm laborers, particularly in Milford township. Lying west of New Ulm, this township was settled early by Reich Germans who valued the flat land because it also offered the amenity of wood that grew along the Cottonwood River. After 1875, however, many of the farm owners there were becoming German-Bohemian. For the few residents of German-Bohemian origin in the city itself in 1870, we find only rural-oriented occupations such as butcher, stone mason, and house carpenter, in addition to domestic servant and day laborer.

Beginning in 1880, as more and more German-Bohemians had to live in the city as opposed to the rural townships, new occupational designations appeared. In 1880 fifty-two Bohemian family heads were residing within the city limits as compared to just 10 in 1870. Because the available land had pretty much been absorbed by 1875, and because the arrivals of Germans from Bohemia expanded rapidly after 1867 when Austria officially permitted emigration, the newcomers had to settle within the city where they could find work. Job representations in the 1880 census therefore expanded rapidly from those listed for 1870. Designations also became more specific, including that all-encompassing unspecific one one for women – "keeping house." Out of the 52 heads of household in the city in 1880 there were 40 ordinary laborers and three retired farmers. Among occupations for German-Bohemian men in the 52 households the category of "laborers" is overwhelming, 17 in all. Most subheadings for their jobs likewise fall into the classification of laborer: work in the flour mill (by which was meant the Eagle Roller Mill) 5; work in the sawmill 1; brewer 1; blacksmith 1; carpenter 2; stone mason 3; teamster 3; butcher, cooper (barrel makers were numerous in the Eagle Roller Mill) 2 each; tailor 1. There was one teacher and one so-called agent (perhaps for the railroad). The tailor, butcher, coopers, masons, carpenters, blacksmith and perhaps the brewer could be ranked as craftsmen. There was but one professional, a teacher by the name of Joseph A. Eckstein who was 22 years old, born in Bohemia, German-speaking, and known from other sources to have been a private music teacher.

In New Ulm City proper, the German-Bohemians were at home in the low-lying river district on the south side, in what became known as Goosetown, but as their economic status improved they often moved up to the city center, especially into the area around Holy Trinity Parish. In part, this "resettlement" was tolerated by the Turners because Father Berghold proved an especially astute negotiator, an even-handed civic booster, and ultimately the one who bridged the

German-Bohemian mill workers: John Lindmeier, Edward Ubl, and Christ Lindmeier. BC

Haberl & Floettl barrel shop – typical names for German-Bohemians or Austrians. BC

Joseph A. Eckstein and wife Mary, nee Koch. According to the New Ulm *Journal, April 10, 1915, Eckstein was born in Bohemia on October 25, 1857 and with his parents came to farm in Sigel township. After attending local schools and then teachers college in Mankato he taught in Home and Milford townships before continuing his study of law and admission to the bar in 1880. For 17 years he was city attorney. BC*

Sausage makers in Saffert's meat market in New Ulm. Both the Saffert and Schnobrich families emigrated from the town of Muttersdorf where they were butchers. Both followed careers in the meat business in New Ulm. BC

gap between the liberal Turner perpetrators of religious intolerance in the city and his flock of conservative Bohemian Roman Catholics. Anti-religious sentiment on the part of the Turners had long been vocal: The *New Ulm Pioneer* had often said, "Many want all church humbug vanished. Others believe to strike out the church entirely is necessary. We are absolutely inclined to the latter opinion. . . . The bible, a mixture of moral truth, moral falsehood, and natural scientific lies . . . is absolutely unfit for scholastic instruction" (1858, Nos. 1,2,3). Turners, of course, despised Catholics! On the one hand they disliked German-Bohemians especially because they were Catholic. But they also disliked Bohemians because they were uneducated members of the peasant class. More subtly, Turners thought of Bohemians as Austrians over whom the image of Metternich and his long suppression of liberalism hovered inauspiciously even after they had come to the United States.

In a similar vein, when 1848 Hungarian freedom fighter Louis Kossuth arrived in New York in 1851 for a tour of tumultuous pro-Hungarian, but quite anti-Austrian, receptions at many sites in the United States, Illinois Congressman Abraham Lincoln eulogized the Hungarians "in their present glorious struggle for liberty," against the Austrians.[13] To the liberal mind of the 1860s and 70s, the Austrian was the enemy. Only grudgingly acknowledging the Bohemians from the Austrian crown colony, the high-minded New Ulm Turners accordingly exhibited behavior consistent with their theories of class, status, and power. According to Max Weber, class stratification occurs in two ways: Isolation via the categories of power, esteem and wealth on the one hand, and the implementation of social groups – parties, status groups, and classes on the other.[14] "Classes are properly at home in the economic order, 'status groups' in the social order, that is, in the sphere of distribution of status; starting from this point, both reciprocally influence each other and influence the legal order and are in turn influenced by it. Parties, on the other hand, are primarily at home in the sphere of power. Their activity is concerned with social power, that is, with exerting influence on communal action, as much as in a 'state.' Communal action by parties as opposed to classes or status groups, always requires the forming of an association."[15] This association in our context was the Turner society.

For over a century in New Ulm, the Turners were better educated than the non-Turners. Being well-educated and acclimated to occupational mobility as a sign of their higher social status, they frequently sought employment outside of New Ulm. This caused their numbers in New Ulm to diminish, especially since World War II. After all, opportunities for professional careers as physicians, lawyers, teachers, and related occupations were rather limited in New Ulm and Brown county. Thus, as sons and daughters married away from the community, the possibilities for maintaining the Turner status in the city diminished.[16]

As late as the 1960s, however, Turners still owned more property, businesses, automobiles, houses, stores, and warehouses than non-Turners. Only about 12% of each Turner generation over a century owned no substantial property aside from their own homes. Turners earned more money on a monthly basis than non-Turners, and consequently they *had* more money than non-Turners. This obviously resulted in Turners occupying class positions superior to those held by non-Turners. In most respects, the forty-eighter Turners were a local class elite. The German-speaking Bohemians functioned at the opposite end of the class spectrum. When George Neuwirth following World War II wanted to borrow money to build his block-sized dance hall and bowling alley in downtown New Ulm, the local bankers refused to support him and he had to turn to big city lending agencies. His parents had come straight from Muttersorf in Bohemia. But for decades thereafter, his dance hall was a nightly entertainment center for his German-Bohemian countrymen, despite Turners and their preference for Turner Hall.

Not that the process remained static. In the 1990s it is fashionable for selected German-Bohemians to become members of the Turnverein. Exterior traditions and rituals make the old elitism appealing for the outsider who wants to demonstrate "arrival." For example nobody enters the Turner facility without a private key given to members who pay their dues. Bohemian members are especially proud to invite their guests through the private key entrance. To raise money, Turner Hall is rented frequently for weddings and other neutral social functions. German-Bohemians schedule their receptions here just like anyone else. The Bohemians also hold their Bohemian Club dances and festivals in Turner Hall. German-Bohemian women pride themselves on working in the Turner Hall serving units. They even try to out do each other raising money for the ordinary needs of the Turn-verein. Bohemians are, after all, recognized for their ability to cook, work hard, and save money.

Over the decades Bohemians displayed their achievements in traditional ways. They gave generously to the Catholic parish for its parochial grade and high schools. Often they sent money home to Bohemia for the transportation of relatives wanting to immigrate.[17] To the north of *Gänseviertel* (Goosetown), the poorest section of New Ulm, lies what Goosetowners call "Rat Town." Non Bohemians allege it was because the Eagle Roller Mill attracted poor working families. Bohemians allege the intended meaning of "rats" was for the lower class non-Bohemians who lived there. Residents teem with stories about the taunting and street fights by the children from Rat Town against those from Goosetown. There is also plenty of lore about the boats that shuttled Goosetowners from the mainland to an island in the river on summer nights for beer parties.[18]

It appears that the Bohemians were especially desirable employees for the Turner Germans from the Reich and the fact remains that Turners did supply many Bohemian immigrants their entry level employment. In return they contributed mightily of their muscle and brawn to the economy of Brown county. In their hardship and struggle to acquire a better life, the Bohemians clung steadfastly not only to the soil, if possible, but to their *Bömisch* dialect of the German language, their traditions, and their ethic for hard work. They neglected, however, to learn English and to recognize that in America both the English language and the educational opportunities it affords were the pathways to greater financial success. According to the census of 1900 quite a few German-Bohemians still could neither read nor write. The Turners, by contrast, as early as 1858 espoused the principle that they would establish schools, initiate German immigrants into American practices, "inculcate in them American ideals," and teach them the new language. To become an American Turner, an immigrant had to at least declare his intention of becoming a citizen of the United States, because often the Turners had political goals they hoped to advance through the ballot box. In short, the American Turners acted as Americanization agencies.[19]

As late as World War I, many German-Bohemians had not yet become citizens. The Turners assimilated rapidly, at least to the degree necessary to assert local control. "Germaness" – that subtle quality of life expressed by local folklore, working habits, polka and waltz music, the traditional crafts, and Old World customs for butchering, making sausage and making lace have been kept alive in New Ulm not by the Turners but by the German-Bohemians. It is no accident that the blacksmiths, stone masons, carpenters, and in particular the two mainstay meat markets (Saffert and Schnobrich) remained in the hands of Bohemians. Moving rapidly up the ladder from ethnic leaders to an Americanized status elite, the well-to-do upper class Turners created lifestyles different from the more simple but also more genuinely German folk of Goosetown and the surrounding farm region. Accustomed to a "stockade" mentality derived from their mode of existence on the German cultural island in the crown colony of Bohemia, the German-Bohemians of New Ulm, now in a replicated "stockade" mentality against the Turners, have clung steadfastly to their accustomed Old World values. The overall heritage in New Ulm today, therefore, is much more German-Bohemian than strictly German. The German language spoken on the streets is flavored by the former German-Bohemian dialects. When the 1970 census reported that 41% of the citizens of New Ulm still spoke German as their mother tongue, the census takers were referring more likely than not to the German-Bohemians.[20]

New Ulm's Heritagefest in July attracts thousands who come to enjoy authentic guest musical groups from Germany, Austria and Bohemia [the Egerland Trachtengruppe came in 1983 and 1991 to represent specifically the Bischofteinitz region] and on the other hand to hear their favorite polka bands from New Ulm. Of the dozens of polka bands that were active in the 1950s, virtually everyone was either led by or highly peppered with German-Bohemian musicians. New Ulm Catholic schools K-12 have survived because the German-Bohemians believe in them. Berger's Jewelry stocks a strong department of its store with religious gifts, such as crucifixes and rosaries, which Turners of Old would certainly not buy. German-Bohemian Marlene Domeier's German Store exclusively sells imports from Germany every day of the week except Wednesday (*Ruhetag*) and thrives. The German-Bohemian Heritage Society offers German lessons in the spoken Bohemian-German dialect, and their subgroup, the Heritage Singers perform beautifully in the Bohemian-German dialect. In a word, the fact that New Ulm is today considered the most German town in the Midwest is not so much due to the Germans but to the German-Bohemians who settled there and perpetuate their version of the German ethnic heritage.

Notes

1. An earlier version of this chapter appeared as the result of a paper presented at October 9-11, 1986 conference, "The Contributions of the German-Speaking Forty-Eighters to U. S. Cultural, Social and Political Life," Max Kade Institute for German-American Studies, University of Wisconsin, and which was published with the title "Status Versus Ethnicity: The Turners and Bohemians of New Ulm," in Charlotte L. Brancaforte, ed., *The German Forty- Eighters in the United States* (New York: Lang, 1989), pp. 257-278. A somewhat different slant and a separate conclusion was reached at that time. See here in particular Noel Iverson, *Germania, U.S.A. Social Change in New Ulm, Minnesota* (Minneapolis: University of Minnesota Press, 1966).

2. See Chapter 11, "The Turners," in Carl Wittke, *Refugees of Revolution: The German Forty-Eighters in America* (Westport, CT: Greenwood Press, 1970; originally University of PA Press, 1952), pp. 147-160, and in general Horst Ueberhorst, *Turner Unterm Sternen Banner* (München: Heinz Moos, 1978).

3. Cf. Don Martindale, *Social Life and Cultural Change* (New York: Van Nostrand, 1962), pp. 397-98, 427 ff.

4. Two books discuss this phenomenon, Richard Jensen, *The Winning of the Midwest: Social and Political Conflict, 1888-1896* (Chicago: University of Chicago Press, 1971) and Paul Kleppner, *The Cross of Culture* (New York: The Free Press, 1970). For an overview of how this aspect of social interaction manifested itself in the Bennett Law Controversy, see my Chapter 4 in *The Immigrant Experience in Wisconsin* (Boston: Twayne, 1985), pp. 43-58. Concerning the Germans from Russia, cf. Richard Sallet, *The Russian-German Settlements in the United States*, tr. La Vern J. Rippley and Armand Bauer (Fargo: Institute for Regional Studies, 1974).

5. La Vern J. Rippley, "Archbishop Ireland and the School Language Controversy," *U.S. Catholic Historian*, 1 (Fall, 1980), 1-16. See also Marvin O"Connell, *Ireland*, op. cit. 322 ff.

6. Iverson, p. 16 ff.

7. For a summary, see Hildegard Binder Johnson, "The Germans" in June Drenning Holmquist, ed., *They Chose Minnesota* (St. Paul: Minnesota Historical Society Press, 1981), pp. 164 ff.

8. In addition to Johnson, see J. M. Strasser, *Chronologie der Stadt New Ulm, Minnesota* (New Ulm: Druck der New Ulm Post, 1899), articles by Alexander Berghold, *Der Deutsche Pionier*, 4: 163 ff., and Elroy E. Ubl, *Historical Notes: A Glimpse at New Ulm's Past* (New Ulm: New Ulm Journal, I: 1982 and II: 1983). See also Hildegard B. Johnson, "New Ulm Failed as Socialist Experiment," *New Ulm Daily Journal* (June 26, 1962), pp. 1, 6, 8.

9. Hermann E. Rothfuss, "The Early German Theater in Minnesota," *Minnesota History*, 32 (Summer and Autumn, 1951), 100-105 and 164-173; La Vern J. Rippley, "Notes About the German Press in the Minnesota River Valley," *Report: Society for the History of Germans in Maryland*, 35 (1972), 37-45; William Pfaender, "Die Pioniere von New Ulm, *Amerikanischer Turnkalender*, (1881), 65-68. *The New Ulm Post* carries many

of the arguments between the Turners. Often anti-Turner in orientation were the *New Ulm Journal* and the *Brown County Review.*

10. Ubl, Notes, I, pp. 33-34. H. B. Johnson, *They Chose Minnesota*, p. 166 attributes this comment to Father Berghold in 1905. However, Berghold left New Ulm in 1890 because of a disagreement with Archbishop Ireland and he remained outside Minnesota until 1899 when he returned as pastor of St. Nicholas Parish in New Market. Here he remained until 1906 when he returned to his native Austria for retirement. Cf. Rippley, "Berghold," 48.

11. These data are taken from a a typed treatise done of the 1860 manuscript census by Frederic R. Steinhauser. It is available in German, and there is an identical version in English with a lengthy chart of the 635 immigrants. However, Steinhauser randomly selected some inhabitants from townships in adjacent Nicollet County and swapped them for the Norwegian township of Hanska in Brown County. His data on the greater New Ulm community is not easily retrievable for a legal unit from which exact data could be gathered to make comparisons to subsequent censuses.

12. For a summary of the origins and philosophy of the Turners, cf. Wittke, *Refugees*, p. 147 ff., Albert B. Faust, *The German Element in the United States*, II (New York: Steuben Society, 1927), pp. 387 ff., and August J. Prahl, "The Turners," in A. E. Zucker, ed., *The Forty-Eighters* (New York: Columbia University Press, 1950), pp. 79-110. A summary is in Iverson, *Germania*, pp. 25-52. See also Ernest Bruncken, "German Political Refugees in the United States during the Period from 1815-1860," *Deutsch-Amerikanische Geschichtsblätter*, 3 (1903), 33-48 and 4 (1904), 35-59.

13. Wilder Spaulding, *The Quiet Invaders. The Story of the Austrian Impact Upon America* (Vienna: Bundesverlag, 1968), p. 45.

14. "Classes, Status Groups and Parties," in *Max Weber: Selections in Translation*, ed., W. G. Runciman (Cambridge: Cambridge University Press, 1978), pp. 43-65 and Max Weber, *Economy and Society*, especially "Status Groups and Classes" (Berkeley: University of California Press, 1978), pp. 302 ff.

15. In Runciman, p. 55.

16. Iverson, Chapter 4, pp. 75 ff.

17. Cf. immigrant letters from the Liebl family of Heiligenkreuz, between Hostau and Weissensulz in Kreis Bischofteinitz, in possession of the author.

18. Interview March 20, 1986 with Hermann Mueller, born in 1903 on Front Street and with George Neuwirth who independently confirmed each other's anecdotes.

19. Ernst A. Weier, *The Work of the Turner Societies* (Indianapolis: American Gymnastic Union, 1919), pp. 10-11 and Arthur a Keuken, *Turnerism is Americanism* (Detroit: National Executive Committee of the American Turnerbund, 1938), p. 7.

20. Evelyn Scherabon Firchow in the German Department at the University of Minnesota with graduate students has studied the German dialects of New Ulm and reported orally at sessions of the Society for German American Studies symposia.

Six

The Folklore of German-Bohemians
In the Old Homeland – Transfer to
Brown County

Nder the heading "folklore," are understood many things. Seeking a definition some authors stress the "lore" which signifies the materials rather than the people, "the folk." Thus they are concerned with origin, form, transmission and function. The transmission of folklore, most scholars agree, must fulfill the criterion that it be communicated in an "oral tradition."[1] By itself, however, an oral vehicle for handing down culture does not result in folklore. Nor is learning from parents how to use tableware or to brush one's teeth a part of folklore. On the other hand, just writing something does not thereby exclude it from the ranks of folklore. Thus if stories, ballads, or spoken dialects are written down and codified they are not thus deleted from the realm of folklore. Additionally, that which is transmitted mainly by body movements rather than speech can still be folklore though it is not orally transmitted. For example, dancing, one's manner of shaking hands, distances people keep when talking to strangers, games like horseshoe and baseball probably belong to oral tradition.

Folklore that is defined from the perspective of the folk often becomes erroneously categorized by the folk themselves as peasant, lower class, rural, or even primitive. Such a definition presumes that folklore is geographical and that it depends on economic or educational status. It relegates folklore to that which is old, from the past, and therefore dead and static. In this chapter the term is used for "any group of people who share a common heritage." It could be a group of lumberjacks, of railroad men, of Jews or Blacks or Catholics; it could also be a military unit, or a college and its students. Subgroups of a "folk" could be those who have their own separate lores, and even a single family that has traits and traditions that were passed down over generations, resulting in folklore. For purposes of what follows, the commonalty is the German-Bohemian heritage.

Generally folklore includes folktales, myths, legends, jokes, proverbs, riddles, blessings, greetings, tongue-twisters, leave taking formulas, folksongs, tunes, speech, language dialects, lullabies, ballads, metaphors (for example the color one paints a barn as opposed to a house), nicknames, place names, epitaphs and grave markings, even foods, recipes, quilting, embroidery designs, fence styles, and many more traditional sounds and conventions.

Within the overall category of folklore is the topic of folklife. Folklife generally includes what is understood as "material culture," an inclusion which extends folklore from the oral tradition to the visible aspects of everyday life. Material culture responds to techniques, skills, recipes and formulas that were transmitted across the generations. Usually, cultural traits were held together by the forces of tradition and embellished by individual variation as was verbal art. How people with a tradition build their homes, make their clothes, prepare their food, go about their farming, harvest their fields, shape their tools or implements, design furniture and process their food belong to the study of folklife.[2] In a word, folklife lags behind and lies in the shadow of modern society. Contemporary folklife presupposes an older, submerged culture.

Somewhere between oral tradition and material culture lie folk customs. This classification implies group interaction rather than individual skills or personal habits. Included are the patterns a people employ for the rites of passage, birth, initiation, marriage and death. In other words, a larger social unit, an extended family, or the whole community may be involved. There might be music, dance, costumes, parades, processions, festivals and the like, which may have both religious and secular ramifications and exemplifications. A further aspect of folklore would be the performance of folk arts. *Volkskunde*, which has been the subject of study for European scholars since the early nineteenth century beginning with the Brothers Grimm, is "the study of the interrelationships between the folk and folk-culture, in so far as they are determined by community and traditions."[3] All of traditional life and behavior from a locale or region are incorporated. Seen in this dimension, not only the material but also the social and spiritual aspects of life are encompassed.[4]

Following the German tradition of *Volkskunde* in the German-Bohemian tradition, we shall interweave the oral with the visible, the material with the spiritual, the religious with the secular, and come up with a regional pattern of life that fits the European background of immigrants to the greater New Ulm region. Of interest are German-Bohemian arts, crafts, handiwork, and attitudes toward work, worship, burial patterns, building styles, annual festivals, weddings, births, funerals, seasonal festivities, liturgical events like Christmas masses, New Year's, Lent, Easter, Corpus Christi, Ascension, All Saints Day and the like.

In this chapter the primary focus is on leisureful folklife; in the succeeding one, it is on work-a-day folklife. First the more festive, later the income-earning dimension. The folklife of the German inhabitants of western Bohemia has been well documented.[5] What follows first is a summary of such practices after which is seen those patterns that persisted after the people reached Brown county.

Annually the Bohemian forest witnessed a sequence of customs and celebrations that were tied to the calendar. To proceed systematically, we begin with New Year's Day. In many villages young men got up early and strolled from house to house wishing in German dialect a happy new year (a glücksöles neis Joua). Cherished sayings were for special villages, usually uttered in rhymes, sometimes forced. In Zemschen and vicinity there was a lengthy "I wish you a cluster of horns, a tree full of corns (kernels), a bag full of gold that will please you manifold" (I wünsch enk an Stoll vulla Harla, an Buan vulla Karla und an Beitl vull Göld, das enk heier reat gföllt). In the Muttersdorf region the wish was even longer, "I wish you a happy New Year, very bright and clear, a newly born baby Jesus, who will take you into Heaven maybe. The year is at an end, I ask for you a present" (I wünsch enk a glückselis neus Joar, recht hell und kloar, ein neugeborenes Jesulein, das wünsch i enk in Himmel hinein. Das Joar hat a End, i bitt um a Gschenk).

New Year's wishes were generally spoken only by men; if women said them it was a sign of bad luck. Traditionally, younger men did the honors and, as in the locution for Muttersdorf, usually worked into it a request for a glass of schnapps. Girls on New Year's followed another custom, that of whipping. Breaking off a small bundle of fresh willow, birch or hazelnut twigs, they proceeded from house to house switching male members of the household with their own special dictum. Those young men who did not get switched ran the risk during the course of a year of drying up and blowing away. The young male always had the option of buying his way out of more than one or two taps, provided he was willing to cough up some money. Since the date of December 28 just past was the males' day to switch, females could now return a few blows to zealous male villagers who had given them one too many four days earlier.

New Year's was important for everyone since it set the tone for the rest of the year. All villagers wanted to get up early, go to church, be kind to their neighbors, pray for good weather, eat well, carry around money in their pockets, and hire industrious help for the farm. To welcome new hired hands, the house wife sometimes laid a broom across the doorway. If the newcomer picked it up, it signified he would be a good worker. Those who were moving on, also did so on January 1, often going through the ritual of saying good-bye, even to the horses, cattle, and house pets.[6]

Epiphany, the feast of the Three Kings, called for young women to melt lead and drop it into cold water, following which they fished out the mysterious shapes and studied them to predict their futures. This custom, common to many European communities, offered young females the capability to estimate their probabilities for marriage during that year. Also on Epiphany, villagers sometimes built little boats from nut shells, loaded them with a small candle and set them afloat on a stream or village pond. The one whose boat first capsized would be the first to die. At mass in the morning, the priest blessed water, chalk, salt and incense, with which, that afternoon in some villages, the residents blessed their houses and fields. With chalk they wrote on each house door the initials of the three kings, accompanied by the year in which the house had been constructed, for example, K (Kaspar), M (Melchior) and B (Balthasar) – 1873. In some cases, young men went from house to house singing or playing music for which they expected to be treated to money or schnapps.

February Second or Candlemass Day was the deadline to wash off the chalk markings for those who wished. In Muttersdorf, an old tradition called for special effort by the villagers to go out at midday with lanterns in search of their beloved Fasching – pre-Lenten festivities, which they found in the form of masked, not very well hidden young fellows. This opened the season for the many balls that took place before the arrival of Ash Wednesday and the conventional season of fasting.

Every social club or work organization was expected to stage a dance: the firemen, veterans, hunters, wood cutters, sometimes even the more cavalier clubs like the "hobos" and "goof-offs." A competition held sway with each organization trying to outdo the other with colorful decorations, special dance orchestras, or excellently performed folk dances. To keep people mindful of the event, tickets were printed, distributed door-to-door, and displayed traditionally at home in a saint's picture corner where everyone saw them readily and would not forget to attend. Frequently a lottery was staged at midnight so all guests would be inclined to remain in attendance. The wood choppers ball was always a specialty. Pine branches decked the hall, colorful lanterns glowed on the walls, silhouettes of woodcutters shone in the windows, and the choppers sometimes staged a special show in the middle of the dance floor, figuratively hacking away to the tune of a wood chopper's march or polka.

All of these activities actually belonged to Fasching, known in the local dialect as "Fosnatnarren" (Pre-Lenten foolishness). Troops of masked young men and women appeared at the different balls where guests tried to conjecture their identity, if possible by getting them to talk or laugh at all manner of jokes, practical or spoken, but usually without success. Only unmarried villagers participated.

Zemschen and Pössigkau celebrated so-called *Tolldonnerstag* (Crazy Thursday), a special peasant ritual. Six *Strohmänner*, fellows decked out in long straw uniforms to more or less resemble huge bundles of grain, were hitched to a plow. Guiding the plow was a farmer wearing a vest of long fur and high boots. Next to him walked a driver cracking his whip violently. Behind them came a young woman supposedly hand-seeding the earth; instead, she threw the grain into the faces of onlookers. Behind her walked another young woman with a rake; finally, a spirited team of horses plodded along pulling a harrow. Sometimes the women were actually young men dressed like females. If the plowmen pulled off some of their many tricks, the draft "horses"

Fasching celebration and costumes in OldWorld village of Natschetin. BS

ran away. Or the plow got stuck in the street. Or they purposely
dragged it into a manure pile, or into the village pond.With variations,
the Muttersdorfers staged similar parades.Weissensulz was especially
known for its jumbo procession that evolved from this tradition. At all
such events, the famous snack of *Schmierkuchen* (fruit filled sweet
breads) was a favorite dish to reward the revelers. Generally *Tolldonnerstag* fell on the last Thursday of the week before AshWednesday.

Fasching Sunday – the last one before Ash Wednesday – offered
specialty foods, dumplings and sauerkraut on fatty meat followed by
the inevitable dance and beer party that evening. Monday generally
brought out a Fasching parade through each village with festive figures dressed in costumes to make fun of someone, perhaps a doctor, a
chimney sweep, a butcher, a policeman, a thief, or some government
official. There was much singing, joking, and reveling in the streets.
Dancing was common, so much so that the evening ball was designated in some villages as just for married folks, the others being by this
time so tired from the whole day that they needed an excuse to stay
home and sleep.

Fasching Tuesday was the most celebrated day of the season. Early
in the morning peasants rose from their beds and began dancing with

each other in the superstitious belief that revelry was good for the flax and other spring crops. For the same purpose, farmers' wives washed their linen skirts and laid them to dry on the manure pile, just to be assured of a good crop. Right after the noon meal, musical dance bands blaring polka beats paraded through the streets, and were quickly joined by women in their Sunday finest. Sometimes this event took on the name *Lösungstag*, that is, a time when the girls had the chance to contribute to the cost of the festivities, meals, music, dance hall, etc. This usually resulted in crazy bargaining with the men. In some villages the dialect name *Ploozmoad* (in high German *Platz-magd*) held special significance. This was the girl who spent the largest sum of money to help cover expenses and in return got the right to open the dancing that evening. Because all wanted to at least watch these events if they could not themselves take part, mothers and grandmothers lined the benches surrounding the dance hall.

The most popular dances were the polka, waltz, Ländler, and to a lesser degree also the *Rheinländer*. Ring dances (*Rojan* or *Reigentänze*) were especially favored. On these occasions young men sometimes gathered near the stage just below the dance band where they sang the ring dance songs that were played by the musicians. This resulted in one large circle alternating from boy to girl with hands joined behind the back of each adjacent partner. Often the ring spun ever faster until at some link it ruptured, causing young people to fly into the corners. Music for these 19th century affairs was often produced by a Dudel-sack, a type of bagpipe, or a primitive accordion accompanied by a fiddle or two. Near the turn of the century brass horns and reed instruments gained prominence. Sometimes it took until the wee hours of the morning for the dancers to have enough, at which time occasionally they were *heimgespielt*, led by the band to their various homes in the village.

By midnight of Fasching Tuesday, the guests were often on their way home, because on Ash Wednesday everyone was to be seen at mass receiving ashes on the forehead, and ready for six weeks of fasting and abstinence. At noon on Ash Wednesday, however, some villagers still gathered for a "beer feast" for which free beer was supplied by the innkeepers in "thanks" for heavy pre-Lenten spending. Young and old had a good time. That afternoon, all gathered for a march through the village to its edge. A life-sized straw doll was born along to this place of the dead where it was ceremoniously torched. Now at last the musicians and innkeepers could look forward to a few days of quiet and recuperation. In the village of Sirb, tradition demanded that the straw doll be torched in the middle of the bridge and then dropped in flames into the water.

Lent was spent in prayer and reflection. Villagers told of gathering after the evening meal to pray the rosary, recite the litany, and offer special supplications to the Lord through the regional patron Saint, Leonhard or, in some places, Wendelin. The season of lent was strictly observed. Of course there was strong beer midway through lent, and sometimes there were extra portions of fish but for the most part the severity of Lenten observances warranted the occasional excesses of the pre-Lenten Fasching.

Palm Sunday marked the beginning of the Easter season. Young boys gathered pussy willows or birch branches and forced early buds by keeping them in warm water vases. On Palm Sunday they carried pussy willow bundles bound broom-like to church where the priest blessed them. Back home children disassembled and delivered them to relatives and friends, in the hope of receiving a few coins or perhaps an early Easter egg for their trouble. The remaining branches were hung behind the crucifix, above a door, or held temporarily in a vase. Anyone suffering from a sore throat or hoarse voice at this time could swallow a few buds from the pussy willows and be instantly "cured."

Holy Week got underway in earnest on Holy Thursday, *Gründonner-stag*. At the 8 A.M. mass, bells rang at the *Gloria* but then were said to have flown to Rome ("nach Rom geflogen"), not to be heard again until Easter morning. School boys especially enjoyed this period of "quiet" because they got to use their clappers and ratchet boxes not only for the ceremonies in church but also when they ran through the village announcing the morning, noon and evening angelus times. Apparently this duty of the school boys was so popular that village craftsmen created elaborate devices to scratch out the noises, and children posed gladly for pictures.[7] An ulterior motive sometimes came into play, for villagers often gave the young fellows coins or eggs for their efforts. Occasionally in larger villages, the troupe of young *Ratschler* slept in a barn on straw at one end of town so as to be able early in the morning to proceed on their trek back to the other side.

The customary village bells meanwhile hung in silence, "gestorben" (dead) in the popular designation.

On *Karfreitag* (Good Friday) services took place at 9 A.M. with a sermon followed by a reading of St. John's Passion. In the afternoon there was a simulated ceremony either in church or at the holy grave. The more pious fasted the entire day until the first stars appeared in the heavens, others only till noon or 3 P.M. Young boys in mass server garb guarded the simulated holy tomb the entire day, changing the guard every two hours.

Karsamstag (Holy Saturday) began about 7 A.M. when the priest lit a small wood-fueled fire in which were burned the old oils and daubs from that year's baptizing. In some instances a straw figure of Judas was also burned. Peasants afterwards took the ashes and mixed them with the wheat seed to prevent fires in the ripened grain, or hid a few powdery ashes in the roof of the houses or barns to protect them from burning all year long. At Gloria time in the mass, bells again were permitted to be rung. At this very moment in the village, fruit growers were supposed to run and shake every fruit tree so that it would awaken from its wintry sleep and bear a good harvest. The bells continued ringing throughout the entire singing of the Gloria. Theoretically when the last gong peeled out, every tree had to be shaken or it would remain barren for the year. In Sirb and a few other villages, young women listened because if a dog barked during the bell ringing, from that direction would come a husband for her.

Easter morning really began in the peasant villages on Saturday evening. Villagers streamed into the churches where they sang, played the organ, and rang out the good news of Christ's resurrection. After mass, the priest carried the monstrance in procession through a village lit by candles from windows in homes. Mass servers rang bells and swung incense censors. In a few villages, the night concluded with men firing shotguns into the air to make loud noises.

On the actual Sunday of Easter, villagers celebrated the risen Christ together with their families. Some got Easter water from the church and symbolically bathed in it to remain healthy throughout the year. Easter Monday was also a day of festivities, only now, sometimes with the phrase *nach Emaus* (going to visit in Emaus), people went forth to call on relatives and friends. In some villages this also called for street dancing.

Osterritt in Weidlitz 1936. BS

In Neustadl near the city of Haid was held the big egg bashing contest. After everyone had gathered around for the *Eierkämpfen* (egg battle) or *Stützen* (egg bumping), challengers could see whose egg, when bumped head to head with an opponent's egg, would survive. Anyone with a broken egg lost and was eliminated from the contest. Another game was for opponents to hold an egg in the fist with only a slit showing between the thumb and index finger. If an opponent could drop a coin on it hitting only the egg, he could take the egg. Otherwise the coin was forfeited. Or the egg was placed a given distance ahead of the two opponents. If a challenger could toss the coin to make it penetrate the shell, he got the egg or lost his coin (usually a *Kreuzer*). Another variation was for many contestants to participate. The egg was set a distance of six meters in front of the players. Only one throw each was allowed. The one whose coin lay closest to the egg upon completion, took all the eggs.

In a few villages, the nine days preceding the feast of St. Walburga of Heidenheim (February 25) were celebrated. She was a Benedictine abbess, the sister of Saints Willibald and Winnebald of Eichstätt, who were reared and educated in England before proceeding at the request of St. Boniface to preach the word of God in Germany. As abbess,

Walburga favored education for German women. After her death in 779 her remains were taken to Monheim in Bavaria and Furness in England. Reportedly an oil deposit still flows on her stone slab from October 12 to February 25 of each year. Because the convent in Eichstätt was later called St. Walpurg in her honor, her name has also been associated with the German tradition of Walpurgisnacht.[8] St. Walburga allegedly had been pursued and tormented by evil spirits in the late winter days, an episode that won her the title of patron of travelers. Farmers leave a window open in the house during the novena to Walburga so that she can find rest if needed. Also, travelers who have strayed at night report her appearing to them as a beautiful woman with fiery shoes on her feet, a golden crown on her long hair, and a mirror in her hand. Behind her are seen knights riding on silvery white horses. She was known to usher in the spring and warm weather, and in some regions also a good harvest in the fall.

Although on occasion Walburga has been confused with the commemoration of *Walpurgisnacht*, the latter has always been celebrated on a fixed date from April 30 - May 1 each year. In the Bohemian German villages, *Walpurgisnacht* depicted the struggle of the gods of winter with those of spring, the latter always victorious. As elsewhere in Germany, this was the time for driving out witches and evil spirits. Whip cracking was generally practiced on the village streets. Almost everywhere houses and barns were decorated with fresh greenery. Some laid the cut grass in the form of a cross ahead of doorways to prevent witches from entering. Occasionally a barn was blocked from entry by strewing cut nettles on the entry way. During the night, young men sometimes did Halloween style pranks – took off the garden gate and threw it in the village pond, tipped over outdoor toilets, pulled farm machinery into a stream, and drew lines with sprinkled sawdust between the house doors of secret lovers.

May was the time to set up a *Maibaum* (Maypole). Most villages elevated and decorated a tall, bark-trimmed pole in the town hall square. A large wreath of evergreen branches topped the pole while ribbons hung from it at many points. Usually there were special dances around the May tree, which, when it had served its purpose, was sold to a local saw mill, the proceeds being used at one of the local taverns. In a few villages May was better known for its evening church services. Also, this was the time for *Bitt-Tage* (prayer days) when the pastor led school children with their parents in a procession of parishioners carrying lighted candles and flags through the fields to pray for a good harvest. At times they also led the farmers out to the fields with their plows or other field implements. At such a time, custom called for the farmer's wife to situate an egg and a piece of bread in the road to be crushed under the wagon wheels to assure a good crop.

Pfingsten (Pentecost) was the time for a special procession on horseback with elaborately decorated draft horses. This joyous event, known as *Pfingstreiten,* was to bless the fields. Thus horsemen rode either initially, or after their trek through the acreage, by way of the village church. Some carried a large crucifix en route. *Fronleichnam* (Corpus Christi) was a related event. On this occasion, young girls dressed in white with crowns of flowers in their hair. These maidens not only processed but also strewed blossoms at each of four altars forming a carpet for the priest to approach with the monstrance being steadily incensed by backward stepping mass servers. At each altar the priest delivered a blessing and perhaps a short sermon. In a few towns, entire street passages were strewn with grass and flowers for the occasion.

In the same spirit, some villages celebrated the feast of St. John (*Johannistag*) on June 25. This was an excuse to turn the summer solstice and its more pagan commemoration into a Christian feast day. Days in advance, people brought twigs and branches to a hill top near the village. As soon as it got dark, a bonfire was lit. Songs, old sayings, much tomfoolery and in some places, burning of scarecrows representing officials did not prevent the people from believing in the more providential benefits of the fire. Charred sticks were stuck into the fields to "guarantee" a good harvest. Also, women sometimes gathered ashes from the embers for their gardens, and in general the salutary effects of the evening outweighed the pagan significance.

Various other feasts of the saints were commemorated throughout the summer. *Jakobistag* on July 25, *Annatag* on July 26, *Bartholomäus* on August 24, and in every village the local *Kirchweihfest* (dedication day of the parish church). Feasting and dancing took place all day. Some villages organized pilgrimages usually dedicated to the Holy Virgin Mary. A few traveled distances out of town to special centers, others simply formed a procession to a statue or image, perhaps a small chapel dedicated to the Holy Mother somewhere on the edge of the village. There were also less religious undertakings: special commemoration of potato harvesting in some villages, a threshing bee festival in another, sauerkraut parties in still others.

As fall approached, special festivities were reserved for All Saints Day on November first, this time with special processions out to the cemeteries to decorate the graves of loved ones. *Andreastag* came on November 10, on November 11 *Martini,* a Thanksgiving Day of sorts. November 25 was *Kathrein* (St. Catherine Day) for which there was always dancing, and on December 4 *Barbaratag.*

But before the Christmas season set in, each village celebrated in one way or another the necessities of life. There were special commemorations for *Schweineschlachten* or *Schlachtfest* (pig butchering day) when neighbors came together to kill, clean, and process the hogs. The tradition of catching the blood to make blood sausage, washing the intestines for casings, and processing other trimmings into liver sausage and head cheese were both hard work and fun for the gathering. At noon the party ate fried brains with sauerkraut and dumplings and relished the special blood sausage soup, to which all the neighbors were invited. Meats were then processed into ham and related cuts. Commonly much of the meat was smoked for purposes both of taste and of preservation.

Another fall duty of considerable festivity was *Federnschleissen,* stripping geese and stuffing feathers into down. Often this duty was accomplished in the evenings with members of an extended family sitting around in a room where a member or neighbor of the family sat playing the zither or accordion while the workers sang nostalgic, sad or gloomy songs. Out of this serious pursuit developed also certain oracles that were played out. For example in Muttersdorf girls took off their shoes, then had to pick them up between their feet with their teeth and throw them backwards over their heads. Supposedly, when the shoe landed, if it pointed in one direction, from there would come a husband. If, however, it pointed in the direction of the cemetery, someone in the family would soon die. Then there was the *Gansprobe* (the goose test), in which a gander was let loose in the living room. The girl whom the gander first attacked grasping her skirt in its beak would be the next to get married. These feather stripping bees moved from house to house, at which time the festivities of the event were repeated.

The Christmas season ended the year. It opened generally on St. Nicholas Day December 6 with a *Nikolaus-Markt* (open air tent sale)

Butchering hogs in rural New Ulm. BC

on the town square where some sold and others bought craft items along with food and heart warming drinks. In Ronsperg and vicinity, St. Nikolaus never made appearances without his *Krampus* or devil-costumed figure who rattled chains and spanked children who had misbehaved. In bishop's garb, St. Nikolaus always demanded that the children say a few prayers, sing a song or two, perhaps utter a wise saying, and then be rewarded with nuts, apples, chocolate and various candies. Names of the bad children were written in Nikolaus' black book and if Krampus was so instructed they got a mild whipping on the spot, or were threatened with being thrown in Krampus' black bag.

St. Luzia Day on December 13 also was actively commemorated in the region of Bischofteinitz. Until the Gregorian Calendar reform of

Smokehouse at 77 N. Spring Street, New Ulm, Allan R. Gebhard.

1582, December 13 was the shortest day of the year. Thus Luzia, or in Latin Lucia, the patron saint also of the Swedes and other northern countries, became famous as the bearer of light. In Latin the word *lux, lucis* means "light" and thus the saint's name is appropriately associated with the winter solstice. In all of Bavaria and southern regions where German was spoken, Frau Berchta, or Perchta, has also been associated with the solstice and in the minds of some, Luzia is but a Christianization of the old Berchta who went about in the winter darkness calling forth spirits of the dead, which the depths of winter sanctioned by its lack of light.

In Bischofteinitz county, Luzia also allegedly would come and slit the stomachs of children who had not eaten bread crumbs and drunk cold milk on the feast of All Souls. Out of that belief came the oft repeated threat to the bad children that if they did not behave, Luzia would slit open their stomachs and stuff them full of straw. A threatening little rhyme was common in the community of Waier, "Kinder, seid nur heute recht brav und ruhig, sonst kommt die heilige Luzia, die schneidet allen bösen Kindern den Bauch auf und steckt Stroh und Fetzen hinein." (Children, be good and quiet today, otherwise St. Lucy will come and cut open all bad children's bellies, and stuff them full of straw and rags.)

Christmas Eve was the greatest of annual festivals. Only on this last day of advent was the Christmas tree erected and decorated with apples, nuts, and candy. Often a creche scene was placed under the tree. In many villages the children strewed some straw ahead of the house door so that when the Christ Child came by on his white horse, the animal would gladly want to stop. Because fasting and abstinence were the rule of the church, the Christmas eve meal consisted of fish, peas, nuts and prunes. As usual on festival days, there was plenty of *Schmierkuchen*. Some families gave extra portions of fodder to their cattle that evening. Many believed that during midnight mass, the cattle would speak with each other and with the heavens. Thus a tradition arose for those who wanted to learn the future, to hide in the barn and listen carefully as the cattle lowed at midnight. Distribution of gifts did not take place until Christmas morning. As was traditional in the whole of Germany, the first day of Christmas, the 25th, was spent in the family. The second day on December 26 was for visiting friends and extended relatives. Also on December 26, after the quiet of Advent, people again could go dancing.

December 28, the feast of the Holy Innocents, was celebrated when young village men switched the girls on their legs, avoided often by their squatting low or by offering coins in order to be spared. New Year's Eve or *Silvester* arrived on December 31 which was generally celebrated with a dance, sometimes the fireman's dance. The hall was beautifully decorated and several dances called for the firemen to see to it that no young women were left without the opportunity to dance. At midnight the musicians played special songs ushering in the New Year and everyone wished each other a Happy New Year. Following a brief pause, girls had the right to switch the young men, in proportion as they had been switched a few days earlier. Because New Year's Day was another big event, folks generally went home shortly afterwards.

Life's milestones, too, were celebrated in special ways in the region. In some communities, these began already during pregnancy. Expecting mothers had to be careful not to be frightened by fire or their child would be affected. Even if a mother witnessed too many ugly things, the child might be endangered. If she passed a man with too large a nose, the child could inherit it. Similar superstitions abounded. Customary circumspect phrases told of the birth event, such as "the woodpile tipped in today." Children in the family were given no explanation of the milestone, not even the stork legend, but that "the new baby was fetched from the village pond." All babies were born at home with the help of a midwife. Because inheriting the *Hof* or home farm was of special concern in the village, it was especially crucial that the next heir be born on the site he would inherit.

Baptism took place in church, with the godparents in charge, after which there was generally a banquet for the relatives and neighbors. This was followed by a re-blessing of the mother six weeks after the child's birth, also in church, at which time the mother held the child while both received a benediction. After quiet years at home, the child of six began formal schooling. At this age, the world of work was taught at the hand of house duties or small chores on the farm. Life in the village was learned easily because from their earliest age children participated in all the festivities of community life.

Eventually courtships developed and couples envisioned the possibility of marriage. Until the current century, a *Kuppler*, or official marriage broker, played a crucial role in mating partners. More recently the parents of the bride and groom simply agreed on their own and went forward with plans for a wedding in church. Usually the bride and groom personally strolled through the village inviting the guests. In turn they brought gifts, presents, and money or food stuffs together on the Sunday before the wedding day. The wedding invariably took place at the home of the bride. Sometimes after the guests had gathered, someone smashed a plate with the saying "Just as this plate will never again be whole, so may this couple never again be apart." Once everything at home was ready, the couple knelt on a white cloth so that the bride's parents could give them their blessing. Thereafter the group went together to church in a procession that was announced to the whole community by firing off some shots from a pistol. Often the bride was dressed in a bridal gown, but weddings also took place in local costumes. After a church ceremony, the couple went with their witnesses to the pastor's house to sign the legal papers.

One popular custom during the pre-dining hours at mid-day was to steal the bride's shoe and auction it off, the money going to one of the cultural organizations of the community. Also on the way back to the site of the festivities, young men often roped off the street with ribbons, through which passage was possible only by the payment of fees. Mostly these processions both to and from church were led by at least a fiddler and bag piper, sometimes by a full band of musicians. The wedding dinner took place with the bridal couple enjoying center stage; that meant in the farm house parlor under the *Herrgottswinkel*, or the place where the crucifix was mounted in the corner of the living room. Food was generous, including liver dumpling soup, beef, pork, goose, duck, many vegetables, topped off with coffee and *Schmierkuchen*.

In the evening there was the traditional wedding dance, at which even villagers not included at the wedding itself were perfectly welcome. The next day or perhaps not until the following Sunday, the neighbors celebrated *Nachhochzeit*, a second day of the wedding, when they gathered to eat and enjoy leftovers. Also on the day after or perhaps several days following the formal wedding, there was a trip on the *Kommerwagen*. At least one team of horses pulled a wagon on which were loaded all the things the bride's family was donating to help the young couple start out on their own. Sometimes it included more than just inanimate gifts, namely cattle, farm implements and the like. Usually the groom drove the team and sat with the bride at his side.[9]

Music, consisting of folk tunes played by a small dance band and folk singers, was an essential part of every Bohemian German wedding. In some villages they played and sang a serenade, one for the bridal relationship, another to the parents and grandparents, and anyone else in the family who enjoyed honorable kinship to the couple to be married the next day. On the wedding day itself, the band often went out playing in the streets to gather the guests, "sie einspielen" (play them together into the church) or just as likely to help fetch the bride for her ride to the church. If so, the musicians received a boutonniere to identify them as part of the overall wedding party. When the bride and groom were from different villages, one half of the musicians went to each house to pipe the partners and their relatives together, colorfully crossing the fields and back roads on foot with music blaring until they met and proceeded jointly to church.[10]

Often gaps between the music were filled with "wise" sayings, the

Kommerwagen [bridal shower wagon] in Pollschütz.BS

likes of "der Ehestand ist ein Wehestand" (the state of marriage is a state of misery). At the church, the musicians lined up in a position of honor guard on both sides of the entry while the bridal couple and attendants marched through their ranks, entered the church and proceeded to the altar. Once the vows and mass had been spoken in church, the musicians again led the entourage, sometimes by way of a tavern where they danced for a while, and then on to the home of the bride or wherever the wedding banquet was being held. There they entertained off and on for the rest of the day. At the banquet there was usually a special table of honor for the musicians, alongside the bridal places. In some instances before the musicians had shepherded the guests home ("sie heimspielen" – play the guests back home), they arranged for a mock "bride" housewife. Temporarily the bride was captured and held behind the scenes. Then entered "das wilde Weib" (the wild wife), a man dressed as a woman and very ugly, carrying a straw stuffed small baby. After the audience had its laughs, this particular musician returned to his instrument and the bride continued dancing until all festivities had ended.

Death in the villages was accepted as an ordinary event of nature. If possible, the dying person received the sacrament of Extreme Unction

Village band in Andreasberg near Krummau in the Bohemian Forest leads a wedding party through the countryside. Note the men in wedding attire: ribbons, flowers in hats, and bride wearing black with white veil. Source: Der Böhmerwaldbauer *(Prague: Calve, 1915).*

and when death occurred the bells of the village tolled his passing. Still in his own house, he was immediately placed on a board, the so-called *Totenbrett* (death board) and kept on it for three days at home. Mirrors were covered and clocks in the house stopped until the time of burial. Neighbors and relatives gathered to hold continuous prayer vigils until interment. The corpse was dressed in fine clothes and a rosary placed in his folded hands. Messengers circled the village with announcements of his passing.

On the actual day of burial, guests gathered at the person's home where they took turns sprinkling the body with holy water. Then he was placed in a coffin which was nailed shut and carried feet first out of the house. In passing through the doorway, the coffin was moved forward and across the threshold three times in the form of a cross. Transported on a horse drawn wagon, the catafalque was driven past the outdoor village crucifix where it was blessed. It then proceeded to the cemetery as the mourners followed, praying the rosary. Sometimes a band played, leading the mourners. At the grave site the pastor spoke a few words of parting and the coffin was lowered. Often a mass for

The 1886 Koester-Wilbrecht Wedding in Brown County. Note the band's many wind instruments and the dark clothes of most guests, including apparently the attendants. BC

Band instruments with Joseph Bier on the dudelsack at the Seifert-Wech wedding. BC

the dead person was offered only the next day. On the day of burial, the mourners all gathered at a Gasthaus where they ate and drank to the memory of the deceased, sometimes until late at night. Mourning was prescribed for parents, brothers and sisters, at least one year. For grandparents, only eight weeks. Women had to wear black clothes, men dark suits, and there was no dancing or festivities during the period of mourning.

Gravestones once were made of wood, then of cast iron or metal formed by blacksmiths. Only in this century did it become common to use stone. The custom of using *Tottenbretter* (vertically positioned death boards) persisted from early times to ours. In memory of the dead person, a board was cut and carved with inscriptions of identification. Frequently they were erected on a pathway or crosswalk or out in a field. In addition to the name and dates of the person, there was often a verse, sometimes humorous, characterizing the individual, or bearing a special message he might have spoken to the living. For example, "Durch eines Ochsen Hornesstoss, kam er in des Himmels Schoss, am 21. Augustus. Gelobt sei Jesus Christus!" (By an ox's gore, he was brought low on the 21st of August. Praise be to Jesus Christ!) The *Tottenbretter* were intended as a device to keep a deceased member of the community in the consciousness of the living. Rarely were they positioned in the cemetery. Perhaps they stood against the chapel there. Rather they were stood in a busy intersection where daily people passed these artistic reminders of their loved ones.[11] A few customs for burial disappeared when modern conveniences arrived, for instance the ride on a horse drawn hearse or, in winter, on a bob sled drawn by a team. Also the practice of musicians leading the funeral procession to the cemetery gradually disappeared during the current century.

In the life of a German-Bohemian farmer there were folkloric occurrences that did not deal with life's milestones as such. However, they were annual landmarks of another kind – rites believed to assure fertility of the fields and the economic stability of the community. Certain plantings had to take place, for instance, according to the sequence of full moon and for most decisions the horoscope was consulted. Throughout, however, there was pious faith in God, "Vertrauend streut der Bauer den Samen in das Land; Doch Segen und Gedeihen kommt von Gottes Hand" (Trusting, the farmer scatters seed on the soil but its germination and growth lies in God's hands).

From the first load of hay each season, farmers crumbled a few dry leaves and pressed them in their wallets for good luck. When grain was threshed, the first bread made from the newly ground flour was served to the hired help. Rather than keeping cats and traps, superstition was invoked to hold back the mice from stored grain. Before the first load was deposited in the granary, the farmer beat against the door three times with his horse whip incanting the words "für die Leute Brot für die Mäuse den Tod" (for the people bread, for the mice death). When threshing was about finished, neighbors sometimes used the last bundles to make a rope, tie up the farm owner, and not release him until he had "bought" his freedom with a goodly supply of beer and schnapps. In most villages there were also festive dances on an evening following the conclusion of the threshing season.

Weather, too, was best dealt with in the framework of folklore. A little holy water fortified with blessed salt offered optimum protection against hail. In some villages hail would stop if the housewife just ran outside, gathered three hail stones and threw them into her cook stove. Some thought it helped prevent hail if you left a hoe lying on the ground with the blade toward the heavens. Hardly more scientific was the local practice in a few villages for men to run outside and shoot into the thick clouds with their pistols. Other housewives found relief in placing a straw basket containing a loaf of bread on top of the manure pile until the storm had passed. If you were caught outside during lightning, you dared not raise your finger or it would attract a strike. Best was to take shelter beneath a hazel nut bush because under this shrub Mary is said to have found protection when fleeing with Jesus into Egypt.[12]

Animals figured large in the folklore of the Bohemian German farmers. Barns had to be protected from witches. Before taking the cows out to summer pastures, farmers made a small hole in the ground, poured some milk in it, then heated a nail red hot and plunged it into the milk to keep their summer milk supply from getting bewitched in one way or another. Palm branches and holy water were stationed in various nooks and crannies of the animal shelters for the same purpose. To keep the cows from suffering too much heat in the summer, the herder took along two hard boiled eggs and threw them between the legs of the lead animal as it headed for pasture. If he missed his throw, that was a bad omen. Newly acquired cows were led into the barn and made to step over a broom so that they would be quickly domesticated to their new surroundings.

Birds held other forebodings for their keepers. If farmers bought chickens, they held them in their hands and scratched the right foot three times into the ground around a table leg to be sure they would stay at their new home. They never positioned a hen to hatched eggs on a Friday, for such an ill-timed setting would surely turn out badly. If ever a hen crowed or even attempted such a masculine maneuver, it was considered a terrible sign of misfortune and her head was chopped off immediately. The first grass cut in the spring had to be fed to the geese to assure second and third crops. A howling dog at night signaled a death; and if the church bell was ringing, the direction of the dog's snout indicated in what direction someone had just died. Cats that became seven years old turned into witches. Most insects were considered a menace, but the spider often brought good luck. Proverbs involving spiders were plentiful, for example, "Spinne am Morgen bringt Kummer und Sorgen; Spinne am Abend bringt Geld und Gaben" (a spider in the morning brings trouble and sorrow, a spider in the evening brings money and plenty).

Inanimate objects were at times treated like living personalities to avoid harm. Baking bread required nine different markings with the sign of the cross in the dough so it would turn out fine in the oven. If furniture creaked during use, it meant someone in the neighborhood would soon die. The fire crackling in the cook stove signaled many things, including when guests were expected to arrive. Breaking a mirror brought seven years of misfortune. If shoes squeaked, they were not yet paid for. If everyone at table cleaned his plate there would be fair weather the next day. If you cut a child's hair before it is a year old, you threw away its intelligence. An old axiom ran, "kalte Hände, warmes Herz" (cold hands mean a warm heart). The first dream in a new bed will always come true.

Plenty of formalized adages enabled usually a mother or housewife to cure most evils. Toothache, headache, common cold, all could be handled with wise rhyming phrases. In the same vein, fires were no problem, because a housewife needed only to write appropriate letters on a plate, throw it into the fire so that it broke, and the fire would go out. Warts could be removed routinely sometimes with secret riddles, sometimes by rubbing on rain water that had been collected from the roof in a hollowed out stone, and then again by rubbing them with earth from the cemetery. The best cure for gout was an egg from a black hen, boiled hard in a pot that cost an uneven number of Kreuzers, wrapped in linen and buried in an anthill. As soon as the ants had devoured the egg, the gout would be gone. Cattle could be cured by similar devices. Thousands of prescriptions and recipes were handed down from generation to generation, offering solutions to most of life's problems. Not many, but some did manage to cross the ocean to Brown county.

In Brown county the Germans from Bohemia did not live in close proximity to enjoy the intimate village life that fostered folklore and folklife practices in the Bohemian Forest. Moreover, their numbers were diminished and the inhibitions associated with the presence of out-group neighbors quickly smothered most of the special customs and traditions of the Old Country. Still, it is a rule of thumb that folklore is, while an echo of the past, a vigorous voice of the present. In this present voice, we now try to find in Brown county echoes of the old Bohemian homeland.[13]

Anecdotes persist in Brown county, for example, the humorous, sometimes derogatory, stories about people in and from the village of Hirschau.[14] One alleges that the mayor of Hirschau traveled to a neighboring village where he met a farmer driving a team of oxen on a narrow road. Facing the oxen and farmer, the mayor said "Should the mayor of Hirschau step aside or should the oxen move over?" Not wanting to get involved, the farmer told the mayor: "I will let you take that up with the oxen." Another anecdote: A Hirschauer was attacked by a bull and after a horn-headed tussle, fled to safety behind the fence with the words, "The more intelligent one always gives in!" Another Hirschauer cut down a tree in his pasture, laid it crosswise on his hay rack and tied it down securely. Reaching his farm yard, he found the tree too wide for the gate through the walled site, so he sawed off each end of the tree.

On another fine day a high official came to Hirschau riding on a white horse and wearing around his neck a golden chain. Though the residents admired it, one said "someone with such a fancy neck piece must surely be a thief!" In another instance, a Hirschauer's cow wandered off to the owner's great dismay until the villagers pitched in to help him find it; after which the farmer replied: "I'm so glad I was not with my cow, otherwise I would have been lost too!" And when the bishop came to Hirschau, four men carried his fancy sedan chair through the village, all others following in procession behind them. But when one of the bearers stumbled and thereby lost his grip, the other three also gave way. Unceremoniously the bishop flew into the ditch minus his tall hat, to which the mayor responded, "Today we have the honor of restoring the bishop to his throne."

The Brown county calendar in festivals is actually not so different from the European setting because as Catholics, the Germans from Bohemia followed a similar set of commemorations. Festivities for the New Year were the same though less vivid because farm life out on the American landscape did not lend itself to village style sharing. Pre-Lenten dancing and partying still are very popular, although the name *Fasching* is no longer directly associated with the affair. However, masked balls once were thoroughly familiar throughout the first half of the 20th century. Easter with its egg games survived as did corpus christi (*Fronleichnam*) processions to outside altars. Saints' days were different here, if they survived at all, but Thanksgiving substituted for other fall festival days. St. Nickolaus with Ruprecht or Krampus in accompaniment paid his visits to the good and bad children. Christmas eve was once a somber time with fasting and abstinence rather than banqueting and the opening of gifts. St. Lucy Day on December 13 seems to have remained more alive in neighboring Swedish communities than in Brown county.

Back in the Old Country of course there was no baseball. Yet this wholly American sport quickly captured the fascination of German-Bohemians. Throughout rural Brown County baseball teams formed, usually in conjunction with a creamery location, though earlier in this century in the Sleepy Eye area the baseballers aptly organized themselves into what was known as the "Pasture League." Once the Stark Township baseball team was made up entirely of Helget cousins and even today the townships of Stark, Albion and Sigel have their own lighted baseball fields out in the countryside, still located on creamery sites that, however, no longer gather milk.

Life's milestones are another matter. As in the Old Country, virtually all children until the mid 1930s were delivered by midwives who perpetuated a tradition that gave way to modern science, although it is now experiencing a rebirth. Baptism is still a liturgical event celebrat-

Fasching party in New Ulm 1916 in front of the tavern then known as "Zur Stadt Prag" (at the City of Prague). BC

ed in the company of family and sponsors. Weddings were the most elaborate. In the early days a *Kuppler* (match maker) handled formalities, though his presence was more a tradition than strictly a function. Always the dinner and reception took place at the home of the bride where the neighbors cooked for days in advance of the celebration. In the tradition of the *Kommerwagen*, the groom was expected to supply some cows and horses, the bride so and so many bushels of grain, chickens, and any housewares not received as wedding gifts.

Always there was music and dancing! In the Old World pattern the band frequently came out to the bride's place before her departure for church. Dancing took place in the barn, or in a shed, always to the tunes of a neighborhood dance band playing the familiar waltzes, polkas and Ländlers. As abroad, there was a second and third day of the wedding, usually a cleanup session with neighbors and friends popping over to help finish off the food. Wedding dresses were elaborate but never white, not even the bride's dress. Rather it retained a folk costume style that reminds us of the European setting. At every wedding there was plenty of draft beer. Parents of the couple often entered the planning for marriage by helping draw up a contract specifying what each child would bring to the fledgling new home.

Several features not known in the European setting but part and parcel of the Brown county wedding was the prenuptial shower for the bride. The shivaree after the wedding is also a New World event that hearkens back to the German *Polterabend* which occurred before the wedding. About two weeks succeeding the wedding in Brown county the couple in their new residence are serenaded with the sounds of pots and pans, horns and shotguns followed by a beer party for the neighborhood. Oddly, no one reports that the shivaree turned into a dancing party. Also, a formal photograph taken the day of the wedding by the German-Bohemians was displayed for years in a box frame embellished with craft work that incorporated part or all of the bride's veil. The tradition of musicians, mass servers or another appointed group stopping the couple or taking them "prisoner" until they bought their freedom with a few coins likewise was practiced in both Old and New Worlds. Sometimes a few shots of brandy sprung the locks as effectively as cash.

Funerals in Brown county were equally traditional. Wakes were conducted strictly in the home, not at a funeral parlor. Usually two men held a vigil in succession with relief members of the family, day and night, until the burial. Commonly the living room served as a depository for the corpse where friends and relatives called, reciting formal prayers and the rosary each evening. Commonly in this century, photographs were taken of the body in the casket. Following the wake at home, the deceased was taken to church for mass and final rites, after which a procession continued to the cemetery for final internment. Sometimes there was music performed by a dance band leading the funeral procession but details are vague. That the burial caravan was an event of considerable proportions is born out by an occasional newspaper report that someone was fined for driving through, or too near, the funeral entourage.[15] Following cemetery rituals, guests retired to the family home or farm for a noon meal, much in the Germanic tradition. The period of mourning was prescribed exactly as in the German villages of Bohemia, signified in particular by the black garb worn in public for weeks or a year, depending on one's relationship to the deceased.

While funeral rites may not belong to the folkloric past the way verbal traditions and annual festivals do, neither are workdays and earning styles central to the narrow definition of folklore. Crafts, building styles, the production of lace, of pillows, masonry, carpentering, and

Wedding of Franz and Maria, nee Gröbner, Schroepfer, who came to Minnesota in 1867 when he was 36, she wearing European native dress typical for such occasions. BC

house designs, while definable in the folklife of a people, are yet separate and therefore more properly suited to be the topic of our next chapter – the role of the German-Bohemians in their workday as opposed to their festival day, is the subject matter of the subsequent pages.

Notes

1. For a broad discussion of the concept of folklore, see two good sources among many, Alan Dundes, *The Study of Folklore* (Englewood Cliffs, NJ: Prentice Hall, 1965), especially the first chapter "What is Folklore?" pp. 1-24, and Richard M. Dorson, *Folklore and Folklife: An Introduction* (Chicago: University of Chicago Press, 1972), especially the "Introduction" pp. 1-50.

2. Dorson, pp. 2 ff.

3. Richard Weiss, *Volkskunde der Schweiz: Grundriss* (Erlenbach-Zürich: Eugen Retsch Verlag, 1946), p. 11.

4. Don Yoder, "Folklife Studies in American Scholarship," in *American Folklife*, ed., Don Yoder (Austin: University of Texan Press, 1976), p. 4.

5. Especially worthwhile are Josef Schramek, *Der Bhömerwaldbauer: Eigenart, Tracht und Nahrung, Haus- und Wirtschaftsgeräte, Sitten, Gebräuche und Volksglaube* (Prague: F.

G. Calve, k. u. k. Hof-und Universitäts-Buchhandlung, 1915); Josef Blau, *Landes und Volkskunde der Tschechoslowakischen Republik* (Reichenberg: Paul Sollors' Nachfolger, 1927); Alois Bergmann, *Die Schmiedkreuze Westböhmens* (Elbogen: Egerlandhaus für Buch und Kunst Karl H. Frank, 1926); Josef Blau, *Böhmerwälder Hausindustrie und Volkskunst,* 2 Vols. (Prague: F. G. Calve, k. u. k. Hof- u. Universitäts-Buchhändler, 1917); Josef Blau "Huhn und Ei in Sprache, Brauch und Glauben des Volkes im oberen Angelthale (Böhmerwald)," *Österreichische Zeitschrift für Volkskunde,* 8 No. 5 (1902), 166-183; Josef Blau, "Hausgewerbe und Volkskunst in Deutschböhmen," *Deutschböhmen: eine Skizze von Land und Volkstum, Geistesart und Wirtschaft,* 5 No. 3/4 (1918), 24-29; Josef Blau, "Der böhmische Bettfederhandel: Kulturgeographisch, statistisch, geschichtlich und volkskundlich," *Mitteilungen des Vereines für Geschichte der Deutschen in Böhmen,* 69 (1931), 56-114; K. Lutz-Metzner, "Erntedankfest in Bischofteinitz," *Glaube und Heimat,* 4 (1952), 6-7; Josef Blau, "Der Typus einer Bauernkirche: St. Leonhard bei Neuern im Böhmerwalde," *Zeitschrift für Österreichische Volkskunde* (Wien), 5 No. 3/4 (1899), 70-79; Josef Blau, "Die Spitzen und die Spitzenklöppelei der Slawen in Böhmen, Mähren, Schlesien und Oberungarn," *Österreichische Zeitschrift für Volkskunde,* 16 No. 4/5 (1910), 160-173.

    6. Among many sources, see *Bischofteinitz,* pp. 693 ff.

    7. *Bischofteinitz,* pp. 705 ff., *Ronsperg,* p. 181.

    8. Concerning St. Walburga, see *New Catholic Encyclopedia* (New York: McGraw-Hill, 1966), XIV, p. 769.

    9. Pictures in *Bischofteinitz,* pp. 733, 737 and *Mies,* p. 103.

    10. See photograph in Schramek, *Der Böhmerwaldbauer,* p. 200.

    11. *Bischofteinitz,* poem and pictures, pp. 740 ff.; Schramek, *Der Böhmerwaldbauer,* p. 226; Rainer Schmeissner, *Oberpfälzer Flurdenkmäler,* Vol. 4 of *Steinkreuzforschung* (Regensburg: Selbstverlag, 1986), pp. 53-56. Additional publications in Schramek, p. 225.

    12. Schramek, *Der Böhmerwaldbauer,* pp. 231-237.

    13. To gather information on this subject, I staged a series of folklore workshops at which we divided the members of the German Bohemian Heritage Society of New Ulm into units and asked them to brainstorm about an assigned topic. These discussions resulted in reports written by the discussion group leader, who in each case was an untrained member of the society. The opinions of over 100 people were thereby brought to bear on a variety of topics. In the following paragraphs and in the next chapter some of their revelations shall be reported.

    14. Rudolf Kutitschek, *Hirschauerstücklein. Ein Volksbuch des Böhmerwaldes,* 3rd ed. (Minterberg, Böhmerwald: Dupert Steinbrenner & Co., 1943).

    15. *New Ulm Review,* June 13, 1888, p. 5.

Seven

German-Bohemians in the World of Work:

Economic and Sociological Perspectives

WORK DEFINES A PEOPLE. In his book on the Bohemian Forest Cottage industry, Josef Blau supplies the advice, *Wer ein Volk kennen lernen will, der muss es bei der Arbeit sehen.* (He who wishes to get to know a people must observe them at work.)[1] His folk aphorism is the motto for this chapter – not just work itself, but work clothes, work conditions, lifetime occupations and fields of employment. The very clothes of work are of significance. Indeed, dress often identifies the American farmer (bib overalls), the cowboy (hat, stirrups, leather pants), lumber men (plaid shirts), railroad firemen (striped overalls with cap), blacksmiths and shoemakers by their aprons, miners by their hats. Thus, even though clothing in the work place may be standard factory output, still the way it is worn might express folk-cultural traditions that adapt the costume selectively to preconceived ideas.

One widespread cottage industry of the Bischofteinitz region that transferred intact to the Brown county area was *Spitzenklöppelei*. At first glance this would seem to be a folk craft that was only done for hobby or pastime occupation. But on further investigation, it is clear that this was considered the most noble of the cottage industries in the Böhmerwald. While *Klöppelei* or lace making is certainly not unique to the Böhmerwald, it did acquire commercial prominence in the region during the 19th century. From two focal points, the one in Muttersdorf and the other in Ronsperg, the industry fanned out to most of the villages from which Brown county immigrants originated.

In Muttersdorf at the time when the emigrants were leaving from 1855-1865, the Spitzenklöppelei commercial and trading company owned by Nikl Schnobrich (House No. 70) exported finished products far and wide in the Austrian empire.[2] Substations supplying Muttersdorf and Ronsperg were especially notable in the villages of Stockau, Metzling and Heiligenkreuz. At the Ronsperg operation in the 19th century at least 200 persons were more or less steadily engaged in lace production. At Schwarzach, the Wartha company was well known for its products that sold all over Europe. By 1900 not just women but whole families, including husbands, had no other income but lace making in which they were engaged in some instances from 5 A.M. to 11 P.M. After World War I the Wartha firm reported employing regularly 1500-1800 lace makers and selling its products not only in Czechoslovakia, Germany and Austria, but in Paris, Brussels, Sweden and Holland, all countries in which there were sophisticated native lace makers. Positioned on the Bavarian border, the Wartha firm was ideally located for shipping its wares, and for employing inhabitants of the border region in its operation.

Many immigrants to Brown county continued the craft of *Klöppeln* after their arrival. Letters exchanged between the families who remained behind in the Bischofteinitz region to those in the southern Minnesota county report often on this activity. In fact, following World War I when the economy of the Böhmerwald plummeted, letter writers stated that about the only way they could keep body and soul together was by making lace on pillow cases and similar products, the only commodity which still brought a reasonable financial return.[3] Perhaps best known for her lace making in the New Ulm area is Dolores (Mrs. Walter) Haas of rural Sleepy Eye, whose ancestry is from Schillikau. As a folk art, local lace makers in Minnesota have received the attention of the media. Preserving the Böhmerwald version of *Klöppeln* is the mission taken by the Neudeker Heimatmuseum in Göggingen near Augsburg in Bavaria.[4]

Klöppeln began first and foremost as folk art. Subsequently trade schools offered formal instruction in the production of fine lace. Although there were several such schools, the best known was the Klöppelschule at Sablat near Prachatitz. Others were at Eisendorf, Heiligenkreuz and Weissensulz.[5] Having received professional status, teachers of *Klöppeln* tried to develop new forms, fancier designs, and

Dolores Haas of Sleepy Eye making lace on Klöppelsack. The art of lace making was passed down to Hass from her grandmother Helget who emigrated from the village of Schilligkau. BC

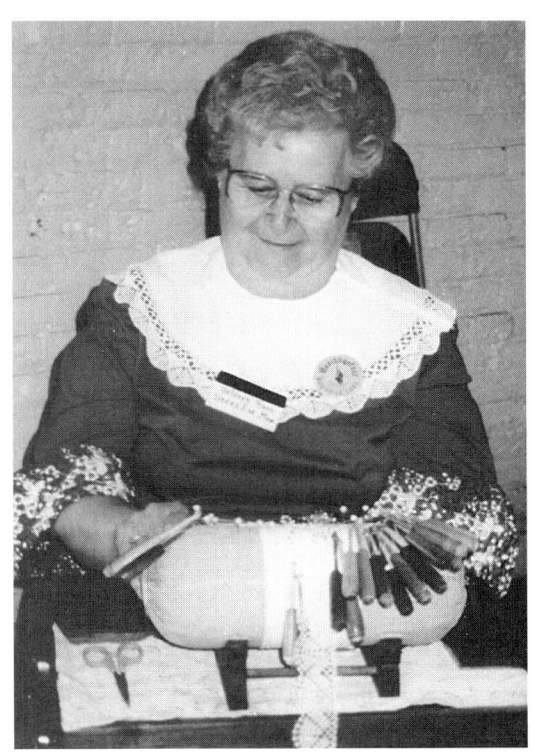

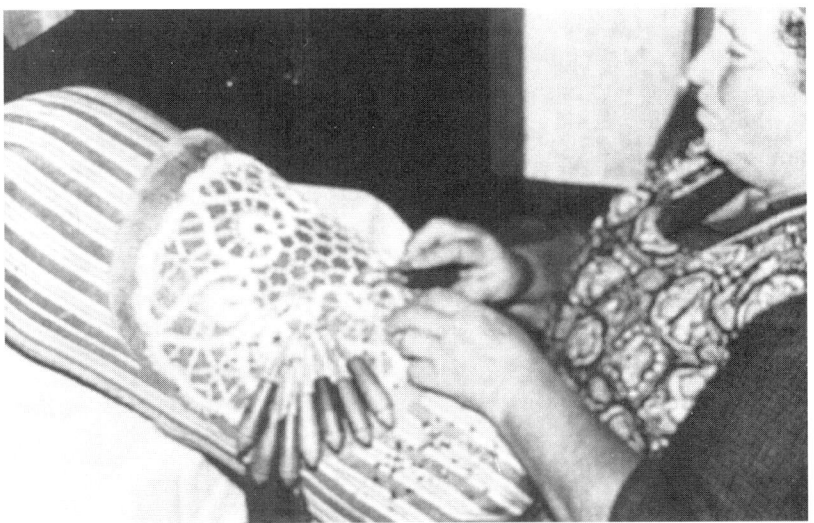

Klöppelsack used by a woman in the Old Homeland, for making lace. BS

more marketable products. Gradually a new vocabulary evolved for the geometric matrixes, colors, patterns, and the designs. Some names are interesting because of the folk origins they illustrate. A few refer to the goose – that beloved fowl of the region – Gänsekragla (goose collar), Gänsetatscher (one who pets and strokes geese), Teufelszähne (devil's teeth), Mäusezähnchen (mouse teeth), Gänsenester (goose nest), Christbäumla (Christmas tree), Ochsenauge (Ox eye), Schnecken (snails), and even Misthäufla (manure pile).

Another folk art that developed commercial standing in Bohemia derives from the goose, namely *Das Federnscshleissen* (feather stripping, down making). While every house supplied its own down needs from local geese, in the Neuern and Klattau areas production gained commercial significance beyond household demand. Dealers bought feathers all over Europe and sent them to Neuern where women and children worked in factories processing them into bed clothes. Children to grandparents worked piecemeal to strip feathers,[6] for it took one person as much as one day to "harvest" a quarter kilogram. But if the commercial production of down was tedious, it was considered an enjoyable folk tradition. The old saying "Wo Töchter sind, da müssen auch Gänse sein" (a family that has daughters must also have geese) meant several things. On the one hand they needed beds; but speaking financially, daughters supplied able hands for tending geese and stripping feathers. Most villagers had a common pasture for the geese and it was the girls who often shepherded them. Besides fulfilling a need in the home, stripping feathers occasioned winter festivity, lightened the boredom of long winter nights, and eased the family budget.

Folk crafts in the agricultural field involved flax. As early as 1800 writers refer to the Bavarian and Bohemian Forests as "a single, overarching linen factory." One called it the place where people survived by spinning and weaving. Another lauds this land where a unitized product kept the family busy in the fields in summer and in their homes spinning in the winter.[7] This cottage industry developed strongly only after the English blockade of Napoleonic Europe, when cotton from the United States and wool from England could not reach the continent. Already well known for its flax, the Bohemian Forest for a time also became famous for the quality and craftsmanship of its spinning wheels. In time, folklore revolved around symbolism of the spinning wheel – spinning to gain heaven, spinning to earn a lover's

Mary Baar-Lindmeier at work Klöppling. BC

hand, as punishment when sentenced to spin for a civil fine. Songs narrate of the spinning wheel as an object of joy or sorrow. There was a *Spinnradtanz* (spinning wheel folk dance) to the music of a local band. Games developed when eight or ten women gathered each day at a household to allay the boredom of spinning alone. Younger women's games often involved young village men. Older women sang melodies with religious overtones. As with *Klöppeln* , there were practical schools to learn the spinning trade.

Weavers were plentiful. In the year 1796 the Bischofteinitz region registered 1,122 professionals. In contrast to spinning, weaving was usually a man's job. Men also created the lore and the jokes that accompanied the trade, not all of them flattering to the profession. For example, the following story gets repeated often: When a traveler was stuck in a highway mud hole during the spring thaw, another happened along and helped him out. On reaching higher ground, the relieved traveler asked the newcomer what was his profession. When he answered " *Weber* (weaver)" the man returned to the mud hole, "I'd never accept the help of a weaver."

Joining in the production of linen, were dye makers. This profession held prominence in the southwestern triangle of Bischofteinitz near

Angeline Portner of rural New Ulm, wearing Homeland dress. RP

Prachatitz, Gratzen and Neuern. Dyeing cloth in a home bound con-catenation of processes was among the first cottage industries to give way to a factory and thus by the middle of the 19th century it had lost its economic importance. There was, however, plenty of longing for the art when it came to making local costumes. Individual peasant clothing gave rise to the saying still heard, "Selbstgesponnen, selbst gemacht ist die beste Bauerntracht" (self spun, self made, results in the best native costume).[8]

Native dress was the pride of both men and women. In matters of fashion each village was distinct, for in its native costumes each village had its own self-created official identity.[9] These were clothes for Sun-day and festive occasions. They varied according to the event being celebrated, such as weddings, for the inviter to the wedding (*Hochzeit-slader* or *Hochzeitbitter*), for the bride usually in native costume rather than in a long white gown, for the parents of the bride, for the cooks,

Native dress for a young woman from the village of Sirb. Each village in the Homeland had its own distinctive Tracht *[costume]*. BS

etc. To some extent the costume also changed with the seasons, from winter to summer.

All these cloth operations were side shows in terms of real income. The farm economy was the real means for people to make a living. Farming was governed more by folklore than by scientific knowledge, at least during the period of emigration to Brown county. Although every one lived in villages, they owned land that was rarely in contiguous pieces. The arable land was always scattered with small fields that usually amounted only to around 5-10 hectares in total. There were farms, however, that consisted of 20-30 hectares but few of as much as 50 hectares. (A hectare contains 2.47 American acres.) At the time the immigrants departed for Minnesota, land ownership was limited by several factors. Forest lands were held by nobility or "in common" by the community. Green fields or pastures were owned "in common" although small farmers were permitted to participate in a pasture's yield up to the limits of its productive capacity. In the overall Bischofteinitz region *Grossbetriebe* or Meierhöfe [large dairy farms still owned by the nobility] continued to employ local day laborers for the benefit of wealthy absentee landowners. Nevertheless, these were progressive units that served as models for the less educated peasantry who farmed the smaller adjacent lands.

Because the climate was relatively mild but cool, crop land accounted for only about half of the land surface. A third was covered by forest and the balance by pastures, wetlands and villages (housing, roads, ponds, gardens, etc.). Winter rye was a primary crop because it thrived in the cool summer weather. Rarely did the temperature sink much below 20 degrees Fahrenheit in winter while in summer it often hovered around 65-70 degrees. Rye supplied flour for ordinary bread although wheat gradually became common as well. Bohemian Red Wheat (Böhmischer Rotweizen) was a well-known strain, not as hardy as the Turkey Red Hard winter wheat that was brought to Kansas by the Mennonites from Russia in 1874, but of locally high quality. Oats, once used also to make bread, in later years came to be used only as animal feed, particularly for horses and cattle. Barley gained steadily in popularity during the 19th and 20th centuries, both as animal feed and for brewing purposes. Potatoes were the most substantial element in the human diet and constituted part of every farmer's planting. Cabbage, carrots, and beets were always popular vegetables. Cabbage produced sauerkraut for easy winter storage. Oil producing plants like soybeans and raps as well as alfalfa hay were unknown at the time of emigration. Farmers sowed clover not only for hay but also for seeds. In the overall productivity of the fields, manuring was dutifully managed. Crops were rotated regularly.[10]

Dairying, no matter how small the scale, was a mainstay of the Bohemian farmer, and this pattern re-duplicated itself in Brown county. Women customarily did the milking, in summer three times a day, at 6 A.M., at noon, and at 7 P.M. Separating milk into skim for the hogs and cream to be churned into butter made small Bohemian as well as Brown county farmers into their own little processing plants. Later when cream was hauled to central processing stations, it was picked up only about once every five days. Skim milk was fed to hogs, used in producing a local soup or for baking various whole grain breads. Sometimes it was hauled to the fields as fertilizer. Many

Otto Hartwick plowing with oxen in rural New Ulm. Oxen were also used for plowing in the hill country of the Old Homeland. BC

housewives made cottage cheese from the skimmed milk (*Quark*) while others baked *Schmierkäs* (creamed cheese) for daily consumption. Different recipes called for caraway seed in the cottage cheese or other flavoring devices in the creamed variety.

As became true for all densely populated regions of Europe, the potato became the mainstay of life for a couple of centuries. *Kartoffel*, *Erdäpfel*, also known as *Derfäpfln* in some dialects, potatoes were served much more even than bread. They could be made into dumplings, noodles, soup, broth – mashed, fried, or baked. Potatoes also produced a fine whiskey.

Sauerkraut also enjoyed a favorite spot in menu planning. For processing the cabbage heads the German-Bohemians developed the *Krauthobel* (cabbage plane), a sliding square box that guided cabbage heads over three or four sharp blades mounted in the base. They shaved thin slices of cabbage as the head was driven across them to yield fine strings of sauerkraut. Eaten as a substitute for soup to begin the meal, sauerkraut according to folk belief fostered better digestion. More likely, this food was inexpensive to grow, the climate was favorable, storing it was easy, inexpensive and safe, and thus it found its way into many folk eating habits.

While foods such as these routinely transferred to Brown county, the Bohemian house and barn styles were less easily brought along. Several theories prevail why structural styles transferred so poorly. One is that simple and quite young immigrants came before they had learned the art and engineering necessary to take the lead in constructing barns, houses, and outbuildings in America. Another is that New World materials did not lend themselves to similar construction. Yet a different version is that by the time the German-Bohemians arrived in southern Minnesota, other settlers had been on site and when these German speakers came they just fell in behind the Yankees and took over what the latter sold or abandoned. Finally, there is the acknowledgement that American settlement required dwellings out on the land rather than in villages. Thus, the compact and joint style of construction that was required to save space within the village was not necessary on the wide open spaces of a 160 acre homestead.

The home style of the Böhmerwald is rather easily traced to its sources in eastern Bavaria. Almost every roof in the old homeland was cut off at its peak to shelter the end gable by means of a deep cut roof. This style is observable in the city of New Ulm and occasionally in neighboring villages but it in no way predominates. Likewise, the pattern of constructing one's home of stone or bricks did not arrive with these immigrants, although many of them built homes of brick in the typical American style. The city of New Ulm is replete with substantial older brick homes, few if any, however, built by the Bohemians.

Access to the Bohemian homestead was through the elegant *Hoftor*, which has no replication in the New Ulm vicinity. Nor did households in Minnesota reconstruct the beautiful *Kachelofen*, a masonry construction that combined a cooking range and open chimney for smoking meats on the barn side of a construction wall, and an extension of the same into the parlor for inner warmth and often for a baking facility on the house side of the wall.[11] Usually there were benches for sitting alongside the *Kachelofen*. Occasionally there were also provisions for hanging clothes above the stove to dry, or even to sleep above and behind the *Kachelofen*. In no instance is a Kachelofen known to have been built and used in Minnesota.

Some pieces of Minnesota furniture hold a resemblance to the Old World styles but for the most part, the frontiersmen did not bother making their own house articles. The Bohemian Forest kitchen table

Typical German-Bohemian home, in this case, of the Andreas Zwach family, who pose before Trohatin No. 24, called "Spitze." The grandson of Andreas, John Zwach, was a long-term Minnesota state representative from the New Ulm area. DZ

was heavy and solid, the beds durable and made usually of wood with decorative paintings on the ends. The kitchen usually housed a sturdy china cabinet (*Schüsselkorb*) in which the daily tableware was stored. In the parlor stood a china cabinet of more elegant style (*Glasskasten*) with doors of glass through which the fine china was on display but seldom put into use. Painted chests were common in Bohemia but few made it across the ocean with the immigrants.

On first consideration it seems that ordinary tools of the farmyard did come across: the standard wooden-wheeled wagon, sleds with their iron-capped wooden runners, the ox yoke, simple wooden wheel barrows and scythes, forks, rakes and plows. On closer examination, though, it appears that these implements were accidentally the same rather than the result of any direct transoceanic transfer. Because the implements available to the farmer were steadily changing throughout the 19th and even more so during the 20th centuries, it was unlikely that agricultural methodology from Bohemia would have lasted more than one generation in the United States.

Another local cottage industry of the Böhmerwald that helped farmers over their economic bridges in the winter and that did repeat, if differently, in America was the woodworking industry. Farmers in the Böhmerwald were available for *Waldarbeit* whenever crops did not command their full attention. Bohemian forests contain mostly softwoods: evergreens mixed with birch, beech and an occasional oak. Trees were felled any time of the year, but winter was the likely season. Winter was the *only* time to move the logs easily, skidding them with ox or horse teams. In some instances woodsmen developed techniques to slip the heavy end of a log onto a skid and guide it down the hillside by hand. Woodsmen also developed a two-wheeled apparatus for summer use, on which they loaded the heavy end of a log and dragged it down the hill, also by hand.[12]

As in Minnesota, logs were moved over greater distances by floating them in streams. Special canals and slips helped get them to larger streams where they could be rafted to sawmills. Each process required skills learned from master wood handlers, and passed down from generation to generation. Out of the wood working industry developed related endeavors like processing wood into charcoal which was needed especially in the glassblowing industry and for blacksmithing. Forest specialists also produced pitch which they distilled into axle grease (*Wagenschmierbrennerei*) to lubricate wagons and other farm implements. Several related industries developed in response to need, one being shingle factories, thin boards for jalousie window shades, matches, and wooden scrub brushes. North of Tachau was a wooden button factory. In a region where wood was plentiful, structures sometimes were decoratively embellished by large roof overhangs and balconies of wood carefully sawed to create a pleasing impression. Today such structures are especially noteworthy in southern Bavaria and in Austria.[13]

In the same vein, fences were constructed of wood, at least around the household. In the wide open pastures, fences were uncommon. Instead, young people were trained to herd cattle, geese and similar domestic animals. Field rotation called for a threefold pattern: winter crop (rye or wheat), summer crop (barley, oats, or potatoes) and *Brache* (fallow). *Gemeinweide* means pasture in common. During the decades of emigration a system of rail fencing prevailed. Sometimes the rails were run horizontally, at other times on a diagonal, the former called *Schrengerzaun*, the latter *Schräger Schwartlingzaun*. Picket

The Alexander Waibl (died 1894) farmstead in Cottonwood township. BC

fences of vertical laths, boards or split small rails were common in the villages. These bore the names *Hachalzaun* and *Spaltenzaun* among others, depending on the local dialect. The *Stachelzaun* or barbed wire fence did not gain prominence until in the twentieth century.[14] In decades past, it was customary to keep the entire village fenced with full sized (sometimes ornate) gates at access points, which facilitated driving cattle to the fields. The village fence also prevented geese, sheep and other animals from leaving the village grounds where they roamed at will during the day.

Minor uses for wood, in terms of the amount required, but not so minor in view of the work involved for production, were simple locally crafted farm tools – rakes, forks, shovels, hoe or axe handles. So were shoes (called *Holanischla*) which were once common with leather upper boots for field work but which gave way to rubber and leather when these materials became commonplace. Both fir and beech wood were suitable and reportedly kept the feet warm and dry better than any other material. Known far beyond their borders for fine quality wooden shoes, the German-Bohemians were called upon especially during World War I when leather was in short supply, to deliver the

City of Frankfurt 10,000 pairs of wooden shoes for the German army. The specifications called for large sizes so that the soldiers could slip their boots inside for protection against wet and frost conditions.[15]

Sometimes shoe carvers developed skills for the higher arts, as evidenced by the many hand carved religious works, altars, statues, pulpits, stations of the cross, candelabra and the like.[16] These were often the same carvers who hand-made the ornate *Hoftor* (gateway to the homestead) and house doors as well as ornamented peasant furniture. Mentioned earlier were the *Totenbretter* which in some cases required the rather sophisticated skills of carvers and painters.[17]

In Brown county, the German-Bohemian farmers carried on their traditions while also adapting their ways to the New World. An analysis of the New Ulm, Sleepy Eye, and Brown county directories does yield a few patterns which point to certain traditions of employment for the immigrants and their descendants away from the farm. A common designation is "bartender" while many worked for the mills, the brick and title companies, in the breweries and as carpenters, masons, and railway workers. Most notable in terms of a profession the immigrants chose, but which was unknown in their homeland, was cigar making. Clearly this required a skill which the newcomers learned to perform satisfactorily. While cigar manufacturing flourished in New Ulm, there is little evidence that a comparable enterprise might have been entertained in either Sleepy Eye or Springfield. Cigar making is among the best examples of a cottage industry in Brown county, and one that was localized to the city of New Ulm. Since no local farms grew tobacco, the leaves had to be imported from Cuba and Sumatra.[18]

For both cooking and heating, for fencing and building, farmers needed wood. Thus in the wooded regions around Brown county there were many five acre wood lots platted to accommodate these needs. Such were most recent in northeastern Cottonwood township near the Minnesota River and along the Little Cottonwood which dissected the township west to east. Always in the townships along the Minnesota there were small plots. In Sigel, Milford, Home, and Stark townships, they were generally along the Big Cottonwood. In cases farther west where the supply of wood was less than adequate, and in later years in the above townships as well, coal was the primary source of fuel in winter. Boosters periodically fantasized about what anthracite finds might do for the local economy.

Wood work in the county meant the production of firewood each winter on the small plots of land along the river valleys. Because lumbering was never an earnest enterprise in Brown county, local farmers brought in traveling saw rigs to cut their logs into boards. Much more common were creameries that gathered milk at distances a team could easily cover each day. One local resident said recently – wherever there was a deep well, there once was a creamery. In the year 1908 there were sixteen such institutions scattered in the county and producing 1.5 million pounds of butter annually.[19] Like their forebears in the county of Bischofteinitz, these farmers operated their dairy farms as cottage industries in which the entire family participated. The skim milk was used to make calves and hogs grow as well as to make cottage cheese and Schmierkäs. Brown county Bohemian farmers also grew a lot of wheat, corn, barley and rye, just as in the Old Country and of course plenty of potatoes to nourish their large families. In the year 1908 the county was home to 10,612 head of horses, 25,113 head of cattle, 14,500 swine and nearly 4,000 sheep. On the land there was much that replicated the Bohemian situation.

The picket fence was once as popular around residences in the City of New Ulm as in the *Böhmerwald*, though they were simpler, less artistic, and generally made of boards sawed commercially rather than split from saplings in the Old World fashion. Before the invention of barbed wire in 1874 the New Ulm countryside remained largely unfenced. Rail fencing was too expensive and too labor intensive and like in the Old World, plenty of young people were available to herd cattle on pasture. Locally harvested wood was important for fence posts and cooking but not of much value for the manufacture of fork, axe, hoe and related handles. These were acquired from more distant commercial suppliers.

One cottage industry that was exclusively in the hands of the German-Bohemians was blacksmithing. Families like Zwach, Hofmeister, Haala, Windschittl and the Gag family still active in the sheet metal business made names for themselves by their iron-working skills. Not only did they produce the equipment for plowing, sowing and horse shoeing, they also made the iron crosses that decorate the graves of Bohemian German Catholics in the region. In the Catholic cemetery at Sleepy Eye a large number of cast and forged iron, rather than stone crosses mark the graves. Adjacent to the Catholic is the Protestant

Iron crosses in Sleepy Eye cemetery.

Iron burial marker in Sleepy Eye cemetery: "Blessed are those who die in the Lord."

burial ground in which there is not a single cross made of iron. Many of these iron monuments to the dead are also visible in the Catholic cemetery at New Ulm, while they occur elsewhere usually only in the context of East Europeans. The Germans from Russia, for example, were noted for their extensive use of iron cross on their graves.[20] Blacksmithing of course served the local farm economy and for decades this trade in Brown county was the exclusive turf of German-Bohemians.

Certain seasons, such as especially threshing time, kindled excitement, community cooperation, and much enjoyment of the folklife that accompanied it. As always in the Bohemian German tradition, working was living. To work was to enjoy life! Group work and cooperation were required to accomplish many tasks. Seven to ten farmers formed a threshing ring and the rig moved from one farm to the next until all had their grain under a roof. At threshing time the whole family helped. A kind of pyramid of importance ranged from rig owner with his steam engine down to the last kid who helped carry water, or

Wagon and blacksmith shop. German-Bohemians often owned or operated the black-smith shops in Brown county. BC

perhaps leveled oats in the grain box. The man standing on top of the thundering, coughing, threshing machine was always boss! And the power of the rig boss derived symbolically from the energy of the mighty machine. Because *its* might prevailed, so did *his*. What he said, was gospel. Men and women organized their lives during those weeks by that one important chief of operations. The rig owner-operator decided when the first teams would load, and when they would start pitching into the machine in the morning. It was also he who signalled when the whistle would blow for dinner and when the first bundle wagons could head home to do their chores. The time when the first teams could retire determined when the last racks would pull in to unload because the cycle had to be completed each day.

During threshing time the women had to cook. And one home maker tried to outdo the next in both taste and plenty so that the word got around who had the finest meals. A kind of ethic, even a sense of awe, held sway over who was permitted to park his heels under the house wife's dinner table during threshing. Meals were cycled, and if

Cemetery in the Bohemian village of Berg. Note the iron crosses produced by local blacksmiths. PB

some out of cycle teamster missed the main crew at the center table, he also missed the jokes, the stories, and the mild ribbing that accompanied this ceremonial repast each day of the threshing season. Nobody ever quite adequately washed up for the banquet that it actually was.

Filling silos in September was less embellished, but a social event nevertheless. Shredding corn in October was a mild substitute of the fun threshing followed in November and December by cutting wood, always in the spirit of neighborly cooperation accompanied by plenty of food and oral tradition. Next ensued ice making in late January and early February. The owner of the ice business in New Ulm was Hermann Regelin who was *not* Bohemian but in Sleepy Eye it was the Windschittls, who were. Whether cutting wood or ice, sawing it or delivering it, the various operations always provided opportunities for work and income, especially for new arrivals who themselves still had not found the resources to become farmers or small businessmen.

Cooking in Brown county was yet another aspect of folk culture determined by Old World traditions. Summer kitchens were once common in Brown county. Excessive temperatures in southern Minnesota

Field cross from the Bohemian village of Neubäu. Found on the Rewitzer farmstead. RP

Stack threshing in rural New Ulm. Note hopper for elevating bundles and wooden separator. BC

made this American invention a phenomenon that was not necessary in rather cooler Bohemia. Usually it stood next to the house, served also as a laundry center in pre-basement times, and has disappeared with the advent of electrical, gas, or microwave cooking ranges that do not heat the whole house when they make the stew.

The outdoor baking oven was impractical in rural areas since access by housewives would have been cumbersome. A village bake oven was not a strong German-Bohemian tradition either. Home baked bread was nevertheless the rule for the Bohemian household, and always there was plenty of *Schmierkuchen*. Rather than pie, which was an English contribution to the American palette, the Bohemians devised a thick yeasted dough on which they layered fruits of various kinds to bring about a filled roll that looked like a squared off piece of pie.

Meats were fried down and stored in large crocks of lard, frequently smoked and then hung up to dry in the attic or made into sausage heavily seasoned for purposes of preservation. Meat was also canned because it could not be frozen. The culinary arts of today's German-Bohemians, except for *Schmierkuchen* (available even today in New Ulm supermarket bakeries) soon developed into a hybrid of many European delights.[21] Constrained by the locally available flour, yeast, salt and spices, the foods gradually acquired a homogenized taste. Breakfasts, in the American tradition for a meat-bolstered workman's' start of the day were once rich in sausages, eggs and milk, but have since given way to American cereals (e.g. cornflakes) that perhaps grew out of the European pattern of serving grains and bread products early in the morning. Pancakes for breakfast seem not to have caught on early with the German-Bohemians. While food may not belong to the oral or folkloric past the way verbal traditions and annual festivals do, neither are workdays and earning styles central to the narrow definition of folklore.

Judging from available pictures, the Bohemians pretty much dressed like the blue collar worker next to whom they performed. Only in their wedding pictures do European native costumes come forth. Yet regardless of the festivity or the labor performed, the rule applied from the German folk saying: *Die Arbeit macht das Leben süss*, "work makes life sweet." Most of the Bohemians amply illustrated this adage in their daily lives and to the present time, few of them seem willing to indulge excessively in leisurely vacation activities. The tradi-

Bauernhochzeit [Farm wedding] in the village of Mukowa. BS

tion of hard work, meaning usually work with one's hands, overrides all of life, and the lack of work suggests guilt in one form or another. There was but one exception: music – which is the story for our next chapter.

Notes

1. Josef Blau, *Böhmerwalder Hausindustrie und Volkskunst*, I (Prague: Calve, k. u. k. Universitäts-Buchhändler, 1917), p. viii.

2. Blau, ibid., II, 1918, pp. 132 ff. See also ibid., "Die Spitzen und Spitzenklöppelei der Slawen in Böhmen, Mähren, Schlesien und Oberungarn," *Österreichische Zeitschrift für Volkskunde*, 16, No. 4-5 (1910), 160-173, and Johann Gröbner, "Das Spitzenklöppeln," *Bischofteinitz* (Furth im Wald: Heimatkreis Bischofteinitz, 1967), pp. 673 ff.

3. Pany letters to the Dolores Gröbner Ludewig family, La Vern J. Rippley, ed. & trans. "The Josefine Pany Letters," Part I & Part II, *Currents: A Minnesota River Valley Review,* 4 & 5 No. 4 & No. 1 (1994-1995), 4-10, 38-41.

4. There are from time to time reunions of German-Bohemians who were expelled from the Böhmerwald at the Heimatmuseum in Göggingen at which *Klöppeln* is demonstrated while the talent is taught to younger generations. Cf. *Heimatbote für die Kreise Tachau und Bischofteinitz*, Vol. 38, No. 3, January 15, 1988, (illustrated with photographs).

5. Blau, *Hausindustrie*, II, p. 142. Photograph of school p. 145. Other institutions, p. 150. General information pp. 132-183.

6. Blau, *Hausindustrie*, II, pp. 195 ff.

7. Blau, *Hausindustrie*, II, pp. 1-132, here p. 3. See also photos in Rudolf Kiefner, *Heimat Jenseits des Böhmerwaldes im süddlichen Egerland – der Kreis Bischofteinitz* (Furth im Wald: Heimatkreis Bischofteinitz, 1987), p. 230.

8. Quoted in Blau, II, p. 132.

9. *Bischofteinitz*, pp. 742-749 with photographs. Josef Schramek, *Der Böhmerwald-bauer: Eigenart, Tracht und Nahrung, Haus- und Wirtschaftsgeräte, Sitten, Gebräuche und Volksglaube* (Prague: F.G. Calv'sche Hof- und Universitäts-Buchhandlung, 1915), pp. 2-49.

10. Johann Gröbner, "Die Landwirtschaft unseres Heimatkreises," in *Bischofteinitz*, pp. 539 ff. See also Schramek, ibid. pp. 43-72. Aerial views of the configuration of fields appear in Kiefner, *Jenseits des Böhmerwaldes*, pp. 111, 130, 201, 280, 316, 471.

11. Sketches and photographs in Schramek, pp. 73 ff. See also the many photographs in Rudolf Kiefner, *Heimat Jenseits des Böhmerwaldes* (Felsberg-Wolfershausen, Germany: Self Published, 1987).

12. In general, Josef Blau, *Böhmerwalder Hausindustrie und Volkskunst*, I, Part Two, pp. 26-90, pictures, 52, 59.

13. Blau, I, pp. 90-199, with photographs. Two useful small volumes in which architectural styles of the county of Bischofteinitz can be studied are by Rudolf Kiefner, *Bezirk Bischofteinitz in alten Ansichtskarten* and *Kreis Bischofteinitz in Ansichtskarten* (Furth im Wald: Heimatkreis Bischofteinitz, both 1981). Note that these pictures were on postcards. They were intended as "famous" sites and exotic places. Therefore, most of the structures are in stone, many in the Baroque styles that dominated the town centers. More illustrative wood uses are in Kiefner, *Heimat Jenseits des Böhmerwaldes*, pp. 192, 200, 234.

14. Blau, I, pp. 199-213, with photographs. For examples of town picket fences, see Kiefner, *Heimat Jenseits des Böhmerwaldes*, pp. 50, 103, 106 (note the combination of split mini-rails and wire), 117, 140, 278-9, 199.

15. Reported from the newspaper *Bohemia* in Blau, I, p. 241.

16. Blau, I, pp. 250 ff., Kiefner, *Heimat*, pp. 76, 77, 151, 154, 155.

17. Blau, I, pp. 300 ff.

18. Cf. city and county Polk directories for New Ulm, Brown county, Sleepy Eye and Springfield, 1901, 1911-12. Elroy E. Ubl, "Cigar Manufacturers Thrived in Early New Ulm," in *Historical Notes* (New Ulm: self published, 1982), I: 17-18.

19. Fritsche, *Brown County*, p. 362.

20. Allois Bermann, *Die Schmiedkreuze Westböhmens. Ein Beitrag zur Geschichte und zum Verständnis alten, deutschen Kunsthandwerks aus Böhmen* (Elbogen: Egerlandhaus für Buch und Kunst Karl H. Frank, 1926); Nicholas C. Vrooman and Patrice Avon Marvin, eds., *Iron Spirits* (Fargo: North Dakota Council on the Arts, 1982) and Timothy J. Kloberdanz, *Cross Makers: German- Russian Folk Specialists of the Great Plains*, unpubl. Ph. D. Dissertation, Indiana University, 1986. See also on this topic La Vern J. Rippley, "Schmiede- und Gußeisenkreuze in Westböhmen und im Südwesten Minnesotas, USA," in Rudolf Kiefner, *Passion jenseits des Böhmerwaldes im südlichen Egerland – der Kreis Bischofteinitz* (Felsberg-Wolfershausen: Self Published, 1991), pp. 417-422.

21. Emmet Hoffmann, *Deutsch-Böhmische Küche* (New Ulm: German-Bohemian Heritage Society, 1991).

Eight

The Music of the German-Bohemians

URING THE COURSE of the 19th century in the region of Bischofteinitz, numerous singing societies with various repertoires came and went. Some performed operas and rendered symphonic or chamber orchestral selections from a European classical repertoire. More commonly, however, they were smaller bands – singing and dance orchestras that resorted to folk music for their own fulfillment and certainly for that of their German-speaking public. Village brass bands were common; so were small accordion groups with brass or woodwinds to accompany them. In this respect, the Germans in Bohemia were not too distinct from their Czech neighbors who likewise loved folk music. On occasion there were Western Bohemian *Sängerfest* celebrations which typified German communities of the United States as well. Since the expulsion of the Germans in 1945/46, considerable effort has been made to re-activate groups that sing and perform the songs of old. An example is the 83-page collection *Liedergruss aus dem Egerland Böhmerwald Erzgebirge,* issued by the Egerländer Trachtengruppe des Heimatkreises Bischofteinitz e. V. in 1973. The same group produced several record albums of songs preserved from the pre-war heritage. Many books published by the expellees include not just the lyrics but in many cases the musical notes for the songs of the region, though in some cases of specific communities only.

The population of Ronsperg in Bischofteinitz county from which

Village band from Rindl. BS

the mainstay of New Ulm German music emanates, was full of folk songs that transferred to New Ulm. In the book *Ronsperg Ein Buch der Erinnerung* the section on music and folk song begins with the famous "Böhmerwald Lied" and continues with dialect versions of other familiar pieces. Overarching all the village and dialect songs is the ever popular "Tief drin im Böhmerwald" [opening lines of the above title] which was long a favorite of the German-Bohemians around New Ulm. The Fezz Fritsche old time band made itself famous by singing it in the German language right up to the end of the master's career in 1979. Most of the *Heimat* books for the various regions include pictures of what might pass for old time bands, at least they demonstrate the presence of a strong musical tradition.[1] Obviously the folk music of the immigrants arrived in Brown county with them. Taken for granted in the early days, music was at first scarcely mentioned. Soon, however, the traditional tunes were combined with more sophisticated numbers after which larger organizations began to render formally what was once taken for granted.

The evidence suggests that in New Ulm itself, there was initially much more attention paid to formal theater, usually in Turner Hall, than to music.[2] Although choral groups appeared in Turner Hall before 1860 it is not until January 12, 1873 that we find formal musical presentations, for instance, the concert at Turner Hall by the Concordia group performing *Das Lied von der Glocke*. On April 26, 1878, however, the *New Ulm Post* reported the founding of a New Ulm Men's Chorus conducted by Robert Nix. The same year, Nix founded the Silver Cornet Band including members Ed Dunkel, Otto Seiter, Armin Steinhäuser, Fred Pfaender, Joseph Galles, Emil Seiter, Tony Olson, Ed Stoeckert, Robert Scherer, Henry Subilia Sr. and Jr., Joseph Eckstein and Fred Windland – all Turner members. During the spring of 1879 local music lovers created a band under the leadership of John Adelbert, a music teacher who lived on North Broadway. Still, theater remained the primary entertainment for Brown County city audiences.[3]

Early in 1882, the Silver Coronet Band was reorganized as the City Band and placed under the leadership of Boniface Gruenenfelder. Born in the Canton of St. Gallen in northern Switzerland, Gruenenfelder developed a series of bands not only in New Ulm but in neighboring St. James, La Salle, Mountain Lake, Lafayette, Gibbon, Winthrop and Westbrook. A member of Holy Trinity parish, Gruenenfelder had much contact with the German speakers from Bohemia, although he was himself not one of them. (Gruenenfelder died in 1933. *Journal*, Sept. 29, 1933). Nor was the Concordia Band, founded by A.F. Reim and later directed by C. G. Reim, the result of Bohemian but of German traditions from the Strassburg area in Southwestern Germany. (*Review*, June 28, 1882; *Review*, Apr. 29, 1911; *Journal*, Feb. 12, 1958).

The German-Bohemian tradition in formal musical organizations got one of its early impetuses from George Gag who organized and directed the St. Aloysious Band at Holy Trinity Catholic School. The Gag family in particular seems to have preserved its strong ties to the Bohemian homeland. The paterfamilias, Peter Gag, born in Trohatin a bit northwest of Ronsperg in 1825 (*Journal*, Jan. 22, 1955 and *Review*, Apr. 26, 1911) emigrated first to New Wien, Iowa in 1855 and then north westward to New Ulm in 1856, bringing along his son, Joseph Gag (born January 20, 1849), the father of musical director, George. Peter was known for most of his life in Brown County as the *Böhmer König* – the Bohemian king (*Review*, Feb. 16, 1916).

Wind instrument band from Searles in Brown county 1901. Notice the similarity between these instruments and those of the band in the Old Country. BC

The tradition of electing a Bohemian king to reign over musical and other festivities was once widespread in the county. On March 26, 1911 the Sleepy Eye paper reported that there was no opposition to the election and crowning of John J. Krueger Bohemian king, even though "our well-known Bohemian friends from Leavenworth suggest that his neighbor, John Youngman, be selected one of the cabinet officers." On March 21, 1919 the Springfield paper headlined that George Wurmstein was once again enthroned Bohemian king. In a typical post World War I mood about world politics, the paper added that "No Bolshevism will go with him either. He wants straight Americanism and lots of it."

A much stronger tradition of Bohemian music in the city arrived in the person of Joseph Hofmeister who conducted and inspired a host of New Ulm bands, including especially the Great Western Band and then the Second Regiment Band, later known as the Hofmeister Band. Hofmeister was reportedly born in the Eger vicinity, the nearest larger administrative city for the Bischofteinitz region of Bohemia, on March 29, 1868.[4] Whatever his exact birthplace, Hofmeister derives from the musical tradition known in Europe as the "Egerländer." As a matter of fact, the contemporary group best known for preservation of

*Boniface Gruenenfelder,
master band music
instructor of New Ulm.
BC*

the music and traditional garb of the Bischofteinitz region calls itself the "Egerländer Trachtengruppe" – Egerland folklore, song and dance society.[5]

Born on March 29, 1868, Joseph Hofmeister immigrated to the U.S. with his parents (some sources say with an aunt) about 1880 and grew up on a farm west of New Ulm in Milford Township. Weekly the boy walked into town to take music lessons from Wenzel T. Eckstein [known in New Ulm officially for his long term of service as a court reporter]. Eckstein was acknowledged for his early contribution to the Bohemian folk music tradition in New Ulm.[6] Joseph Hofmeister's first wife, Anna Manderfeld,[7] bore him three children: Josephine (Mrs. Albert Hacker), Haydn, and Frank. On September 30, 1902 Hofmeister married Maria Hackl who had been born at Neuern in Kreis Pilsen September 28, 1876. (*Review*, Oct. 6, 1933 and Mar. 2, 1955). Of this second marriage were born the following seven children: Ludwig, Walter, Peter, Hugo, Otto, Theodore and Anthony. Trained for musical careers by their father, all nine sons became professional

Joseph Hofmeister, undoubtedly New Ulm's greatest musician. Born near Eger, he received his music training in Bohemia. BC

instrumentalists. Before coming to New Ulm, mother Marie Hackl sang for operatic productions in Kreis Pilsen.[8] A certain fame came to the family when five of the boys simultaneously were playing for the Whoopee John Wilfahrt old time orchestra, with the result that this famous dance band at one point was all but in name a Hofmeister undertaking.

Joseph Hofmeister's musical career took a major leap forward when he became director of the combined Star Band, Concordia, and City Bands which merged in 1896 to become the Great Western Band, directed at first by Boniface Gruenenfelder. When Hofmeister succeeded the latter he used musicians with family names who would later become known on the New Ulm old time music circuit, including at that time Henry Kitzberger, John Kopetzki, Lorenz Flor and John Mathiowitz (Ray Meidl typed manuscript, p. 2). Hofmeister's fame as a music director was propelled to new heights when he helped pick up and then directed the new Regimental Band after the New Ulm troops returned in 1899 from service in the Spanish-American

Hofmeister Band of New Ulm about the year 1917. BC

War. Organized with the help of Joseph Bobleter and Louis G. Vogel, the Regimental Band reportedly competed brilliantly until 1917 as the best marching band in Minnesota.[9] For many years the Second Regiment Band performed eight concerts annually in New Ulm's German Park. Although under contract to the city, the band at times had to resort to donations by businessmen to acquire the new and modern instruments needed to keep it ahead of its competition in neighboring cities (*Review*, July 30, 1913). While still in New Ulm, Joseph Hofmeister also directed the Joseph Hofmeister Boys Chorus.[10]

Due to complications following U. S. entry into World War I, the Second Regiment Band was officially discontinued and reorganized as the Hofmeister Band, with Joseph continuing as director. In 1923 the name changed again, this time to the Pioneer Band of New Ulm. A.P. Boock then fronted the band through several name changes, initially the Fifth Minnesota National Guard Band until 1929 when Benjamin Kitzberger took on the task, followed by A.C. Amann. Later Raymond M. Meidl, another German-Bohemian, took charge until 1940 when all members not eligible for regular military service were discharged from what by then had become known as the 205th Infantry Band. The new unit was inducted into regular service as the

Second Regiment Band marches down New Ulm's Minnesota Street in 4th of July parade. BC

215th Artillery Band on January 6, 1941 and served until the end of World War II.

As early as 1920 Springfield city fathers prevailed on Hofmeister to come and direct the Orpheus Band, known for its outstanding professional performances in southern Minnesota.[11] For about ten years Hofmeister's career in Springfield continued to exemplify his love for Bohemian music until his son Walter took over the baton. Besides the Springfield and New Ulm bands, Hofmeister directed a municipal band at Morgan, gave lessons on string and band instruments to local musicians and composed or arranged countless numbers. His "Springfield Sauerkraut Boosters" number remains as a special tribute to the people of Springfield. When Hofmeister died his funeral became a musical event reminiscent of such German-Bohemian experiences in the Old World. Before services at St. Raphael in Springfield, the American Legion as well as the Orpheus Band escorted the cortege from his home to church and from thence to the edge of New Ulm. At that point it was met by the 205th Infantry band, which led the mourners to the Catholic cemetery on the western edge of the city. Pall bearers were various band directors of the two cities. In tribute to his achievements, the Springfield *Advance-Press* obituary said:

> Captain Hofmeister had the soul of a musician. His musical activities engrossed his attention during his thirty-five years of residence at New Ulm and Springfield. His character harmonized with his profession. He was gentle and forbearing, always ready to serve others and asking little for himself. He lived a useful life. He earned the praises that have been and will continue to be bestowed on him and his work (Oct. 5, 1933).

Two decades later the Hofmeister family of musicians was heralded by the *St. Paul Musician* (Vol. 12, 1953, pp. 5-8). From this remarkable family of nine performers, the following minutia can be recounted. For a time in 1923 there existed in addition to old time, the Hofmeister Brothers modern dance band which performed in many communities throughout southern Minnesota. Haydn played clarinet, went on Mexican border service, and was band drum major of the 136th Infantry Band during World War I. He served as assistant band director in France, toured Germany with the 23rd Infantry Band and later was a member of the 150th Field Artillery Band which toured the U.S. South. Back in Minnesota he directed the Comfrey city band, played with four of his father's bands and settled in St. Paul.

Ludwig was in the original Hofmeister orchestra, played trombone, banjo and piano and assisted in three of his father's bands. Frank was a trumpet player with the Hofmeister orchestras and subsequently played with the Whoopee John band on piano, bass and violin. He also served with the modern dance Orient Orchestra of New Ulm and played trumpet during his service on the Mexican border. He was in three of his father's bands. Peter, a clerk for much of his life at the St. Paul Public Library, played drums. He performed alternatively also on valve instruments and the violin, and served in three of his father's orchestras. Hugo started with the Al Menke modern dance band of Fairmont then in 1928 he too joined the Whoopee John dance band and continued for several decades. A reed man, Hugo handled the saxophone clarinet group and himself wrote and arranged a lot of music. In St. Paul he played with the Elks' band and with two of those managed by his father.

Otto Hofmeister started out as an alto player, then switched to bass. He played so well according to popular accounts that people on the dance floor used to throw silver dollars into the bell of his big sousaphone. Subsequently he learned the trumpet, played piano, clarinet, saxophone and accordion. In St. Paul he performed with the Troubadours, directed the St. Francis De Sales band, the Hilex Drum and Bugle Corps, and the Fire and Marine Drum and Bugle Corps. He served in Europe during World War II and helped with two of his father's bands. Theodore started on the baritone sax in school, was elevated to the city band, and learned clarinet from his brother while on the road. During World War II he played with the 8th Army band, had been on two of his father's bands, and gave lessons on clarinet, sax, and trombone. The youngest of the brothers was Anthony who played trumpet both in local city bands and for dance groups as well as for two of his father's orchestras.[12]

Although the Bohemian musical tradition in Brown County and southern Minnesota is epitomized in the Hofmeister family, the most authentic exemplification of the folk traditions and tunes that infused a lasting style in Minnesota is the so-called old time dance band. Since the time of their first arrivals in the late 1850s, small dance bands epitomized German-Bohemian family celebrations. While documentation of such musical dance bands is scant, one of the early bands was the original "Goosetown Band" which was organized and fronted by John Lindmeyer. Lindmeyer had directed bands in his native Schwarzach before immigrating to New Ulm.[13] John Lindmeyer was born in Bohemia in 1860, married Katherine Schroepfer there in 1886 and came to the United States in 1892 (*Review*, Oct. 5, 1939). Members of this early "Goosetown" band included John's sons – John Jr. who played clarinet, Wenzel Vogl tenor horn, Anton Lindmeier b-flat clarinet, Christ Lindmeier alto horn, Frank "Swift" Lindmeier coronet, and John "Boom Boom" Bauer the bass horn.

Usually band members switched and swapped to maximize their playing time. For example Henry Kitzberger who played with the Concordia, the Star, the Great Western, the Second Regiment, the Hofmeister, the Pioneer and the 205th Infantry bands, also managed and played in his own old time band. He began on the accordion at about age 12 and later played the clarinet. The original Kitzbergers (Anton and Barbara Kitzberger) immigrated in about 1869 from

The Star Band of New Ulm. BC

Bohemian Neumark where Anton had been a brick maker. Using clay and straw for binding materials, this pioneer built his home in Lafayette Township of similar material (*Journal*, Sept. 12, 1949). Typical of the German-Bohemians, he not only married another Bohemian but one from a musical family, Anna Hackl from New Ulm in 1903, the sister of the second wife of Joseph Hofmeister, with whose famous bands he also played throughout much of his life (*Journal*, March 4, 1932). Which illustrates a prominent fact about nearly all of the old time orchestras: Countless band members were related by blood or by marriage. And around the turn of the century, almost all were Catholic.

Members of the Whoopee John Wilfahrt dance band demonstrate this phenomenon. Before he gained fame on the radio and dance circuit out of St. Paul, John Wilfahrt relied on his brother and his cousins to produce the music that boosted him to fame. Born on the farm owned by first generation immigrant Joseph Wilfahrt in Sigel Township on April 3, 1871, John Wilfahrt Sr. married Barbara Portner in Holy Trinity Catholic Church in 1892. The Portner family originated in Rindl along the Ronsperg to Schwarzach road straight west of Trohatin and Berg.

Johann Portner (born Feb. 23, 1820 in Rindl) married Maria Hoffmann in the old homeland before coming to New Ulm with their nine children about 1873. Barbara Portner was born in Bohemia on June 16, 1867. In the early years of their married life, John farmed on the Portner place (Sec. 14 of Sigel Township) but moved into the city in November 1927. The Wilfahrt family, according to the best evidence stems from the village of Schüttwa a bit southwest of Ronsperg (*Journal* April 27, 1953). John Wilfahrt Sr. had been a member of the township school board, was a director of the Sigel Cooperative Creamery and was by trade not only a farmer but also a carpenter. While his wife Barbara died on Jan. 11, 1937 he lived many more years in New Ulm retirement until his death on April 28, 1953.

John Anthony Wilfahrt Jr. (Whoopee), one of eleven children, was born in 1893 and grew up on the farm in Sigel Township on the southwest edge of Clear Lake in Section 14. On June 14, 1914 he married Bertha Gertrude Hillesheim (born Sept. 18, 1889) his neighbor in Sigel township. In the early years he conducted not only his dance band but also ran a tire shop and then a music store. Later the tire shop was taken over by his brothers Charles and Ernst, while the music shop was phased out in favor of Brown's Music Store. Of the eleven children of John Wilfahrt Sr., half were married to people whose names eventually turn up as members of old time bands, for example Helget, Wiltscheck, Schmid and Reinhart.

In a 1952 interview with Glen Reed of Radio Station WMNE in Menomonie, Wisconsin, Whoopee John tells about his humble beginnings as a musician. A portion of the text was later reprinted on the jacket of a record album entitled "Whoopee John the Great One." Accordingly, when John was a boy of eleven he received a three-dollar accordion from his mother. "We did not have a radio or phonograph, and I was too young to go to dances. The only music I could pick up was folk songs that my mother (Barbara Portner) used to sing around the house. So I made up original music and played it on the accordion until my father, tired of all that noise, told me to practice somewhere else. I tried the kitchen pantry for a while but that didn't work, so I ended up practicing my accordion in the barn."

By the time young John was fifteen he was playing at Sunday night house dances for the German-Bohemian neighbors in Sigel and adjacent Cottonwood townships. His first house dances were commissioned in 1908. Soon it was time for a bigger instrument, a double 12-

Johann Portner 1820-1900, who immigrated to the New Ulm area in 1873 from the village of Rindl. BC

bass player, and then a 76-key concertina which John bought from a neighbor in 1911. Spurred by success, Whoopee dared to ask his father (John Sr.) for a 102-key concertina, which the senior Wilfahrt capitalized for him at $150. In 1912 John's brother Eddie began accompanying Whoopee on the clarinet. Soon a first cousin from a neighboring farm, Edward Kretsch, the son of George Kretsch and Katrina Portner, a sister of Barbara (*Review* July 18, 1923 and *Journal* August 24, 1950) came forward to play trumpet and with that the band was on its way.[14]

Old time music in the German-Bohemian tradition was transmitted in the way that folk music and folklore are always passed down, by the oral-aural approach. Some say that John wanted to honor his grandmother (Maria Hoffmann Portner) when he chose as his theme song the *Mariechen Waltz*, which was the melody for the old German folk song, *Mariechen sass weinend im Garten*. Although the Whoopee John dance band seldom sang the words to the lullaby, one of the original members of the orchestra, Otto Stueber, in July 1986 shortly

Whoopee John Wilfahrt and Mary Hillesheim wedding photo taken June 14, 1914 of celebrants on the home farm on the southern rim of Clear Lake in Sigel township. The bride and groom sit in the first row. To the right of John is Eddie Wilfahrt, a small girl, then the parents of John & Eddie. In the second row holding the horns are two Kitzbergers, then two unknown gentlemen followed by Mrs. Hillesheim. LR

before his death was still able to render several verses. It should be noted that Otto Stueber, born in Sigel Township in 1899, was the son of Christ and Elizabeth (Portner) Stueber, a first cousin to John through the Portner line (*Journal* September 3, 1986).

In 1924 when the state's Catholic societies held a convention in New Ulm, the Whoopee John band played for the celebration under their then current name the "Böhmische Dorfmusikanten" (Bohemian Village Musicians). In the band at that time and on the photograph so captioned, are the musicians, Eddie Wilfahrt with clarinet, Ed Stueber with another clarinet, Whoopee John with his concertina, Otto Stueber with trombone, John "Boom Boom" Bauer with bass, and Emil Domeier with trumpet. True to pattern, all the band members except for Bauer were related, the Stuebers being first cousins as was Emil Domeier, whose paternal grandmother also was a Portner. John Bauer – born in 1871 in Muttersdorf northwest of Ronsperg – came to

the U.S. in 1888 and in the course of his very long life played in virtually every orchestra in the New Ulm sphere.[15] Although only the
Whoopee John orchestra labeled itself as the "Böhmische Dorfmusikanten" most of those who played with Whoopee under that title
in 1924 at one time or another fronted their own Bohemian style
bands. Eddie Wilfahrt performed almost as frequently as did John in
the early days. A 1929 poster for Okeh-Odeon under the heading "Der
Deutsche Heimats-Rekord" features the Eddie Wilfahrt Concertina
Orchestra with Norman Vogel on trumpet, Otto Stueber on trombone, (Eddie with clarinet), George Arndt on bass horn, Ben Bauermeister on the concertina, Grant Schlottmann on drums and Garnett
Schlottmann on banjo and violin. The Schlottmanns later had their
own band.

Emil Domeier started with the John Wilfahrt band about 1915 but
in the 1920s shifted to the Eddie Wilfahrt band, returning to John in
the late 1920s, only to launch his own Emil Domeier Band in 1929.
Until his death in 1957 the Emil Domeier Dance Band traveled con-
stantly through the six state area. Two of his regular players were
immigrants, Ernst Zimmerman and Hermann Abel, the latter known
as Piccolo Pete. During the 1930s, Emil, with Ray Ries and Curtis
(Swede) Johnson, broadcast daily from the KYSM Studio in New
Ulm's Turner Hall, under the caption "Three Hired Hands." Later in
the 1940s and 50s, Domeier was billed on dance posters as Dumphy
the Boss. One of his daughters, Bernice, married Donald Morris who
in turn had his own dance band, "The Jolly Germans" reinforcing the
pattern that German-Bohemian musicians were interrelated. His
daughter Marlene owns and operates New Ulm's German Store on
South Minnesota Street.

The Domeier family traces its roots to the original immigrants,
Josef Domeier and Maria Heinl who, from Trohatin, a few kilometers
south of Muttersdorf, arrived in New Ulm on May 10, 1872. Like so
many others in the New Ulm area, they were members of the Berg
church in Bohemia, and in New Ulm joined Holy Trinity. Born in
1830 to Johann Domeier and Maria Eckstein (quite likely a relative of
the Eckstein family of musicians prominent in late 19th century New
Ulm), Josef came to New Ulm – according to family lore – at the invitation of Anton Gag. Anton Gag is known as the father of the famous
artist, Wanda Gag.[16] Perhaps it should be reiterated that in all of these

The Eddie Wilfahrt band. Russell "Sandy" Sandhoefner, LeRoy "Slivers" Dewanz, George Arndt, Donald Wilfahrt, Duane Schlottman, Eddie Wilfahrt with accordion and Lenore "Lala" Wilfahrt. LR

The Emil Domeier band at the Hilltop Ballroom. Ray Ries, Emil Domeier with bass horn, Carl Kittleson, Swede Johnson with accordion, Victor Lindeman on drums and Paul "Lefty" Alexander. LR

early bands, there was a Portner. Maria Portner married George Domeier, and was the grandmother of Emil Domeier, the band leader. Elisabeth married Christ Stueber, and was the mother of Ed and Otto Stueber, early members of either the John or the Eddie Wilfahrt bands. Katherine married George Kretsch, giving us Edward Kretsch who early on played with John Wilfahrt. And Barbara was Mrs. John Wilfahrt, the mother of the famous Whoopee John. In turn, John Wilfahrt's grandmother was a Hoffmann, while Emil Domeier's mother was also a Hoffmann, illustrating the intergenerational intertwine of the families who spawned the bands. Portners were also married to Sellner (Clara – the sister of Katherine, Barbara and Maria – was married to John Sellner) a family which yielded its share of musicians.

During the early years from around 1910 to 1950, most of the bands played by ear only. As a matter of fact, a good many never did learn to read notes much less to write their own music. Whoopee John at first relied on his players Leo "Pinky" Schroepfer, a barber at Sleepy Eye, who gradually wrote down the notes for Whoopee and the band. Later John Wilfahrt hired the respected note arranger for university and professional bands, James "Red" McLeod, who was under contract during the later 1930s and 1940s to produce numbers for the Whoopee John band.[17] McLeod reports that John Wilfahrt was a fine ear-driven musician who could not write or arrange music, and was able to read it only with difficulty. McLeod was also under contract to interview prospective musicians who applied to play with Whoopee John, while his related obligation called on him to write two arrangements for the band per week. Often, according to McLeod, the band leader would hum the basic tunes which he wanted arranged for his ten piece band. At times when the old master did not get time to hum a few tunes McLeod would just generate his own polkas, waltzes, schottisches, and ländlers. In the words of McLeod, "during this process the band grew away from John."[18]

In the 1950s when five Hofmeister sons were playing for Whoopee John, the band also had in its entourage professionals like Joseph Scholl of Schmidt Music Company, Willi Stephenson, Norman Staska, Don Anfinson, Harold Anderson, Roy Boyle (the polio victim who did voice comedies for John), John Thomas, Leon Benicke, and others who by their talent for music all out-classed the band leader. Many college graduate music majors and high school band directors also played with him for shorter periods of time giving the band technical skills that surpassed the master. But perhaps Whoopee's most loved "music" was not that written and played by the professionals but rather that which he produced earlier in his career, when the folk tunes were still fresh and "un-professionalized" by the experts. It is these earlier numbers that continue to enjoy a sort of classical position within the old time music repertoire.

Another highly skilled and well-known arranger for the ear-driven veterans was LeRoy "Silvers" Dewanz, a professional piano tuner who enjoyed writing, playing, and arranging band music for many orchestras over the years. Dewanz also became the instigator behind a professional musicians union that helped local players achieve better financial rewards for their performances.

The previously mentioned were by no means the only German-Bohemian bands, nor is it possible to mention all of them. However, the following are described briefly to establish that most of the old time New Ulm bands did originate from roots in Bohemia. The Sylvester Liebl band formerly of New Ulm but later of West Salem, Wisconsin came from the Heiligenkreuz community northwest of Hostau and Muttersdorf. The Helget family with its many branches including concertina master Johnny Helget, derives from the same area in western Bohemia.[19] Christy Hengel (whose father was born in Sigel Township in 1892), although born on a farm near Wanda, Minnesota, is of Bohemian origins. Builder in his in downtown New Ulm home of the Hengel concertina, Christy in 1989 was named a National Heritage Fellow with an award of $5,000 for his contribution to German-American folk art.[20]

In 1953 the following old time bands were playing out of New Ulm: The Six Fat Dutchmen, Fezz Fritsche, Babe Wagner, Don Frank and the Skinny Dutchmen, Elmer Scheid, the Jolly Brewers, Bruno Randles, Clem Brau and the Jolly Lumberjacks, Lester Nott, Blue Gordon, Gordon Schlottmann, Schell's Hobo Band, Eddie Heck, the Slim and Eddie Kalz Band, Arlie Rolloff and the Roamers, Hilbert Martens Band, Ann Sailor's Accordion Band (successor of Emil Domeier), Big Schreyer's Trail Riders, and the Harold Welter Band.[21] These bands were not necessarily German-Bohemian in name but often had a majority of musicians with German-Bohemian names, a

Christy Hengel in his shop and home at 403 North Minnesota street, exhibiting reeds for a concertina he is constructing. Taken in September 1989 when Christy was honored with the national folk arts award. LR

Christy Hengel "shouldering" a wood carved replica of himself at his home in New Ulm. LR

few of whom include: Zwach, Kopetzki, Kitzberger, Fischer, Kalz, Gag (Norbert Gag once played with Fezz Fritsche and others), Henle, Lindmeyer, Krzmarzick, Seifert, Wiltscheck, Mathiowitz and others. Likewise, the current day bands by Peter and Paul Wendinger of St. George and Erwin Suess of North Mankato are also German-Bohemian. To acknowledge his debt to Whoopee John, Suess recently re-recorded John's theme song the *Mariechen Waltz*, this time adding a vocal by son Duane of the original German folk song "Mariechen sass weinend im Garten."

Mostly the Bohemian players were ordinary working men during the day and musicians at night. Harold Tastel and Alfred Kopetzki were such individuals. Tastel played with the early John Fritsche band, then with Whoopee John in the pre-St. Paul period, next with Eddie Wilfahrt and Emil Domeier.[22] Proudly Tastel speaks of the music lessons he took from the Kitzberger family, from Edward and Benjamin as well as their father Henry. Involved with most of the ensembles previously mentioned, the Kitzbergers derive from paterfamilias, Anton, who hailed from Bohemian Neumark.[23] While attending Holy Trinity school, Tastel bought a concertina from Wenzel Fischer, another Bohemian. Unlike many of his contemporaries, Tastel learned to read notes well but liked best playing the Bohemian folk tunes by ear and always felt most at home in Goosetown. "Rather in *Gänseviertel* than in *Hundeviertel* (better to be in Goosetown than in dog town)" – a reference to the upper neighborhoods of the city and its society.

Alfred Kopetzki, a plasterer by trade, began playing with John and Eddie Wilfahrt in 1924, keeping a hand written ledger of where, on which date, and how much, he earned each evening. If we take the month of May, 1924 he performed beginning on the 2nd of May at Stewart and almost nightly as follows: Courtland, Plato, New Ulm Armory, Alex Hillesheim farm, Cologne, Norwood, Lafayette, New Auburn, Searles, Winthrop, Lake Jefferson Pavilion, Stewart, Courtland, Chaska, Robert Wilfahrt farm, New Ulm Armory, Cologne, Glencoe, Cobden, Gibbon, Waconia, New Ulm Armory, Prokosch barn dance, Nicollet and New Auburn, a total of 27 nights that month, all within a manageable radius of New Ulm, and with revenue of $188. That means he averaged $7.00 a night which was common during the 1920s but was not again achieved by the musicians during or after the depression until following World War II. Many monthly

Louis Vogel, Ben Bauermeister, unknown, John Fritsche, Henry Kitzberger, Ray Macho. LR

paychecks in the late 1920s earned Kopetzki $200 except during March when obviously the Catholic Lenten season dampened dancing across the region.

To work an ordinary shift during the day and to play music during half the night including travel time was no easy assignment. If the bands played within easy driving distance from New Ulm then "two job" status was acceptable. If the distances became greater than an hour's driving time, then sooner or later one job had to be sacrificed. During the late 1920s the Wilfahrt bands were in transition from "two-job" status to full time performance. John made it while Eddie did not. No records for the Wilfahrts exist for this period. But the transition can be illustrated with the Kopetzki dates for service in the Whoopee John – sometimes Eddie – Wilfahrt bands for the month of January, 1928 beginning on the second and including 25 engagements: Cologne, New Richland, Jackson, Winthrop, New Auburn, New Ulm Armory, Sleepy Eye, St. Paul WCCO at Lowry Hotel, Belle Plaine, Mankato, Waconia, Arlington, North Mankato, Le Sueur, Norwood, New Auburn, St. Peter, Sleepy Eye, Morgan, Belle Plaine, Welcome, Mankato, Hamburg, New Ulm, and New Richland. All of the assignments were still within a 100 mile radius of New Ulm, but the distances were expanding. Without exception during this period,

The Slim Kalz Bohemian band. Ray Meidl, Louis Vogel, Joseph "Sepp" Schneider, Edwin "Slim" Kalz, Wenzel Fischer, Alfred Kopetzki. LR

all the dance sites were German communities.[24] In fact the belt stretching southwest to northwest between Brown County and New Ulm up to St. Paul and including a distance of 50 miles on either side of the Minnesota River in general equates precisely with both the most densely German settled areas of the state and with the places where the Wilfahrt orchestra(s) most often played.

In these early years the Whoopee John Orchestra was creating a pathway to big city success by a combination of two technological breakthroughs. First, vehicles became available to transport an orchestra over what was then fairly long distances, as well as improved roads on which to run them. Secondly, there was radio to bring the music to a much larger audience than was possible through personal appearances only. In the above mentioned March 1952 interview with Glen Reed of WMNE in Menomonie, Wisconsin John looked back with great pride to his 28 consecutive years broadcasting on radio. His favorite was WCCO – with Clelland Card and Cedric Adams announcing – but he also played on WTCN, WDGY, WEBC and

WEPG often in the Nicollet Hotel in Minneapolis or the Lowry in St. Paul.[25] In the 1930s the Wilfahrt band also appeared on WNAX in Yankton, South Dakota.

Due to the stress experienced from the need to appear live twice weekly on radio programs, Whoopee John moved to St. Paul in 1930, leaving behind his "two-job" players and expanding his territory considerably through the decade of the 30s and 40s. Picking an arbitrary period of August 1942 we can learn patterns of the operation from business ledgers of the Whoopee John orchestra.[26] Even though the musicians were now full time, they earned $5 per engagement and included in addition to John, his piano player and business manager Edna Istel, son Pat Wilfahrt, Roy Boyle the handicapped Polio victim, Harold Anderson, Earl McNeal, Quentin Hartwick and the aforementioned Hofmeister brothers – Hugo, Frank, Otto, and Theodore. Beginning on the 1st of August and with the 17th open, the band played successively in the towns of Neillsville WI, St. Paul (WTCN Radio), Cleveland, Rice Lake WI, Kettle River, Searles, Watson, Menomonie WI, Sherburn, St. Paul, Gibbon, Alma WI, Tintah in Traverse County, Millville in Wabasha County, Rochester, Hersey, New Ulm, St. Paul, Coates Station, Farmington, Clayton WI, St. Cloud, New Ulm (two nights at fairgrounds), St. Paul, Bixby, Alta Vista IA, Bloomer WI, Neillsville WI, Durand WI, Ellsworth WI, Chaska, St. Paul, Rockford in Wright County, and Rice Lake in Dodge County. While the band now was moving well beyond the Minnesota borders, the principle of playing in German-American communities pretty much holds.

Earnings for this highest paid of the old time orchestras remained no better than during the 1920s. During the Great Depression of the 1930s, musicians' earnings dropped to $3 or $4 per night, and even $2.50 for an engagement. Not until well into the days of World War II did wages per night climb back to 1920s ranges, between $6 and $8 per engagement. It took until the 1950s, by most accounts the pinnacle period for old time bands, for nightly remuneration to reach $10. The figure rested here until in the 1960s when it came in around $15. During August 1942 tickets sold for between $.45 and $.75 with the most common entry fee $.50. Receipts per night ranged from $100 to $200 depending, of course, on attendance. With a total revenue for the month at $3,866.60 the financial outlook for the band seemed secure.

235

The Whoopee John band, originating as the Bömische Dorfmusikanten [Bohemian Village musicians] back in New Ulm during the 1920s, here become the big city band playing probably at the Marigold Ballroom in Minneapolis for their Monday night radio broadcast around 1950. John "Skinny" Thomas, Elmo Marx, Don Anfinson, Roy Boyle, Doug Hancock, William Bundy; dancers unknown. Note Decca recording labels. LR

But in addition to $1,300 monthly for musicians, there were expenses for the halls which ran just over $400 for the month followed by advertising at about $150. Admission taxes claimed another $267 while union dues hovered at about $50 for the month. Not counting payment to family members, Whoopee John ended up with an income of about $1,650 for the month of August, 1942 not counting costs for transportation, meals and lodging. Overall estimates lead to a conclusion that the band business was not lucrative. All engagements for WTCN were without pay. As best can be determined, the band generally returned nightly to St. Paul where the musicians resided privately. A glance at the map indicates that commitments at the Twin City radio stations meant the band never could never travel too far from this all-important promotional opportunity. Essentially the band continued traveling in an ellipse out either east or west (most often west) from St. Paul, a bit more south than north, and always to areas heavily settled by German immigrants and their descendants.

A July 1951 (the last month for which the business records are available) profile of the Whoopee John Wilfahrt orchestra, exemplifies more promotional performances both on WTCN radio and on WTCN TV which was sponsored by the Twin Cities Chevrolet dealers. During this period John was still playing also for WCCO Radio, with Saturday night half hour broadcasts from the American House (formerly the Deutsches Haus) near the Capitol on Rice street in St. Paul and Monday night stands from the Marigold Ballroom in Minneapolis. This was his heyday! Band members included in addition to John himself and Edna Istel, also James Leverett, Roy Boyle, Eugene Karels, William Bundy, Leon Benike, Frank Hofmeister, Donald Anfinson, Willard Stephenson and son Pat Wilfahrt. Surprisingly, many of the same geographic points were reached in 1951 as in the corresponding earlier decade in 1942. The ellipse enlarged a little but the shape persisted.

Always needing to be back in the Twin Cities for the broadcasts, the band now sometimes played on the radio in the afternoon and for a dance the same evening, for instance on radio WTCN on July 1, 1951 and the same evening for a dance at Lake Sarah. Then it was back to Minneapolis for the regular Monday night performances at the Marigold Ballroom and the broadcast on TV on July 2. From there the band traveled on successive nights to Eau Claire WI, Hersey WI, then Mayville ND, Beardsley and on Saturday, July 7 at the American House in St. Paul. Sunday the 8th was at Sauk Center and back to Minneapolis for the TV show at the Marigold. Now the band slipped down to Mankato, up to Breckenridge SD, over to Grand Rapids, then to Detroit Lakes (all in northern Minnesota) and back to St. Paul for the regular busy weekend of broadcasting and a Sunday night dance at Millville MN. During the week of July 16 John left from Minneapolis on Tuesday to Denning and out to Rugby ND, to Bisek ND, over to Barrett MN and back into the Twin Cities. On Sunday night the band went a short way south to Coates Station and back for the Monday performances in Minneapolis before heading down to Perry, Des Moines, and Schleswig IA with a return stop at Sioux Valley MN before weekend engagements in St. Paul and Minneapolis. A Sunday night appearance at Oak Center was sandwiched in between. The next week it was off to Kettle River MN concluding the month on July 31.

Spanning the years from January 1940 to the end of 1952, transcripts of the radio broadcasts furnish the musical numbers as well as lists of the musicians who performed for each engagement. Announcers during these years are also indexed, Ted Crea and Pete Lyman in the early years followed by Jack Bell, Max Henderson and Marv Conn succeeded by Curt Edwards who in later years was the most prominent. The musicians in the 1940s involved the famous Hofmeister brothers, Hugo, Frank, Otto and Ted as well as Harold Anderson, Eddie Istel (brother of Edna) and Whoopee John. By 1945 Lawrence Malmberg had joined the band with an accordion, Roy Boyle was there, as was now Lawrence Grivina with second trumpet and Albert Smith. Edna Istel continued on the piano supported variously by Hugo, Frank and Otto Hofmeister. By the end of 1952 only Frank Hofmeister was regularly present along with Boyle, Karels, Bundy, Benike, Leverett, Anfinson and Stephenson.

Following World War II, the radio and television broadcasts were sponsored by the Scott Briquet Coal Company. So that the on-air performances would help the record sales, the strategy called for playing those numbers which Whoopee John had most recently recorded. Although these were the Red McCleod authored pieces, the band also played many old fashioned Bohemian and German tunes, sometimes with new names under spruced up arrangements. Always the Mariechen Waltz opened and closed each program.

Other excellent old time bands had fewer German-Bohemians in their lineup of musicians. Ellsworth "Babe" Wagner, born in 1914 at Essig just west of New Ulm moved to the city before he was one year old. After his youth in New Ulm where his father worked as a policeman, Babe went to Minneapolis where he played trombone for the Gene Krupa band. In 1946 he returned to New Ulm and with his brother Virgil "Swede" Wagner began the Babe Wagner Band which enjoyed nightly engagements, and cut 24 sides with Columbia records before Babe died at the early age of 35 in 1949. There was no direct German-Bohemian blood in the Wagner family but there were a few Bohemian musicians, Pat Zwach who played saxophone in 1948, and Christy Hengel who played the concertina.[27]

Harold Loeffelmacher started his "Six Fat Dutchmen" in 1930,

The Babe Wagner band, which recorded in the early 1950s on Columbia labels. Elsworth "Babe" Wagner, Pat Zwach, Adolph "Red" Kahle, Russell Sandhoefner, Russell Heling and Don Ross. LR

apparently naming the group with reference to the Whoopee John orchestra which in early times was referred to as the "Nine Fat Dutchmen."[28] Harold's father was born on a farm in Nicollet county's West Newton township in 1861, thus the family's roots intertwined with the German-Bohemian style of music in the New Ulm region (*Journal* March 19, 1937). Harold himself was born at Fairfax in 1905 but as a youth took music lessons from A.P. Boock, New Ulm's director of the Hofmeister Band (*Review* January 1, 1961, *Post-Review* February 8, 1988). In his earlier days, Loeffelmacher played with the the bands of Earl Hunt, Whoopee John, Eddie Wilfahrt, and John Fritsche (*Journal* 1959). From 1940 to 1946 Harold recorded on the Columbia label then switched to RCA for 14 more years. He died in 1988 (*Journal* February 2, 1988; *Entertainment Bits*, 16 April-May, 1988).

The name remembered across the Midwest as leader of the

Harold Loefellmacher's Six Fat Dutchmen band. Taken at the Webcor Building at 17th North and Minnesota Street in New Ulm, now the 3M Company, probably in the mid 1960s. Harold Loefelmacher with the bass horn, Vern Bottenfield, Charles Silcox, LeRoy "Slivers" Dewanz, John "Skinny" Thomas, Emil Milbret, Willard Gulden, John Arsers, Roland Wolf and Jack Lance. LR

"Goosetown Band" was Victor "Fezz" Fritsche who grew up and spent much of his life in the very bone marrow of Goosetown. That means on the farmstead facing Front Street at the lowest point of the city adjacent to the Minnesota River. Around him on all sides were the German-Bohemians along Valley and Front Streets. When Fezz was born there on March 7, 1908 approximately 500 German-Bohemian households lived within a half mile of his birthplace.[29] His Front Street home was the heart beat of this branch of the Fritsche family. Born in 1834 at Alunburg in German Saxony-Anhalt, family founder Ernst Fritsche imbibed the traditions of the region just north of the mountains which form the northern rim of Bohemia. As the crow flies he derived from a district less than 50 miles from the Bohemian cities of Eger, Pilsen and the lands surrounding them. Historically there had always been considerable migration of Germans from Saxony into the Bohemian territory and vice versa. Culturally there was also much interchange. Suffice it to say that the Fritsches in Europe were not alien to the tradition of the German-Bohemians among whom they lived so amicably in America.

The Fezz Fritsche Goosetown band in the mid 1950s. Front row, Wayne "Jake" Jaeckel, Donald DeDon, Victor "Fezz" Fritsche, Florian "Tex" Prahl who played the accordion, and Donald "Spike" Beak; back row, LeRoy Jorgenson, Clarence "Clancy" Prahl, Norman Hofmeister and Pat Ford. LR

Arriving in Chicago in 1854, Ernst Fritsche (the grandfather of Fezz) joined the Chicago Landverein that left the following year for New Ulm. Listed as a carpenter by the 1860 census taker, Ernst married Christine Schumacher in 1860 and began farming in Cottonwood township (on the southeast 80 acres of Section 8) immediately south of New Ulm. All of his immediate neighbors were from the region around Bischofteinitz with family surnames like Schnobrich, Gag, Dietz, Gröbner, Pechtl, Seifert, Helget and others. Ernst sired John Fritsche, the father of Fezz, and also Louis who lived for decades in Minneapolis.[30] In 1893 Ernst left the Bohemian community in Cottonwood township for the Bohemian community in New Ulm at the Front Street home which is still in the Fritsche family. Ernst died there in 1921 (*Review*, September 21, 1921).

John Fritsche, one of Ernst's nine children, was born on the Cottonwood farm in 1877 where he grew to manhood with the Bohemians. In 1897, however, he moved to Lamberton and then to Walnut

Grove, but in 1900 came back to Lamberton where he married Laura Timm in 1901. Both Lamberton and Walnut Grove, on Highway 14 west of New Ulm, were daughter settlements of the Bohemians in rural New Ulm. Then in 1903 John returned to New Ulm where he farmed on Front Street and worked on rural telephone lines until his death in January 1940. John loved all types of music. For over 20 years he played with the 205th Infantry Band, was a close associate of the elder Hofmeister, and at various times operated his own dance band. John was also a citizen well known for his leadership of the Infantry Band, as chairman of the Brown County board of commissioners, and in similar civic affairs.

Born in New Ulm's Goosetown on March 7, 1908 Victor "Fezz" Fritsche married Myra Radtke of Springfield in 1939. In the meantime he absorbed the music and traditions of his beloved Goosetown. More than any other individual Fezz turned the nickname into a point of pride calling his old time band "Fezz Fritsche and his Goosetown Band." Most Fezz Fritsche fans affectionately called him "The King of Goosetown" and he loved it. More than any other band leader, Fezz epitomized the Bohemian musical tradition! He sang German folk songs and was the first band to popularize the "Böhmerwald" song with his German-language vocal rendition. He was also known for his German-dialect rendition of "Tante Anna," a number mocking the marital aspirations of a "beautiful" spinster.

German-Bohemian music in its Minnesota reincarnation won the hearts of millions through the performances of Whoopee John, Harold Loeffelmacher, and Fezz Fritsche, each of whom in his own way, was a King of Goosetown. These giants and their many imitators sprang from the German-Bohemian tradition even if they were not all from Bohemia. It was primarily these three who made New Ulm into the Polka capital of the nation. Of course several other factors facilitated the self-styled designation, a major one being the city's new radio station KNUJ which broadcast the major old time bands live during "dinner bell time." Beginning in the early 1950s, Loeffelmacher Fritsche and others each had their own live 60-minute noon hour and half hour Sunday programs where they did their own announcing, advertising and performing (*Journal*, Nov. 18, 1979).[31] Another popular figure from that era to ours was Elmer Scheid who developed what came to be known as the Hoolerie Style, unfortunately either

The Elmer Scheid Hoolerie band around 1960. John Arsers, Curt Boettger, Leopold Preisinger, Quentin "Doc" Hartwick, Roman Kahle, Jerry Drusch, Marty Schonrock and Elmer Scheid. LR

misspelled or mispronounced, for it is always written "ie" but pronounced Hoolerei. This is what might be called an early German-Bohemian woodwinds emphasis characteristic of the early Whoopee John, but further developed by Scheid, himself half Bohemian, into a high range audio that typifies also certain pieces of Erwin Suess, his co-star of Hoolerie. Erwin Suess in particular deserves credit for recording songs like the Böhmerwald in their original German for American audiences.

A second boost for German-Bohemian old time music in southern Minnesota came from Polka Day celebration which began in 1953 when the city re-paved Minnesota Street. The initial success made it into an annual event that lasted for the next 19 years. In the first year, 21 bands participated and with each succeeding year as the crowds grew so did the participating bands until it became impossible to move in downtown New Ulm (*Journal*, Sept. 30, 1979). The more

The Babe Wagner band in the mid 1950s. First row John Schradel, John Arsers, Cliff Mathiowetz and Julie Helget; back row Milt Abrahamson, "Swede Wagner," James Bertleson and Ron Carver. LR

subdued Heritage Fest that has supplanted Polka Day today is held on the fair grounds where crowd control is facilitated by gate fees and chain-link fences. The last Polka Day street dance occurred in New Ulm on July 26, 1971.

A third boost to German-Bohemian old time arrived in the form of large ballrooms. As the tradition of the big band grew during the 1930s so did the facilities – and not just in Minnesota. Across the Midwest and, for that matter the nation, the dance hall became more essential to working people in American communities than the city hall. Big cities, small towns, and isolated spots in the countryside invariably had their baseball diamond and their dance hall. Following World War II the large dance hall experienced its heyday. Whereas the bands, especially in the German-Bohemian tradition, earlier played in barns, at home, in a garage for an all day wedding and in seasonal pavilions, the grand ballroom came into wide scale service in the 1940s and lasted about two decades. In this respect a catalyst in New Ulm was the erection of George's Ballroom. Begun in 1946, it occupied an entire city block right downtown and included several dance floors, a bowling alley as well as various food and liquor services. George claimed it represented "the ultimate in hardwood maple flooring that had *spring* and *give* so the dancers never tired."[32]

A died in the wool German-Bohemian, George Neuwith like Fezz Fritsche was born and raised in the thick of Goosetown by parents who had immigrated in 1888 from Muttersdorf in Kreis Bischofteinitz. Like hundreds if not thousands of their countrymen, the Neuwirths came to New Ulm at the invitation of earlier arrivals, and began life as domestic help and farm hands, gradually working their way to success. In George's view of himself, his greatest triumph in life has been supplying his hometown with the massive dance hall, that easily accommodated 5,000 guests. With this facility, George served not only himself by acquiring considerable wealth but also his beloved countrymen who at George's had found the space they desired to dance traditional old time German-Bohemian music. Today the facility languishes though some of the well-known German-Bohemian bands, among them the German-Bohemian Wendinger brothers not only fill the air waves with Bohemian but also German-language folk songs of Bavarian origin. The Wendingers frequently also organize tours for their fans back to the Old Homeland.

Included finally, are a few songs today's German-Bohemian Heritage singers routinely perform as entertainment at social gatherings. The first is entitled "Ötza spann i mein Rössla vorar (d) Kutschn." Here a young man hitches his team of horses to the coach, Rössla being a smaller team bred to pull buggies and light coaches. He is headed to pay his girl friend a visit and as he passes her window, she tells him to come in. In the second verse the young girl asks her young beau to come in for a while. She then reveals that because of him she has been crying a lot due to the fact that her father and mother do not approve of their seeing each other. In the third verse, the young man asks his girl friend to step on into his coach and they will drive over to her father and pay him a visit. The young man then goes on to say that they should also speak very nicely to her mother and that if both still do not approve of him, then they will simply gone off and elope with each other.

Another popular song bears the title "Öitza howe ma(n) Heisl mit Howastroah deckt." Once upon a time a young man covered his house

Peter and Paul Wendinger band in 1979. Paul Wendinger, Peter Wendinger, Gary Bleisner and Joleen Wendinger. LR

with oat straw but when he gets married he will get rid of the oat straw roof. In the second verse he has indeed gotten married and asks what he gets out of it. Little more than a room full of children and a wife who can not do anything. So in the third verse he builds a house out in the woods. But here the crows keep looking into his windows. In the fourth, he warns that he will really stick it to the crows if they don't watch out, and will cut off their wings so they will never fly again. In the fifth and final verse he claims that his father's house will some day be his but that it has open ends in front and in back and so the wind blows in one end and out the next.

Although many of the songs are favorites, the prize among them all remains Andreas Hartauer's "Tief drin im Böhmerwald." In this one, the poet remembers that it was back in the Bohemian Forest that his cradle rocked, and that it has been a long time since he has gone away. But he guarantees that he will certainly never for get it. The chorus repeats that his cradle stood in the beautiful Bohemian Forest. In the second verse he addresses his beloved childhood to which happy period he would someday like to return, where his father's house stood in the green meadow and from which he could look out over his wonderful Fatherland. In the final verse he prays that some day he may be permitted to return to this wonderful home in the beautiful Bohemian Forest, to see the hills and valleys, for then he will return and call out happily, "keep yourself beautiful, O Bohemian Forest, for now I am going to stay here at home."

German-Bohemian songs are kept alive by the New Ulm German-Bohemian Heritage Singers who collect, render and preserve the songs of old. Not as long standing as the Heritage Society of which they are a subgroup, the singers started when Kretsch brothers Ernie, Pat and Paul rendered a few old numbers at the society's annual fall picnic in 1988, to the musical accompaniment of Norbert and Arlene Woratschka. Soon additional members, Arty Dietz, Kurt Eisen and Marilyn Sellner, joined the pioneers at various functions in and around the city, until 1991 when the group gained two instrumentalists and nine more vocalists. Woratschkas usually hosted the performers for practice, language lessons and their sound system. Decked out in costumes characteristic of the Egerländer Trachtengruppe of Melsungen, Germany, the group responds increasingly to demands for their performances. In mid 1994 the group released its first tape cassette "Preserving the Heritage," mostly in German-Bohemian dialect and in 1995 they performed at the Heimat Kreistreffen in Furth im Wald.

Notes

1. *Unser Heimatkreis Bischofteinitz*, pp. 846 ff. 694 ff. 717 ff. The section on folk songs begins p. 813. *Bezirk Hostau: Hei. 1at zwischen Böhmerwald und Egerland*, offers pictures pp. 142 ff. 254 ff., p. 420, with a section on the folk song pp. 510-546. Franz Lang, *Linz im Böhmerwald: Chronik einer alten Siedlung* (Tauberbischofsheim: Fränkische Nachrichten, 1986), offers photos, pp. 173, 180 as does *Ronsperg, Buch der Erinnerung*, pp. 192-200 and 292 ff. Rudolf Kiefner, *Heimat Jenseits des Böhmerwaldes im südlichen Egerland – der Kreis Bischofteinitz* (Felsberg-Wolfershausen, self-published, 1987) also offers pictures of old musical groups and organizations especially toward the end, including photographs in color of current replications of former musical groups.

2. J. H. Strasser, *A Chronology of New Ulm, Minnesota 1853-1899*, revised and edited by Elroy E. Ubl (New Ulm: MMI Graphics, 1978), p. 6.

3. The history of musical organizations in New Ulm and its vicinity appears in

Elroy E. Ubl, *Historical Notes: A Glimpse at New Ulm's Past*, II (New Ulm: Local History, 1983), pp. 187 ff. In most respects Ubl follows a type-written manuscript in the Brown County Museum library which was written by Ray Meidl. Additional references appear in newspaper articles, especially "Band History Reviewed at Dinner Meet," *New Ulm Review*, Jan. 29, 1948; "Pioneer Band Members Feted. Old Band History Recalled" *New Ulm Review*, May 15, 1952; "40-60 Years Music Brings Honors to Six Musicians" *New Ulm Journal*, Aug. 10, 1942; "This Old Time Orchestra in Demand for Celebrations!" *New Ulm Journal*, July 25, 1942; "Here's the Story of New Ulm Music and Man! How they Played It" *New Ulm Review*, April 20, 1950; "Municipal Band Notes 20th Anniversary" *New Ulm Journal*, July 17, 1966; "Local Band History Dates Back to 1878," *New Ulm Journal*, July 17, 1966; in addition, the newspapers carried the obituaries of the many band members, which amplify our knowledge of the musical involvement of individuals and usually report their European heritage, birth, education, dates of immigration, etc.

4. While Eger is located in Bohemia at the point farthest west from Prague still within Bohemian territory, it is possible that Hofmeister actually came from an area farther south and nearer the Bischofteinitz district. People from Bischofteinitz sometimes gave their state capital, i. e. Eger when they meant actually the smaller region, Bischofteinitz. *Review*, Oct. 6, 1933; *Review*, Feb. 19, 1955.

5. Kiefner, *Heimat Jenseits des Böhmerwaldes*, 1987, pp. 700 ff.

6. Wenzel Eckstein was born in Sigel township on Feb. 2, 1867 shortly after his parents Mr. and Mrs. John Eckstein had immigrated from Bohemia in 1865 (*Journal*, Nov. 22, 1943).

7. They were married at Holy Trinity Catholic Church on April 25, 1892. She died in 1900.

8. *St. Paul Musician*, 12 (1953), 5-8.

9. Ubl, *Historical Notes*, II, p. 188.

10. New Ulm *Daily Journal*, August 13, 1954, IX (Centennial edition) carries photographs of several bands Hofmeister directed. The Brown County Museum in New Ulm also has many photographs of his bands in its collection.

11. *Springfield Advance-Press*, Oct. 5, 1933 front page.

12. In addition to the newspapers cited in the text, I interviewed Peter Hofmeister at his home in St. Paul on March 6, 1986. See also the centennial edition, Section IX of the *New Ulm Daily Journal*, August 13, 1954 for photographs and name listings of members in each of the city's bands. Most of the information comes from the Ray Meidl typed manuscript in the Brown County Museum. A biography of Joseph C. Hofmeister appears in L.A. Fritsche, *History of Brown County* (1916), II, pp. 473-475.

13. Lying too close to the Bavarian border, the Bohemian part of Schwarzach was razed by Communist guards. It once lay on a line westward from Ronsperg, through Berg, Schilligkau, Rindl and Waier, from which district many immigrants to "Goosetown" had departed.

14. Edward Kretsch married Martha Sellner, who was the daughter of John and Clara Sellner. Clara Sellner, in turn, was born with the maiden name, Clara Portner, a sister of Barbara, Whoopee John's mother. Mariann Treml reports that Elizabeth Soukup Goblirsch was a first cousin of Martha, and that this Elizabeth served as bridesmaid at Edward and Martha Kretsch's wedding. The interrelationship of the musicians is sometimes multi-sided and hence complex.

15. Bauer was considered a sensation still in 1954 when *Colliers* (August 20, 1954) came to New Ulm to feature some of the city's 500 musicians in its "color camera" sec-

tion. Bauer had himself immigrated from the heart of the Bohemian villages, the Muttersdorf marketing center for the many of the original New Ulm Bohemians. It can be assumed there was much cultural interchange from the surrounding villagers of Berg, Schilligkau, Trohatin, Wasserau, Rindl, etc.

16. There are problems with this information: the Domeiers report arrival in the U.S. in 1872, the Anton Gag family in 1873, even though there were Gags among the very earliest settlers in Cottonwood township, a Peter Gag family (wife Anna) and seven children (1860 U.S. Federal manuscript census). By 1870 neither the Domeier nor the Anton Gag family appears in the censuses, although a few Gag individuals seem to have joined the Peter Gag household by 1870. Concerning Wanda Gag, see Alma Scott, *Wanda Gag* (Minneapolis: University of Minnesota Press, 1949), who on p. 4 reports the birthplace of Anton Gag as Neustadt bei Heid – which is a short distance from Trohatin; and Wanda Gag, *Growing Pains* (St. Paul: Minnesota Historical Society, 1984), biographical data p. xiii.

17. Interview with James Red McLeod, February 13, 1986; interview with Leo Pinky Schroepfer November 8, 1986; interview with Roy Boyle March 6, 1986.

18. The full story of the Whoopee John Wilfahrt band is available with over thirty photographs in the book by La Vern J. Rippley, *The Whoopee John Wilfahrt Dance Band. His Bohemian-German Roots* (Northfield, MN: St. Olaf College Press, 1992).

19. The bands that operated out of Lonsdale and New Prague, such as the Roman Rezac, Ben Barta, Joe Novotny, George Dusek and other family groups, were of ethnic Czech background. Interestingly, in southern Minnesota there seems to have always been a close relationship both in style and in personal contact between the ethnic Czechs and the ethnic Germans from Czechoslovakia.

20. Marjorie Hunt and Boris Weintraub, "Masters of Traditional Arts," *National Geographic*, 179 (January, 1991), 75.

21. New Ulm *Journal* centennial edition, (August 13, 1953) Section IX p. 8

22. Interview March 20, 1986

23. *New Ulm Review* February 7, 1906, *Journal*, March 4, 1932, *Review* December 26, 1917.

24. Maps in *They Chose Minnesota*, ed. June Drenning Holmquist (St. Paul: Minnesota Historical Society, 1981), pp. 153 ff.; Hildegard B. Johnson, "Factors Influencing the Distribution of the German Pioneer Population in Minnesota," *Agricultural History*, 19 (January, 1945), 39-57 and ibid., "The Distribution of the German Pioneer Population in Minnesota," *Rural Sociology*, 6 (March, 1941), 16-34.

25. The Kopetzki ledgers confirm the WCCO airings at the Lowry Hotel in St. Paul beginning on November 3, 1926 and continuing regularly until Kopetzki quit playing with Wilfahrt in the early 1930s. Oral tradition reports that Wilfahrt never made any money for his radio broadcasts in the early days, which is confirmed by the Kopetzki ledgers which draw blanks for radio income appearances until late 1928 when he began to receive $5 per radio performance even though $6 and $7 was earned for a night stand elsewhere.

26. Whoopee John's son and bus driver-ticket taker, Dennis Wilfahrt, of St. Paul has the business records from 1942 to 1953 and radio transcripts from 1946 to 1957, which he loaned to me for this information.

27. *Journal* September 16, 1949, *Journal* April 8, 1981.

28. Letter from Edna Istel dated April 21, 1986 about the Whoopee John Band. She later married G.H. Olson of West St. Paul.

29. See Frederic R. Steinhauser, "New Ulm Minnesota Germans. Adults of Ger-

man Birth Settled in New Ulm and Surrounding Areas 1860." Privately printed, 1979. (Households are judged from the R.L. Polk *Directory* of 1910-1911.)

30. A brother of Ernst by the name of Frederick farmed in Nicollet county north of the Minnesota River, and fathered among others Louis Albert Fritsche who became a physician. In 1916, this Fritsche authored the book, *History of Brown County, MN.* His biography appears on p. 368 ff.

31. Whoopee John at this time was in the Twin Cities and therefore was not doing local noon hour shows.

32. Interview with George Neuwirth of New Ulm, March 27, 1985.

Nine

The German-Bohemians and National Events

GERMAN-BOHEMIAN ATTITUDES toward various national events derive from voting data that correspond to civic boundaries rather than to ethnic neighborhoods and thus are only approximate. Likewise, the data are often available only for the county and are not broken down by township let alone by ethnic neighborhood. Even returns for the city of New Ulm are imprecise because ward boundaries shifted with time. In considering the city of New Ulm, however, the German-Bohemians were strongest in Ward 1, followed by Ward 2. This can be illustrated from the U.S. census, especially for the years 1900 and 1910 which not only record data by ward but also by the categories on nativity "place of birth of this person," "place of birth of father of this person," and "place of birth of mother of this person." On this basis, the most Bohemian section of New Ulm was the First Ward or, Goosetown. The Second Ward was also quite Bohemian. The most densely concentrated Bohemian voting units outside the city of New Ulm were the village (later city) of Sleepy Eye and the townships of Sigel (where they held a majority), Cottonwood, Stark, Mulligan, Milford and Albin. In other townships their percentage was too small to be statistically considered. An occasional mention will also be made of the townships of Lafayette and West Newton in Nicollet county.

In 1860 when there were 2,339 people in the county, Brown returned 409 for Lincoln vs. 91 for Douglas.[1] Scholars have suggested that a large majority of Germans voted strongly in favor of Lincoln and this held true for Brown.[2] Due to the Indian scare of 1862, Brown county's population by 1865 had declined to 2,211. In the election of 1864, therefore, the county returned a smaller vote, but nevertheless strongly in favor of Lincoln with 326 to McClellan's 58. By the time Ulysses Grant met a challenge from Horatio Seymour in 1868, Brown county gave lopsided support to Grant, 654 to 152.[3]

For the balance of the 19th and early 20th centuries, Brown county was dominated by the Republican party, though the Democrats commanded respect in the German-speaking pockets. In neighboring Nicollet county, the triumphs of Lincoln over Douglas (1860) and McClellan (1864) and of Grant over Seymour were far less overwhelming than in Brown. Confusing the issue at all the local levels, however, was the perennial presence from 1869 until 1916 of Prohibition party candidates, always hated by the Germans. Also on the scene offering opposition to both traditional parties was some form of liberal party, even at times a Communist party.[4]

Following are the presidential returns with breakdowns by county as supplied in *Minnesota Votes*. Since 1872, Brown county voted for presidents as follows: The ★ marks the national winner.[5]

Year	Republican	Democrat
1872	★Ulysses S. Grant (R) 802	Horace Greeley (D) 437
1876	★Rutherford B. Hayes (R) 832	Samuel J. Tilden (D) 682
1880	★James A. Garfield (R) 1,297	Winfield S. Hancock (D) 708
1884	James G. Blaine (R) 1,159	★Grover Cleveland (D) 1,169
1888	★Benjamin Harrison (R) 1,285	Grover Cleveland (D) 1,489
1892	Benjamin Harrison (R) 1,080	★Grover Cleveland (D) 1,174
1896	★William McKinley (R) 1,807	William J. Bryan (D) 1,469
1900	★William McKinley (R) 1,695	William J. Bryan (D) 1,471
1904	★Theodore Roosevelt (R) 2,073	Alton B. Parker (D) 869
1908	★William H. Taft (R) 1,518	William J. Bryan (D) 1,536
1912	William H. Taft (R) 472	★Woodrow Wilson (D) 1,359
	Theodore Roosevelt (Progressive) 944	
1916	Charles E. Hughes (R) 2,078	Woodrow Wilson (D) 1,101
1920	★Warren G. Harding (R) 5,841	James M. Cox (D) 796
1924	★Calvin Coolidge (R) 2,255	John W. Davis (D) 270
	Robert La Follette (Progressive) 944	
1928	★Herbert Hoover (R) 3,611	Alfred E. Smith (D) 5,341
1932	Herbert Hoover (R) 2,027	★Franklin Roosevelt (D) 6,716
1936	★Alfred Landon (R) 2,679	★Franklin Roosevelt (D) 3,678
	William Lemke (Union Party) 899	
1940	Wendell Willkie (R) 7,533	★Franklin Roosevelt (D) 3,678
1944	Thomas E. Dewey (R) 7,018	★Franklin Roosevelt (D) 2,842

1948	Thomas E. Dewey (R) 5,068	*Harry S. Truman (D) 4,804
1952	*Dwight Eisenhower (R) 8,152	Adlai Stevenson (D) 3,129
1956	*Dwight Eisenhower (R) 7,965	Adalai Stevenson (D) 3,067
1960	Richard M. Nixon (R) 7,084	*John F. Kennedy (D) 5,353
1964	Barry Goldwater (R) 5,851	*Lyndon B. Johnson (D) 6,069
1968	*Richard M. Nixon (R) 7,039	Hubert H. Humphrey (D) 4,585
	George Wallace 703	
1972	*Richard Nixon (R) 7,791	George McGovern (D) 4,374
1976	Gerald R. Ford (R) 7,479	*James Carter (D) 5,792
1980	*Ronald Reagan (R) 8,051	James Carter (D) 4,915
1984	*Ronald Reagan (R) 8,399	Walter Mondale (D) 4,469
1988	*George Bush (R) 6,898	Michael Dukakis (D) 5,109
1992	*William Clinton (D) 4,278	George Bush (R) 5,390

Although the table speaks for itself, it is noteworthy that Brown county gave a large plurality to Republican Theodore Roosevelt in 1904 followed by a dramatic shift to Democrat Wilson in 1912, with a respectable 944 votes going in that year once again to the popular Teddy Roosevelt and his progressives. Quite dramatic was the shift back to the Republicans in 1916 when "German candidate" Charles Evans Hughes unsuccessfully challenged Wilson. At work while World War I raged on the Continent was the persistent effort by Wilson to paint Hughes in the Kaiser's image. As was characteristic elsewhere, especially in the German counties of Minnesota (Blue Earth, Nicollet, Carver, Sibley, Stearns, Wabasha, Wright), German-speaking citizens turned out large pluralities for Hughes over Wilson. In 1916 Hughes was perceived as the man who would keep the U.S. out of a war against Germany.[6]

In 1920 Brown county gave a plurality to Republican Harding in part because Democratic candidate James M. Cox, as governor of Ohio in 1919 had sponsored a bill in his state legislature calling for abolishment of the German language in schools because it was "part of a plot by the German government to make school children loyal to it."[7] The Republican party that year also appealed successfully to German ethnic voters by reminding them that Wilson had first declared war against the immigrants in this country, then against Germany, and then had raped their homelands at the Versailles peace conference. Jingoistic Cox meanwhile invited his enemies – "every traitor" in America – to vote for Harding. The Democratic National Committee hurt its own candidate by charging in campaign pamphlets that the

Republicans were appealing "to pro-Germans, hyphens, Bolshevists, and everything else un-American in the United States."[8]

The 1924 vote invites attention not because of the large plurality Republican Coolidge won over Democrat Davis but for the triumphal victory over all contenders in Brown county of Wisconsin Senator Robert M. La Follette. Securing 4,515 votes, La Follette beat Coolidge with a 100% total vote victory, by far the largest plurality for La Follette in any Minnesota county. Even strongly German Stearns county offered him only 45% more than it gave Coolidge. This was, of course, the Robert Marion La Follette who championed the Progressive cause in the Midwest from the time of his election as governor of Wisconsin in 1900 to his candidacy for president in 1924.[9] Endearing himself forever to German-Americans, Senator La Follette rallied nine of Wisconsin's eleven Congressmen to vote with him on April 6, 1917 against a declaration of war on Germany.

Always, the Brown county newspapers were somewhat embarrassed about how the local Germans, German-Bohemians in particular, bucked national trends. In 1924 when La Follette more than doubled the take from the traditional parties (4,515 for La Follette to 2,255 for Republican Coolidge and only 270 for the Democratic Davis), the *Brown County Journal* prevaricated in its headline "Republicans in Big Landslide: Coolidge Elected by Biggest Popular Vote in History of the United States Tuesday" (Nov. 7, 1924). And the writer editorialized:

> "... La Follette, independent candidate for president, had a plurality in Brown County of but 2,168. This was far below the expectations of the La Follette supporters as well as of the opposition. La Follette garnered 4,498 [the state auditor said 4,515] votes in the county while Coolidge received 2,330, more than 50 percent. Brown county did far better than New Ulm, which gave La Follette a three to one plurality. Davis, the Democratic candidate, polled but 281 votes [state auditor gave him only 270]. The Democrats are so few in Brown county that it takes a spy glass to find them."

In the Bohemian voting units the pluralities for La Follette were especially high, for instance in Sigel township 138 for La Follette vs. only 8 for Coolidge and none for Davis. While the 1924 returns were otherwise strongly Republican, Brown county in 1928 was heavily in favor of Democrat Alfred E. Smith when the preferences were expressed on religious grounds. The Catholic German-Bohemians tipped the scale because the Minnesota Lutheran German counties (Carver, McCleod, Sibley, Wright) strongly favored Herbert Hoover while the Catholic German counties (Stearns in particular) went overwhelmingly with Brown for the Catholic Smith. The 1932 election, however, witnessed a Brown county landslide for Franklin Roosevelt along with the rest of Minnesota counties (none went for Iowa-born Hoover).

The 1936 figures compel our attention due to the candidacy of former Nonpartisan League activist William Lemke. A Union Party candidate from North Dakota, Lemke was born of Prussian immigrants in Minnesota's German Catholic Stearns county, but moved to North Dakota early in life. There Lemke served as legal counsel to, and an officer in, the Nonpartisan League and as attorney general in North Dakota, from which office he was elected to Congress. Respected for authoring the Farm Mortgage Act, Lemke attracted Brown county votes by his invitation to then famous radio orator, Father Charles E. Coughlin [the "Detroit Fascist Priest"] to become a member of his White House staff. Lemke also appealed to isolationists by linking Roosevelt's New Deal to communism and his own party to Americanism, advocating "that we eat, drink, wear and buy American products."[10]

Lemke got 10% of the Brown county vote and was spectacularly successful in Stearns county where he garnered nearly 25%. In both Hennepin (Minneapolis) and Ramsey (St. Paul) counties he garnered 18,468 (8% of the total vote) and 13,200 (11.3%) respectively. Ramsey was much more noted for its German constituency than Hennepin. Although Lemke drew well among German-Bohemians, he received no pluralities in any of the Bohemian voting units. He did get 73 votes in Cottonwood, 44 in Stark, 41 in Mulligan, and 17 in Sigel with a county total of 899 (*Brown Co. Journal*, Nov. 6, 1936).

Although Roosevelt carried Brown county in 1932 and 1936, he lost it in 1940 with astonishing deficits in the city of New Ulm and the Bohemian voting districts. The 1944 loss was equally devastating while the near Truman victory in 1948 was likewise remarkable. Seen in tables are the results for 1940, 1944, and 1948:

German-Bohemian Strongholds with Norwegian Lake Hanska and City Total as control units

1940						
New Ulm Ward 1	Cottonwood	Mulligan	Sigel	Stark	Lake Hanska	City Totals
Wilkie	602	227	118	184	139	98	2,817
Roosevelt	293	63	77	32	63	208	1,400

1944							
New Ulm Ward 1	Cottonwood	Milford	Mulligan	Sigel	Stark	Lake Hanska	City Totals
Dewey	498	222	191	94	163	157	91	2,809
Roosevelt	279	26	59	60	40	6	151	918

1948							
Dewey	397	102	114	43	73	88	72	2,081
Truman	512	168	125	188	117	41	147	1,580

Three weeks previous to the 1940 election the *Brown County Journal* headlined "Registration for Draft: Men Between 21 and 35 Must Report for Draft" (Oct. 10, 1940) and "First Seventy-Five in County May Be Affected By Draft, Names Listed" (Oct. 31, 1940). On Nov. 7, 1940 the *Journal* commented tersely, "The reversal of Brown county [from 1936] is laid largely to the war question, the international situation, and the draft." In this situation, not surprisingly, the Norwegian stronghold of Lake Hanska township held loyally to Roosevelt despite threats of war or the drafting of its young men. It was the German-Bohemians who were of quite different opinions concerning Roosevelt's intentions. In 1944 the situation repeated itself with even more naked results (the exception being again Lake Hanska). Only in 1948 with the absence of Roosevelt did the Bohemians trickle back to the Truman Democratic party, though not overwhelmingly (*New Ulm Review*, Nov. 9, 1944 and Nov. 4, 1948).

Because Germans feared that Roosevelt as early as his 1940 campaign against Wendell L. Willkie was positioning the U.S. for entry into the European war against Germany, they fled from Roosevelt like the plague. Brown county was no exception, more than doubling its vote against Roosevelt in 1940. Brown county German-Bohemians accelerated their flight in 1944 when third term Roosevelt met Thomas E. Dewey giving 68% more votes to Dewey than to the sitting president. In 1948, however, when the German-despised Roosevelt was out of the race and Truman had won back the German-American vote by his Marshall Plan and Berlin airlift, Brown county still did not return to the Democratic fold (although the vote was close) the way other Minnesota German counties did with massive pluralities for Truman. This was the "Germans for Truman" scenario as explained by Samuel Lubell.[11] As with the national situation, here too, the German-Bohemians did revert to the Democratic slate once Roosevelt, the person negative to the German situation, had been removed from the available choices.

From 1952 to the present Brown county has demonstrated its rather strong Republican tendencies at the polls, with the exception of 1964 when Lyndon Johnson captured Brown county over Goldwater by a mere 218 votes. The same year Stearns county Germans favored Johnson by over 6,000 votes. Having gone for Richard Nixon against Kennedy in 1960, Brown reiterated a 53% preference for Nixon in 1968 when the Democratic opponent was Minnesota's own Hubert Humphrey. The interesting case here was the candidacy of Governor George Wallace who got 703 or 6% of the total vote, virtually the same as in Stearns county and significantly above the Alabaman's take in Minnesota's other counties. These maverick votes seem to characterize the German-Bohemian strongholds of Minnesota as a bit racist. For the balance of 20th century presidential elections, Brown held to a pattern of strong Republican returns.

In non-presidential 20th century elections as well, Republicans always tended to have the advantage. As far back as 1912, Brown county liked Republican Senate candidate Knute Nelson, and in 1916 favored Frank B. Kellogg, then rejected him when he competed with the popular Henrik Shipstead in 1922. Farmer-Labor candidate Shipstead, the dentist from Glenwood, seems to have been popular in all German areas, ever since his first unsuccessful House candidacy against prohibitionist Andrew J. Volstead in 1918. In 1922 Shipstead ran on the Nonpartisan League ticket, which linked him ideologically to La Follette causes (MLM, 1923, p. 614). After many successful elections and huge pluralities in Brown county, Shipstead switched parties with the result that in 1940 on the Republican ticket he trounced his Farmer-Labor opponent Elmer A. Benson as well as the Democrat John E. Regan. It is interesting to note that in the Bohemian election units of Brown county, Shipstead in 1922 ran extremely well. He trounced Kellogg in New Ulm's First Ward [Bohemian

Goosetown] by a vote of 456 to 99. In [Bohemian] Sigel, Farmer-Labor candidate Shipstead's outcome was likewise overwhelming, 160 to 10, in Stark 140 to 22, in Cottonwood 166 to 23. This is the period, we must remember, when Republican presidents were carrying the county by 5 to 1 margins.

Ernest Lundeen was likewise popular with Brown county voters when first elected to the Senate in 1936 (MLM 1937, p. 494). He not only carried the county by a 50% plurality 6,195 to 3,023 but whizzed through New Ulm's First Ward Bohemian concentration 696 to 215. In the townships of Cottonwood (252 to 54), Sigel (124 to 43) and Stark (103 to 50) the results were equally favorable. Farmer-Labor candidate Lundeen was in the U.S. House of Representatives during America's vote to declare war on Germany and won the lifelong fidelity of German-Bohemians by voting against both U.S. entry into World War I as well as against the conscription of men to fight in a foreign war. Unfortunately Lundeen died before his six year Senate term had elapsed.

In 1917 New Ulm was the site of draft protests on this very matter.[12] That summer nearly 8,000 people from Brown and Nicollet counties listened to speeches following a parade of 2,000 young men to Turner Park in the city of New Ulm. Mayor Louis A. Fritsche addressed them as did city attorney Albert Pfaender and others. At the rally, Adolph Ackermann, president of Dr. Martin Luther College was quoted by the local paper:

> our representative in Congress [Republican Franklin F. Ellsworth] does not work in the interests of the voters. More than 80% of the voters are of a different opinion about his duty than he is. Loud applause followed this remark and Professor Ackermann replied: 'I do not give a snap for your applause if you do not go to the polls and see to it that this representative is not re-elected' (*New Ulm Review*, August 1, 1917).

Coincidentally, the *Review* concluded its coverage with the comment that the German-Bohemian "Hofmeister's Band which occupied the band stand, played patriotic airs after each of the speeches. At the close of the program the band played *America* while the audience sang the words." For their activities that evening, the Minnesota Public Safety Commission removed from office all three speakers, Fritsche, Pfaender and Ackermann.[13]

When Democrat Hubert H. Humphrey ran for the Senate in 1948 he lost Brown county to Senator Joseph H. Ball, lost the county again in 1954 to Val Bjornson, and again in 1960 to P. Kenneth Peterson. Throughout all three elections however, German-Bohemian Sigel did give a handsome plurality to Humphrey as did New Ulm's First Ward second precinct, reflecting the DFL chieftain's magnetism for at least some of the German-Bohemians. Humphrey carried Cottonwood in '48 and '60. Senator Eugene McCarthy lost Brown county to the popular Northfield farmer, Republican Edward Thye, in 1958. He just barely won over Republican Wheelock Whitney in 1964. Nor does the George Wallace candidacy for president in 1968 seem to have had an egregious appeal for the German-Bohemians. Wallace got 56 votes in Ward 1 of New Ulm, 28 votes in Sigel, 37 in Cottonwood and 14 in Stark.

In other issues the German-Bohemians were strongly against national trends. As might be expected they opposed prohibition in the many forms in which it raised its head for three quarters of a century. We must reiterate that in every gubernatorial election in Minnesota from 1869 to 1916 the Prohibition Party offered a candidate, though none was ever successful. The real test came with the 1918 returns, however, when the prohibition amendment was on the ballot in Minnesota. As might be expected it lost in Brown county 1,284 to 2,607. The table below contains the German-Bohemian voting units, including control unit Norwegian Lake Hanska (MLM, 1921, p. 528).

1918 Prohibition Act	New Ulm Ward 1	Cottonwood	Milford	Mulligan	Sigel	Stark	Lake Hanska	City Totals
Yes	63	27	32	16	14	25	91	1,384
No	324	106	106	76	102	90	39	2,607

Here it is interesting to observe that in Nicollet county, the German-Bohemian farmers in Lafayette township voted against prohibition 106 to 44 while the Swedes in Lafayette village voted in favor 67 to 14. West Newton's German-Bohemians around St. George also turned it down 125 to 18. Courtland township directly across the river from New Ulm, likewise produced a solid negative 101 to 24 vote.

Prohibition became the law of the land in spite of German and

Bohemian opposition to it. Interestingly, the legislation banning all alcoholic beverages resulted from an act drafted by Minnesota's Andrew J. Volstead, a Norwegian from Goodhue county, who had studied at St. Olaf College and later became a representative to the U.S. Congress from Granite Falls. Backed also by Minnesota's Swedish Governor Joseph A. A. Burnquist, the German-despised 18th Amendment became the law of the land with the Amendment's ratification of in 1919. Minnesota, however, was among the earliest state legislatures to vote for its repeal in 1933.

As a rule, none of the Germans in Minnesota took an active part in politics, especially when it came to running for higher political office. Until the elections of Senators Rudy Boschwitz and David Durenberger there were no senators and few U.S. congressmen from Minnesota with German names. An overwhelming number were of Norwegian, Swedish and Yankee origins. In evidence also is a fair share of Irishmen though clearly the names of Anderson, Christianson, Olson, Nelson, Johnson, Gunderson, Benson, Mondale, Peterson, and Youngdahl, overwhelmingly surpass names like Murphy, Gallagher, Sullivan, Humphrey and McCarthy. The only "O" Irish name to be found in state politics was Joseph P. O'Hara, the 1941-1959 Representative to the U.S. Congress from the Second District .

No German-Bohemians reached a state, let alone a national, post. There were a few who served as county commissioner. Mostly in Brown county if Germans held office at all, it was the more sophisticated Turner group that was successful. For instance, Julius Berndt, architect of the Hermann monument, was county surveyor for years ever since 1883. Fred Pfaender was steadily register of deeds since late in the 19th century. Always there were Turner surnames like Pfaender, Steinhäuser, Fritsche and for years Louis G. Vogel as auditor. He was not from the Bohemian branch of Vogels. So too, Carl P. Manderfeld was clerk of court for a generation. The earliest German-Bohemian to hold an office was Andrew Eckstein who was county commissioner from Sleepy Eye already in 1900. In 1923 his son W.T. Eckstein became county attorney and Joseph J. Sperl from Searles was a county commissioner. Joseph G. Tauer also served through the 1930s as a county commissioner as did Albert L. Gag in the office of county treasurer through the 1940s. John Fritsche from Goosetown was commissioner from 1937 until his death in the early 1940s. John G. Domeier replaced Fritsche in 1941 and continued in office for more than two decades. As the 20th century wore on, other names appeared on the county rosters, such as surveyor G. R. Schnobrich and commissioners Denis J. Warta and Clarence Tauer. Likewise from time to time there were representatives from the German-Bohemian community on the city council and appearances on town boards within the county. Albert Flor was both a commissioner and mayor of the city. Daniel Beranek was a member of the city council. Still, the names in politics do not tally up to the German-Bohemian deserved representation on a percentage basis. Nor was political involvement in any way expected of the Bohemians since the Germans as a whole were also absent from most lineups.

We might ask in closing what were the reactions of the German-Bohemians to the annexation of the Sudetenland by Germany in 1938? The best evidence suggests that it was enormously positive. The slogan "Heim ins Reich" (Come home to the German Empire) had always been the feeling of the German population in Bohemia. To be sure contacts between the Brown county German-Bohemians and the homeland by then had diminished. Illustrating well the contacts that remained at least faintly were the many letters received in Brown county after the war when German-Bohemian refugees all over West Germany wrote with requests for CARE Packages to whomever they could still remember. Letters arrived in considerable numbers. Often such devices served to resurrect lost relatives with whom contacts have thrived through mutual visits in the 1990s.[14]

Notes

1. Generalizations that follow about how the Bohemians in Brown county voted on national and state events are based mostly on the *Minnesota Legislative Manuals*. C.D. Tuthill, *Minnesota Legislative Manual*, 1869 (St. Paul: Office of the Press Printing Co., 1869). The *Legislative Manual* appeared every two years under the authorship of the Secretary of State. Henceforth cited in the text by year of appearance with the initials MLM.

2. Hildegard Binder Johnson, "The Election of 1860 and the Germans in Minnesota," *Minnesota History*, 28 (March, 1947), 20-36, esp. 36.

3. Because the MLM biennial publications are skimpy on national office elections, these results are gleaned from the compilation by Bruce M. White, Jean A. Brookins, Burt Cannon, Carolyn Gilman, June D. Holmquist, and Dorothy P. Kidder, *Minnesota Votes: Election Returns by County for Presidents, Senators, Congressmen, and Governors, 1857-1977* (St. Paul: Minnesota Historical Society, 1977).

4. See in general G. Theodore Mitau, *Politics in Minnesota* (Minneapolis: University of Minnesota Press, 1960).

5. The first decades are in *Minnesota Votes* by county. For the years following 1888, township and ward breakdowns are available in MLM. For gubernatorial and lower office results MLM has tables for counties and their townships beginning in 1888.

6. The best source on this entire topic is Frederick C. Luebke, *Bonds of Loyalty: German Americans and World War I* (Dekalb: University of Northern Illinois, 1974). For an analysis of the German vote see *New York Times* Nov. 9, 1916.

7. John B. Duff, "German-Americans and the Peace, 1918-1920," *American Jewish Quarterly*, 59 (January 1970), 424-44, quote 438.

8. Duff, p. 440.

9. Carl H. Chrislock, *The Progressive Era in Minnesota 1899-1918* (St. Paul: Minnesota Historical Society, 1971). On the La Follette speech in St. Paul, pp. 149-153.

10. La Vern J. Rippley, *The Immigrant Experience in Wisconsin* (Boston: Twayne, 1985), p. 137 and David O. Powell, "The Union Party of 1936: Campaign Tactics and Issues," *Mid America*, 46 (April 1946), 126-141, esp. 134.

11. La Vern J. Rippley, *The German Americans* (Boston: Twayne, 1976, reprinted University Press of America, 1984), pp. 210 ff. See also Samuel Lubell, *The Future of American Politics*, 3rd. ed. (New York: Harper & Row, 1965), pp. 134 ff.

12. *New Ulm Review*, August 1, 1917 reports and argues the case of the July 25, 1917 rally. For a discussion of this fracas see my article "Conflict in the Classroom: Anti-Germanism in Minnesota Schools, 1917-19," *Minnesota History*, 47 (Spring, 1981), 170-183. See also Martin H. Steffel, "New Ulm and World War I," unpublished M. A. thesis, Mankato State College, 1966 and Charles Quimby, "German-Americans March in Protest: Don't Send Us to War Against the Kaiser," *Review* (St. Cloud, July, 1975), 16-18.

13. Ora A. Hilton, "The Minnesota Commission of Public Safety in World War I, 1917-1919," *Bulletin of the Oklahoma Agricultural and Mechanical College*, 48 (May 15, 1951), 14.

14. Rudolf Kiefner, *Heimat jenseits des Böhmerwaldes im südlichen Egerland des Kreis Bischofteinitz* (Felsberg-Wolfershausen, 1987), pp. 623 ff. and ibid., *Passion jenseits des Böhmerwaldes* p. 448 ff.

Conclusion

Simon Mathiowetz family, taken May 31, 1910 on wedding day of John D. Mathiowetz to Agnes Kainz, at the home farm in Eden Township. L-R sitting: Simon and Kathrina Mathiowetz, standing: John D., Joseph S., Mary (Mrs. Joseph Goblirsch), Elizabeth (Mrs. Joseph Treml), and Frank G.

N CONCLUDING THIS TREATISE, it can be noted that the German-speaking Bohemians, who were an inarticulate group with a specific heritage in Minnesota, had been neglected if not totally forgotten. Confused at times about the exact nature of their ancestry, they had put on the identity of Bavarians and have perpetuated this adopted patrimony.

With Robert Paulson's founding of the German-Bohemian Heritage Society in the mid-1980s, however, descendants of these once-shy immigrants to the Brown County area of Minnesota have gradually gained a more precise awareness of their legacy. By 1995 members of this birthright had made numerous visits to their counterparts who,

The Church of St. Mary's in Sleepy Eye 1876. BC

because of their 1945-46 expulsion from Czechoslovakia, now live in Germany, and since visa-free accessibility across the Czech Republic border commenced in 1990, visits to the once-German villages have been frequent. In many respects, these sites today are more reminiscent of the "Old Country" than are comparable hometown villages in Germany because "time" in rural Bohemia for more than a half century has more or less stood still. Thus not only are houses often still intact, but they have remained approximately as they were when the emigrants departed.

In New Ulm a statue pays tribute to the German-Bohemians while the newly organized singers in original costume perpetuate the melodies and by their appearances outside the local area instruct the general public about their cultural fountainhead. Gradually a group of once quiet immigrants is proudly reclaiming its inaugural contribution to America.

Downtown Sleepy Eye 1898. BC

New Ulm's German Store on South Minnesota Street, owned by Marlene Domeier. BC

German-Bohemian Heritage Singers of New Ulm. EC

Tief im Böhmerwald.

Dort tief im Böhmerwald, da liegt mein Heimatort, es ist gar lang schon her, daß ich von dort bin fort. Doch die Erinnerung, die bleibt mir stets gewiß, daß ich den Böhmerwald gar nie vergiß. Es war im Böhmerwald, wo meine Wiege stand, im schönen, grünen Böhmerwald; es war im Böhmerwald, wo meine Wiege stand, im schönen, grünen Böhmerwald.

O holde Kinderzeit, noch einmal kehr' zurück, wo spielend ich genoß das allerhöchste Glück, wo ich a.n Vaterhaus auf grüner Wiese stand und weithin schaute auf mein Vaterland. Es war im Böhmerwald, wo meine Wiege stand, im schönen, grünen Böhmerwald; es war im Böhmerwald, wo meine Wiege stand, im schönen, grünen Böhmerwald.

Nur einmal noch, o Herr, laß mich die Heimat seh'n, den schönen Böhmerwald, die Täler und die Höh'n, dann kehr' ich gern zurück und rufe freudig aus: „Behüt dich Böhmerwald, ich bleib' zu Haus." Es war im Böhmerwald, wo meine Wiege stand, im schönen, grünen Böhmerwald; es war im Böhmerwald, wo meine Wiege stand, im schönen, grünen Böhmerwald.

Postcard triptych with three verses of the folksong "Dort tief im Böhmerwald."

266

John and Thomas Kretsch in 1876. The Kretsch family immigrated to the New Ulm area in 1858, just four years after founding of the city. John Kretsch, born in 1851 in the Old Homeland, died in New Ulm November 2, 1898. Thomas Kretsch, according to his obituary in the New Ulm Post, *March 11, 1881, died at the age of 60 having participated back in Europe in military campaigns in Italy under Austrian General Radetzky.*

Authors La Vern Rippley and Robert Paulson interviewing Edward Meidl, concerning letter exchanges the family had with the Old Homeland.

Index